Mastering Selenium 3.0

Second Edition

Boost the performance and reliability of your automated checks by mastering Selenium WebDriver

Mark Collin

BIRMINGHAM - MUMBAI

Mastering Selenium WebDriver 3.0
Second Edition

Acquisition Editor: Shweta Pant
Content Development Editor: Onkar Wani
Technical Editor: Prajakta Mhatre
Copy Editor: Safis Editing
Project Coordinator: Devanshi Doshi
Proofreader: Safis Editing
Indexer: Priyanka Dhadke
Production Coordinator: Shraddha Falebhai

First published: August 2015
Second edition: June 2018

Production reference: 1270618

Published by Packt Publishing Ltd.
Livery Place
35 Livery Street
Birmingham
B3 2PB, UK.

ISBN 978-1-78829-967-1

www.packtpub.com

Contributors

About the author

Mark Collin has been working in the software industry since 2001. He started his career in the financial sector before moving into consultancy. He has an eclectic range of skills and proficiencies, which include test automation, security and penetration testing, and performance testing. Mark is the creator and maintainer of driver-binary-downloader-maven-plugin, and the Query library used in this book. He is also a core contributor to jmeter-maven-plugin, a tool that allows you to run JMeter tests through Maven. He has also contributed code to the core Selenium code base.

A big thank you to all the core Selenium committers, especially David Burns, Jim Evans, and Luke Inman Semerau. Without these determined individuals, the Selenium project would not be where it is today.

Thank you to Raúl Ireneo García Suárez for being a sounding board and pointing me in the right direction many times.

Finally, I'd like to thank my wife and family for giving me the time to put all of this together.

About the reviewers

Pinakin Chaubal is a B.E.(computer science) from Dharamsinh Desai Institute of Technology (affiliated with Gujarat University). He is a PMP certified professional and is certified at ISTQB foundation level. He has also done HP0-M47 QTP 11 certification. He has 17+ years of experience in the IT world and has been working with companies such as Patni, Accenture, and L&T Infotech. He is the creator of the Automation Geek channel on YouTube, which teaches about PMP, ISTQB, Selenium WebDriver (integration with Jenkins), page object model using Cucumber, and JavaScript (including ES6).

> *I would like to thank my parents for encouraging me in this endeavor, the author (Mr. Mark Collin), and the project coordinator (Ms. Devanshi Doshi).*

Nilesh Kulkarni is a staff software engineer, currently at PayPal. Nilesh has extensive experience of working with Selenium. Nilesh developed frameworks on top of WebDriver in different programming languages and is an open source contributor. Nilesh has actively worked on PayPal's open source UI automation framework, nemo.js. Nilesh is passionate about quality and has worked on different developer productivity tools. He often hangs out on Stack Overflow.

Packt is searching for authors like you

`mapt.io`

Mapt is an online digital library that gives you full access to over 5,000 books and videos, as well as industry leading tools to help you plan your personal development and advance your career. For more information, please visit our website.

Why subscribe?

- Spend less time learning and more time coding with practical eBooks and Videos from over 4,000 industry professionals

- Improve your learning with Skill Plans built especially for you

- Get a free eBook or video every month

- Mapt is fully searchable

- Copy and paste, print, and bookmark content

PacktPub.com

Did you know that Packt offers eBook versions of every book published, with PDF and ePub files available? You can upgrade to the eBook version at `www.PacktPub.com` and as a print book customer, you are entitled to a discount on the eBook copy. Get in touch with us at `service@packtpub.com` for more details.

At `www.PacktPub.com`, you can also read a collection of free technical articles, sign up for a range of free newsletters, and receive exclusive discounts and offers on Packt books and eBooks.

Table of Contents

Preface

This book is going to focus on some of the more advanced aspects of Selenium. It will help you develop a greater understanding of Selenium as a test tool and provide you a series of strategies to help you create reliable and extensible test frameworks.

In the world of automation, there is rarely only one correct way of doing things. This book will provide you with a series of minimalistic implementations that are flexible enough to be customized to your specific needs.

This book is not going to teach you how to write bloated test frameworks that hide Selenium behind an impenetrable veil of obscurity. Instead, it will show you how to complement Selenium with useful additions that fit seamlessly into the rich and well-crafted API that Selenium already offers you.

Who this book is for

If you are a software tester or a developer with working experience of Selenium and competency with Java who are interested in automation and are looking forward to taking the next step in your learning journey, then this is the book for you.

What this book covers

Chapter 1, *Creating a Fast Feedback Loop*, explains how to build a basic test framework that enables you to get started quickly. You will then focus on setting up a project using Maven to download your dependencies. Then you will learn about the advantages of running tests in parallel with multiple instances of the same browser in TestNG. Next, you will learn how to make your test code portable by automatically downloading the driver binaries using a Maven plugin and run your tests without interruption by running them in headless mode.

Chapter 2, *Producing the Right Feedback When Failing*, explores how to cope when tests start failing. This chapter gives you a good understanding of why reliability matters and how to configure your tests to run in a Maven profile. You will get an understanding of continuous integration, continuous delivery, and continuous deployment, and set up a test build in a continuous integration server. You also learn how to connect to Selenium-Grid, how to take screenshots of test failures, and investigate the causes of test failures by reading the stack trace.

Chapter 3, *Exceptions Are Actually Oracles*, provides a great deal of insight into what has gone wrong with your automated checks. You will explore the various exceptions generated by Selenium and understand what they mean. Further, you will gain a good understanding of how WebElement is a reference to an element in the DOM, understand the basic architecture of Selenium, and learn how it sends commands to the browser.

Chapter 4, *The Waiting Game*, explains the most common causes of test failures in automation and also various wait solutions in Selenium. You will explore how waits work in Selenium and how you should use them to ensure that you have stable and reliable tests.

Chapter 5, *Working with Effective Page Objects*, discusses page objects and explains how to use them effectively without letting them get out of control. It also teaches you how to use your page objects to reduce duplication, which in turn will help you make your code concise and your automated checks more readable. Then we will finish off the chapter by understanding how to build fluent page objects.

Chapter 6, *Utilizing the Advanced User Interactions API*, explains how to use the Advanced User Interactions API. You will learn how you can automate challenging scenarios such as hover menus and drag-and-drop controls. You will also explore some of the problems that you may come across when using the Advanced User Interactions API.

Chapter 7, *JavaScript Execution with Selenium*, helps you understand how to use the JavascriptExecutor class. This chapter explores how you can use it to work around complex automation problems. You also learn how to execute asynchronous scripts that use a callback to notify Selenium that they have completed the execution.

Chapter 8, *Keeping It Real*, shows you the limitations of Selenium. You then explore various scenarios that demonstrate how to extend Selenium to work with external libraries and applications so that you will be able to use the right tool for the job.

Chapter 9, *Hooking Docker into Selenium*, looks at how you can use Docker with Selenium. You will understand how easy it is to start spinning up your own grid in Docker. You will also look at how you can integrate Docker into your build process.

Chapter 10, *Selenium - the Future*, has a look at machine learning and artificial intelligence. You will then learn how to leverage some of that technology with Applitools EYES.

Appendix A, *Contributing to Selenium*, explores ways in which you can help the Selenium project.

Appendix B, *Working with JUnit*, explores the changes required to switch from TestNG to JUnit.

`Appendix C`, *Introduction to Appium,* explains how to create a basic Appium test framework.

To get the most out of this book

The following software is required for the book:

- Oracle JDK8
- Maven 3
- IntelliJ IDEA 2018
- JMeter
- Zed Attack Proxy
- Docker
- Mozilla Firefox
- Google Chrome

Generally, the more the browsers you install, the better. You will be able to perform all the exercises in this book if you have at least Mozilla Firefox and Google Chrome installed.

The community edition of IntelliJ IDEA is free, but it's certainly worth purchasing a license to get access to the full functionality. You can use the older versions of IntelliJ IDEA or another IDE according to your preference. The code for this book has been written in IntelliJ IDEA 2018.

Download the example code files

You can download the example code files for this book from your account at `www.packtpub.com`. If you purchased this book elsewhere, you can visit `www.packtpub.com/support` and register to have the files emailed directly to you.

You can download the code files by following these steps:

1. Log in or register at `www.packtpub.com`.
2. Select the **SUPPORT** tab.
3. Click on **Code Downloads & Errata**.
4. Enter the name of the book in the **Search** box and follow the onscreen instructions.

Once the file is downloaded, please make sure that you unzip or extract the folder using the latest version of:

- WinRAR/7-Zip for Windows
- Zipeg/iZip/UnRarX for Mac
- 7-Zip/PeaZip for Linux

The code bundle for the book is also hosted on GitHub at `https://github.com/ PacktPublishing/Mastering-Selenium-WebDriver-3.0-Second-Edition`. In case there's an update to the code, it will be updated on the existing GitHub repository.

We also have other code bundles from our rich catalog of books and videos available at `https://github.com/PacktPublishing/`. Check them out!

Conventions used

There are a number of text conventions used throughout this book.

`CodeInText`: Indicates code words in text, database table names, folder names, filenames, file extensions, pathnames, dummy URLs, user input, and Twitter handles. Here is an example: "`groupId` should be a domain that you own/control and is entered in reverse."

A block of code is set as follows:

```
public class BasicTest {

    private ExpectedCondition<Boolean> pageTitleStartsWith(final
    String searchString) {
        return driver -> driver.getTitle().toLowerCase().
        startsWith(searchString.toLowerCase());
    }
```

Any command-line input or output is written as follows:

```
mvn clean verify -Dwebdriver.gecko.driver=<PATH_TO_GECKODRIVER_BINARY>
```

Bold: Indicates a new term, an important word, or words that you see onscreen. For example, words in menus or dialog boxes appear in the text like this. Here is an example: "Click on the **Projects** button on the top left."

 Warnings or important notes appear like this.

Tips and tricks appear like this.

Get in touch

Feedback from our readers is always welcome.

General feedback: Email `feedback@packtpub.com` and mention the book title in the subject of your message. If you have questions about any aspect of this book, please email us at `questions@packtpub.com`.

Errata: Although we have taken every care to ensure the accuracy of our content, mistakes do happen. If you have found a mistake in this book, we would be grateful if you would report this to us. Please visit `www.packtpub.com/submit-errata`, selecting your book, clicking on the Errata Submission Form link, and entering the details.

Piracy: If you come across any illegal copies of our works in any form on the Internet, we would be grateful if you would provide us with the location address or website name. Please contact us at `copyright@packtpub.com` with a link to the material.

If you are interested in becoming an author: If there is a topic that you have expertise in and you are interested in either writing or contributing to a book, please visit `authors.packtpub.com`.

Reviews

Please leave a review. Once you have read and used this book, why not leave a review on the site that you purchased it from? Potential readers can then see and use your unbiased opinion to make purchase decisions, we at Packt can understand what you think about our products, and our authors can see your feedback on their book. Thank you!

For more information about Packt, please visit `packtpub.com`.

Creating a Fast Feedback Loop 1

One of the main problems you hear people talking about with Selenium is how long it takes to run all of their tests; I have heard figures ranging from a couple of hours to a couple of days. In this chapter, we will have a look at how we can speed things up and get the tests that you are writing to run both quickly and regularly.

Another problem that you may come across is getting other people to run your tests; this is usually because it is a pain to set up the project to work on their machine and it's too much effort for them. As well as making things run quickly, we are going to make it very easy for others to check out your code and get themselves up and running.

How does this create a fast feedback loop?

Well, first of all, allow me to explain what a fast feedback loop is. As developers change or refactor code, it's possible that they may make a mistake and break something. The feedback loop starts off when they commit code and is complete when they know whether their code changes have worked as expected, or something has been broken. We want to make this feedback loop as fast as possible, so ideally a developer will be running all of the tests that are available before every check in. They will then know whether the changes they made to the code have broken something before the code leaves their machine.

Eventually, we want to get to the point where developers are updating tests that fail because the functionality has changed as they go. The eventual code to turn the tests into living documentation, we will talk about a bit more about in Chapter 2, *Producing the Right Feedback When Failing*.

In this chapter, we are going to start by creating a basic test framework. What am I going to need? The software and browser versions used to write the code in this chapter are as follows:

- Java SDK 8
- Maven 3.5.3
- Chrome 66
- Firefox 60

It's a good idea to make sure that you atleast update to these versions to make sure everything works for you.

Making it easy for developers to run tests

Ideally, we want our tests to run every time somebody pushes code to the central code repository; part of doing this is ensuring that it's very easy to run our tests. If somebody can just check out our code base and run one command and have all of the tests just work, it means they are far more likely to run them.

We are going to make this easy by using **Apache Maven**. To steal a quote from the Maven documentation:

> *"Maven is an attempt to apply patterns to a project's build infrastructure in order to promote comprehension and productivity by providing a clear path in the use of best practices."*

Maven is a tool that can be used to build and manage Java projects (including downloading any dependencies that you require) and is used in many companies as part of the standard enterprise infrastructure. Maven is not the only solution to this problem (for example, **Gradle** is a very powerful alternative that is on par with Maven in many areas and exceeds it in a few), but it is one that you are most likely to see on the ground and one that most Java developers will have used at some point in their careers.

One of the major plus points is that it encourages developers to use a standardized project structure that makes it easy for people who know Maven to navigate around the source code; it also makes it very easy to plug into a CI system (such as Jenkins or TeamCity), as all the major ones understand Maven POM files.

How does this make it easy for developers to run tests? Well, when we have set our project up using Maven, they should be able to check out our test code and simply type `mvn clean verify` into a Terminal window. This will automatically download all dependencies, set up the class path, and run all of the tests.

It doesn't really get much easier than that.

Building our test project with Apache Maven

Getting a full working Maven install up and running is not within the scope of this book. It's okay though, don't panic! The Apache Software Foundation has you covered, it has a guide to setting up Maven up in just five minutes! See the following link:

`http://maven.apache.org/guides/getting-started/maven-in-five-minutes.html`

If you are running the Debian derivative of Linux, it is as easy as using this command:

```
sudo apt-get install maven
```

Or if you are running a Mac with Homebrew, it is just this code:

```
brew install maven
```

Once you have Maven installed and working, we will start our Selenium project with a basic POM file. We are going to start by creating a basic Maven directory structure and then creating a file called `pom.xml` in it. Take a look at the following screenshot:

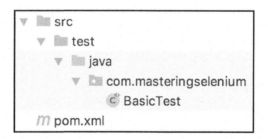

There are two main testing frameworks that you will come across in a Java environment; **JUnit** and **TestNG**. I personally find TestNG to be easier to get up and running out of the box, but I find JUnit to be more extensible. TestNG certainly seems to be popular on the Selenium mailing list, with many threads asking questions about it; you don't often see JUnit questions any more.

I'm not going to suggest either one as the right choice, as they are both capable frameworks that you will probably come across in the enterprise world. Since TestNG seems to be the more popular option, we will focus on a TestNG implementation in this chapter.

If you prefer JUnit, you will want to have a look at *Appendix 2, Working with jUnit*. In this, we will implement the same base project, but we will use JUnit instead of TestNG. This means instead of worrying about which one is best, you can have a look at a TestNG implementation and a JUnit implementation. You can then choose which one you prefer and read the relevant section.

So, to start with, let's have a look at a basic POM code for a TestNG-based Maven project:

```
<?xml version="1.0" encoding="UTF-8"?>
<project xmlns="http://maven.apache.org/POM/4.0.0"
         xmlns:xsi="http://www.w3.org/2001/XMLSchema-instance"
         xsi:schemaLocation="http://maven.apache.org/POM/4.0.0
         http://maven.apache.org/xsd/maven-4.0.0.xsd">

    <groupId>com.masteringselenium.demo</groupId>
    <artifactId>mastering-selenium-testng</artifactId>
    <version>DEV-SNAPSHOT</version>
    <modelVersion>4.0.0</modelVersion>

    <name>Mastering Selenium TestNG</name>
    <description>A basic Selenium POM file</description>
    <url>http://www.masteringselenium.com</url>

    <properties>
        <project.build.sourceEncoding>UTF-
        8</project.build.sourceEncoding>
        <project.reporting.outputEncoding>UTF-
        8</project.reporting.outputEncoding>
        <java.version>1.8</java.version>
        <!-- Dependency versions -->
        <selenium.version>3.12.0</selenium.version>
        <testng.version>6.14.3</testng.version>
        <!-- Plugin versions -->
        <maven-compiler-plugin.version>3.7.0</maven-compiler-
        plugin.version>
        <maven-failsafe-plugin.version>2.21.0</maven-failsafe-
        plugin.version>
        <!-- Configurable variables -->
        <threads>1</threads>
    </properties>

    <build>
```

```xml
        <plugins>
            <plugin>
                <groupId>org.apache.maven.plugins</groupId>
                <artifactId>maven-compiler-plugin</artifactId>
                <configuration>
                    <source>${java.version}</source>
                    <target>${java.version}</target>
                </configuration>
                <version>${maven-compiler-plugin.version}</version>
            </plugin>
        </plugins>
    </build>

    <dependencies>
        <dependency>
            <groupId>org.seleniumhq.selenium</groupId>
            <artifactId>selenium-java</artifactId>
            <version>${selenium.version}</version>
            <scope>test</scope>
        </dependency>
        <dependency>
            <groupId>org.seleniumhq.selenium</groupId>
            <artifactId>selenium-remote-driver</artifactId>
            <version>${selenium.version}</version>
            <scope>test</scope>
        </dependency>
        <dependency>
            <groupId>org.testng</groupId>
            <artifactId>testng</artifactId>
            <version>${testng.version}</version>
            <scope>test</scope>
        </dependency>
    </dependencies>

</project>
```

What you are seeing here is mainly Maven boilerplate code. The `groupId`, `artifactId`, and `version` are subject to standard naming conventions, which are as follows :

- `groupId` should be a domain that you own/control and is entered in reverse
- `artifactId` is the name that will be allocated to your JAR file, so remember to make it what you want your JAR file to be called
- `version` should always be a number with `-SNAPSHOT` appended to the end; this shows that it is currently a work in process

We have added the Maven compiler plugin so that we can define the version of Java that is required to compile the code we are going to write. We have opted to require Java 8, since this is the minimum version of Java currently supported by Selenium.

Next, we have the libraries that our code depends upon; these are stored in the dependencies block. To get us started, we have added a dependency for Selenium and a dependency for TestNG. Note that we have given them a scope of test; this ensures that these dependencies are only loaded into the classpath when tests are run and are never packaged up in any artifacts that are generated as part of the build process.

We have used Maven properties to set our dependency versions. This is not required, but it's a common Maven convention. The idea is that it's easier to update the versions of things in your POM if they are all declared in one place. XML can be very verbose and wading through the POM finding each dependency or plugin version that we want to update can be time consuming, especially when you start using Maven profiles.

You can now open up this POM file using your IDE (in this book, I'm assuming that you are using **IntelliJ IDEA**, but any modern IDE should be able to open up a POM file and create a project from it).

We now have the basis of our Selenium project. The next step is to create a basic test that we can run using Maven. Start by creating a src/test/java directory. Your IDE should automatically work out that this directory is a test sources directory. We then need to create a new package in this directory called com.masteringselenium. Finally, inside this package, we will create a file called BasicTest.java. Into this file we are going to put the following code:

```java
package com.masteringselenium;

import org.openqa.selenium.By;
import org.openqa.selenium.WebDriver;
import org.openqa.selenium.WebElement;
import org.openqa.selenium.firefox.FirefoxDriver;
import org.openqa.selenium.support.ui.ExpectedCondition;
import org.openqa.selenium.support.ui.WebDriverWait;
import org.testng.annotations.Test;

public class BasicTest {

    private ExpectedCondition<Boolean> pageTitleStartsWith(final
    String searchString) {
        return driver -> driver.getTitle().toLowerCase().
        startsWith(searchString.toLowerCase());
```

```
    }

    private void googleExampleThatSearchesFor(final
    String searchString) {

        WebDriver driver = new FirefoxDriver();

        driver.get("http://www.google.com");

        WebElement searchField = driver.findElement(By.name("q"));

        searchField.clear();
        searchField.sendKeys(searchString);

        System.out.println("Page title is: " + driver.getTitle());

        searchField.submit();

        WebDriverWait wait = new WebDriverWait(driver, 10, 100);
        wait.until(pageTitleStartsWith(searchString));

        System.out.println("Page title is: " + driver.getTitle());

        driver.quit();
    }

    @Test
    public void googleCheeseExample() {
        googleExampleThatSearchesFor("Cheese!");
    }

    @Test
    public void googleMilkExample() {
        googleExampleThatSearchesFor("Milk!");
    }
}
```

These two tests should be quite familiar; it's the basic Google cheese scenario with all the main grunt work abstracted out into a method that we are able to call multiple times with different search terms. We now have everything we need to run our tests. To kick them off, type the following command into a Terminal window:

```
mvn clean verify
```

You will now see Maven downloading all of the Java dependencies from Maven central. When it is completed, it will build the project and then run the tests.

If you have problems downloading the dependencies, try adding a -U to the end of the command; this will force Maven to check the Maven central repositories for updated libraries.

You will now see Firefox load up and then your test will fail, since with Selenium 3 all of the driver binaries (the part that actually drives the browser) are no longer bundled with Selenium. You will now have to download the relevant binaries to be able to run your tests.

For now, we will download a binary and then pass an environmental variable into the JVM so that we can get this initial test running. Later on, we will take a look at a slightly more streamlined way to do this that will automatically download the required driver binaries.

We are running our tests against Firefox, so we will need to download the **geckodriver binary**; the latest one is available at `https://github.com/mozilla/geckodriver/releases`.

Now that we have a usable driver binary, we need to tell Selenium where to find it. Luckily, the Selenium team have already provided us with a way to do this. When Selenium starts up and tries to instantiate a driver object, it will look for a system property that holds the location of the required executable. These system properties are in the format `WebDriver.<DRIVER_TYPE>.driver`. To get our test working, all we need to do is pass this system property on the command line:

```
mvn clean verify -Dwebdriver.gecko.driver=<PATH_TO_GECKODRIVER_BINARY>
```

This time, Firefox should load up correctly, run your tests without any error, and finally give you a pass.

If you are still having problems, check the version of Firefox that you are using. The code in this chapter has been written against Firefox 60. If you are using earlier versions, you may suffer from patchy geckodriver support, and you may see some errors.

We now have a very basic project set up to run a couple of very basic tests using Maven. Right now, this will run very quickly, but as you start adding more and more tests to your project, things are going to start to slow down. To try and mitigate this problem, we are going to utilize the full power of your machine by running your tests in parallel.

Running your tests in parallel

Running your tests in parallel means different things to different people, as it can mean either of the following:

- Run all of your tests against multiple browsers at the same time
- Run your tests against multiple instances of the same browser

Should we run our tests in parallel to increase coverage?

I'm sure that when you are writing automated tests, to make sure things work with the website you are testing, you are initially told that your website has to work on all browsers. The reality is that this is just not true. There are many browsers out there and it's just not feasible to support everything. For example, will your AJAX-intensive site that has the odd flash object work in the Lynx browser?

Lynx is a text-based web browser that can be used in a Linux Terminal window and was still in active development in 2014.

The next thing you will hear is, "OK, well, we will support every browser supported by Selenium." Again, that's great, but we have problems. Something that most people don't realize is that the core Selenium teams official browser support is the current browser version, and the previous version at the time of release of a version of Selenium. In practice, it may well work on older browsers and the core team does a lot of work to try and make sure they don't break support for older browsers. However, if you want to run a series of tests on Internet Explorer 6, Internet Explorer 7, or even Internet Explorer 8, you are actually running tests against browsers that are not officially supported by Selenium.

We then come to our next set of problems. Internet Explorer is only supported on Windows machines, and you can have only one version of Internet Explorer installed on a Windows machine at a time.

There are hacks to install multiple versions of Internet Explorer on the same machine, but you will not get accurate tests if you do this. It's much better to have multiple operating systems running with just one version of Internet Explorer.

Safari is only supported on OS X machines, and, again, you can have only one version installed at a time.

There is an old version of Safari for Windows hidden away in Apple's archives, but it is no longer actively supported and shouldn't be used.

It soon becomes apparent that even if we do want to run all of our tests against every browser supported by Selenium, we are not going to be able to do it on one machine.

At this point, people tend to modify their test framework so that it can accept a list of browsers to run against. They write some code that detects, or specifies, which browsers are available on a machine. Once they have done this, they start running all of their tests over a few machines *in parallel* and end up with a matrix that looks like this:

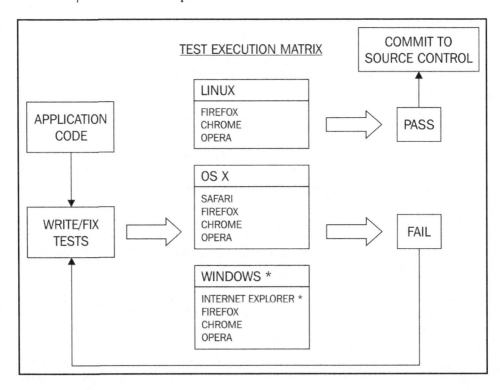

This is great, but it doesn't get around the problem that there is always going to be one or two browsers you can't run against your local machine, so you will never get full cross-browser coverage. Using multiple different driver instances (potentially in multiple threads) to run against different browsers has given us slightly increased coverage. We still don't have full coverage though.

We also suffer some side effects by doing this. Different browsers run tests at different speeds because JavaScript engines in all browsers are not equal. We have probably drastically slowed down the process of checking that the code works before you push it to a source code repository.

Finally, by doing this we can make it much harder to diagnose issues. When a test fails, you now have to work out which browser it was running against, as well as why it failed. This may only take a minute of your time, but all those minutes do add up.

So, why don't we just run our tests against one type of browser for the moment. Let's make that test run against that browser nice and quickly, and then worry about cross-browser compatibility later.

It's probably a good idea to just pick one browser to run our tests against on our development machines. We can then use a CI server to pick up the slack and worry about browser coverage as part of our build pipeline. It's probably also a good idea to pick a browser with a fast JavaScript engine for our local machines.

Parallel tests with TestNG

The TestNG examples used in this chapter will be using TestNG Version 6.14.3 and the Maven Failsafe Plugin Version 2.21.0. If you use older versions of these components, the functionality that we are going to use may not be available.

To start, we are going to make some changes to our POM file. We are going to add a `threads` property, which will be used to determine the number of parallel threads used to run our checks. Then, we are going to use the Maven Failsafe Plugin to configure TestNG:

```
<properties>
    <project.build.sourceEncoding>UTF-8</project.build.sourceEncoding>
    <project.reporting.outputEncoding>
    UTF-8</project.reporting.outputEncoding>
    <java.version>1.8</java.version>
    <!-- Dependency versions -->
    <selenium.version>3.12.0</selenium.version>
    <testng.version>6.14.3</testng.version>
    <!-- Plugin versions -->
    <maven-compiler-plugin.version>3.7.0
    </maven-compiler-plugin.version>
    <maven-failsafe-plugin.version>2.21.0
    </maven-failsafe-plugin.version>
    <!-- Configurable variables -->
```

```
            <threads>1</threads>
    </properties>

    <build>
        <plugins>
            <plugin>
                <groupId>org.apache.maven.plugins</groupId>
                <artifactId>maven-compiler-plugin</artifactId>
                <configuration>
                    <source>${java.version}</source>
                    <target>${java.version}</target>
                </configuration>
                <version>${maven-compiler-plugin.version}</version>
            </plugin>
            <plugin>
                <groupId>org.apache.maven.plugins</groupId>
                <artifactId>maven-failsafe-plugin</artifactId>
                <version>${maven-failsafe-plugin.version}</version>
                <configuration>
                    <parallel>methods</parallel>
                    <threadCount>${threads}</threadCount>
                </configuration>
                <executions>
                    <execution>
                        <goals>
                            <goal>integration-test</goal>
                            <goal>verify</goal>
                        </goals>
                    </execution>
                </executions>
            </plugin>
        </plugins>
    </build>
```

 When using the Maven Failsafe Plugin, the `integration-test` goal will ensure that your tests run in the integration test phase. The verify goal ensures that the Failsafe Plugin checks the results of the checks run in the `integration-test` phase, and fails the build if something did not pass. If you don't have the `verify` goal, the build will not fail!

TestNG supports parallel threads out of the box; we just need to tell it how to use them. This is where the Maven Failsafe Plugin comes in. We are going to use it to configure our parallel execution environment for our tests. This configuration will be applied to TestNG if you have TestNG as a dependency; you don't need to do anything special.

In our case, we are interested in `parallel` and the `threadCount` configuration settings. We have set `parallel` to methods. This will search through our project for methods that have the `@Test` annotation and will collect them all into a great big pool of tests. The Failsafe Plugin will then take tests out of this pool and run them. The number of tests that will be run concurrently will depend on how many threads are available. We will use the `threadCount` property to control this.

It is important to note that there is no guarantee in which order tests will be run.

We are using the `threadCount` configuration setting to control how many tests we run in parallel, but as you may have noticed we have not specified a number. Instead, we have used the Maven variable `${threads}`, this will take the value of the `maven` property `threads` that we defined in our `properties` block and pass it into `threadCount`.

Since `threads` is a Maven property, we are able to override its value on the command line by using the `-D` switch. If we do not override its value, it will use the value we have set in the POM as a default.

So, if we run the following command, it will use the default value of 1 in the POM file.:

```
mvn clean verify -Dwebdriver.gecko.driver=<PATH_TO_GECKODRIVER_BINARY>
```

However, if we use this next command, it will overwrite the value of 1 stored in the POM file and use the value 2 instead:

```
mvn clean verify -Dthreads=2 -
Dwebdriver.gecko.driver=<PATH_TO_GECKODRIVER_BINARY>
```

As you can see, this gives us the ability to tweak the number of threads that we use to run our tests without making any code changes at all.

We have used the power of Maven and the Maven Failsafe Plugin to set the number of threads that we want to use when running our tests in parallel, but we still have more work to do!

If you run your tests right now, you will see that even though we are supplying multiple threads to our code, all the tests still run in a single thread. Selenium is not thread safe, so we need to write some code that will make sure that each Selenium instance runs in its own isolated thread and does not leak over to other threads.

Previously, we were instantiating an instance of `FirefoxDriver` in each of our tests. Let's pull this out of the test, and put browser instantiation into its own class called `DriverFactory`. We will then add a class called `DriverBase` that will deal with the marshaling of the threads.

We are going to now build a project structure that looks like this:

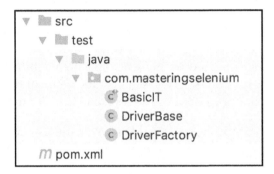

First of all, we need to create our `DriverFactory` class by using the following code:

```
package com.masteringselenium;

import org.openqa.selenium.firefox.FirefoxDriver;
import org.openqa.selenium.remote.RemoteWebDriver;

public class DriverFactory {

    private RemoteWebDriver webDriver;

    private final String operatingSystem =
    System.getProperty("os.name").toUpperCase();
    private final String systemArchitecture =
    System.getProperty("os.arch");

    RemoteWebDriver getDriver() {
        if (null == webDriver) {
            System.out.println(" ");
            System.out.println("Current Operating System: " +
            operatingSystem);
            System.out.println("Current Architecture: " +
            systemArchitecture);
            System.out.println("Current Browser Selection:
            Firefox");
            System.out.println(" ");
            webDriver = new FirefoxDriver();
```

```
        }

        return webDriver;
    }

    void quitDriver() {
        if (null != webDriver) {
            webDriver.quit();
            webDriver = null;
        }
    }
}
```

This class holds a reference to a WebDriver object, and ensures that every time you call getDriver() you get a valid instance of WebDriver back. If one has been started up, you will get the existing one. If one hasn't been started up, it will start one for you.

It also provides a quitDriver() method that will perform quit() on your WebDriver object. It also nullifies the WebDriver object held in the class. This prevents errors that would be caused by attempting to interact with a WebDriver object that has been closed.

Note that we are using driver.quit() and not driver.close(). As a general rule of thumb, you should not use driver.close() to clean up. It will throw an error if something happened during your test that caused the WebDriver instance to close early. The close-and-clean-up command in the WebDriver API is driver.quit(). You would normally use driver.close() if your test opens multiple windows and you want to shut some of them.

Next, we need to create a class called DriverBase by using this command:

```
package com.masteringselenium;

import org.openqa.selenium.remote.RemoteWebDriver;
import org.testng.annotations.AfterMethod;
import org.testng.annotations.AfterSuite;
import org.testng.annotations.BeforeSuite;

import java.util.ArrayList;
import java.util.Collections;
import java.util.List;

public class DriverBase {

    private static List<DriverFactory> webDriverThreadPool =
```

```
        Collections.synchronizedList(new ArrayList<DriverFactory>());
    private static ThreadLocal<DriverFactory> driverThread;

    @BeforeSuite(alwaysRun = true)
    public static void instantiateDriverObject() {
        driverThread = new ThreadLocal<DriverFactory>() {
            @Override
            protected DriverFactory initialValue() {
                DriverFactory webDriverThread = new DriverFactory();
                webDriverThreadPool.add(webDriverThread);
                return webDriverThread;
            }
        };
    }

    public static RemoteWebDriver getDriver() {
        return driverThread.get().getDriver();
    }

    @AfterMethod(alwaysRun = true)
    public static void clearCookies() {
        getDriver().manage().deleteAllCookies();
    }

    @AfterSuite(alwaysRun = true)
    public static void closeDriverObjects() {
        for (DriverFactory webDriverThread : webDriverThreadPool) {
            webDriverThread.quitDriver();
        }
    }
}
```

This is a small class that will hold a pool of driver objects. We are using a `ThreadLocal` object to instantiate our `WebDriverThread` objects in separate threads. We have also created a `getDriver()` method that uses the `getDriver()` method on the `DriverFactory` object to pass each test a `WebDriver` instance that it can use.

We are doing this to isolate each instance of `WebDriver` to make sure that there is no cross contamination between tests. When our tests start running in parallel, we don't want different tests to start firing commands to the same browser window. Each instance of `WebDriver` is now safely locked away in its own thread.

Since we are using this factory class to start up all our browser instances, we need to make sure that we close them down as well. To do this, we have created a method with an @AfterMethod annotation that will destroy the driver after our test has run. This also has the added advantage of cleaning up if our test fails to reach the line where it would normally call driver.quit(), for example, if there was an error in the test that caused it to fail and finish early.

Note that our @AfterMethod and @BeforeSuite annotations have a parameter of alwaysRun = true set on them. This makes sure that these functions are always run. For example, with our @AfterMethod annotation this makes sure that, even if a test fails, we will call the driver.quit() method. This ensures that we shut down our driver instance which will in turn close the browser. This should reduce the chance of you having some open browser windows left over after your test run if some of your tests fail.

All that is left now is to clean up the code in our basicTest class and change its name to BasicIT. Why have we changed the name of the test? Well, we are going to use the maven-failsafe-plugin to run our tests in the integration-test phase. This plugin picks up files that end in IT by default. If we left the class with a name ending in TEST, it would be picked up by the maven-surefire-plugin. We don't want the maven-surefire-plugin to pick up our tests, that should really be used for unit tests, we want to use the maven-failsafe-plugin instead, so we will use this code:

```
package com.masteringselenium;

import org.openqa.selenium.By;
import org.openqa.selenium.WebDriver;
import org.openqa.selenium.WebElement;
import org.openqa.selenium.support.ui.ExpectedCondition;
import org.openqa.selenium.support.ui.WebDriverWait;
import org.testng.annotations.Test;

public class BasicIT extends DriverBase {

    private ExpectedCondition<Boolean> pageTitleStartsWith(final
    String searchString) {
        return driver -> driver.getTitle().toLowerCase()
        .startsWith(searchString.toLowerCase());
    }

    private void googleExampleThatSearchesFor(final String
    searchString) {

        WebDriver driver = DriverBase.getDriver();
```

```java
        driver.get("http://www.google.com");

        WebElement searchField = driver.findElement(By.name("q"));

        searchField.clear();
        searchField.sendKeys(searchString);

        System.out.println("Page title is: " + driver.getTitle());

        searchField.submit();

        WebDriverWait wait = new WebDriverWait(driver, 10, 100);
        wait.until(pageTitleStartsWith(searchString));

        System.out.println("Page title is: " + driver.getTitle());
    }

    @Test
    public void googleCheeseExample() {
        googleExampleThatSearchesFor("Cheese!");
    }

    @Test
    public void googleMilkExample() {
        googleExampleThatSearchesFor("Milk!");
    }
}
```

We have modified our basic test so that it extends DriverBase. Instead of instantiating a new FirefoxDriver in the test, we are calling DriverBase.getDriver() to get a valid WebDriver instance. Finally, we have removed the driver.quit() from our generic method as this is all done by our DriverBase class now.

If we spin up our test again using this code, you won't notice any difference.:

```
mvn clean verify -Dwebdriver.gecko.driver=<PATH_TO_GECKODRIVER_BINARY>
```

However, if you now specify some threads by running this code, you will see that, this time, two Firefox browsers open, both tests run in parallel, and then both browsers are closed again.:

```
mvn clean verify -Dthreads=2 -
Dwebdriver.gecko.driver=<PATH_TO_GECKODRIVER_BINARY>
```

If you want to be completely sure that each test is running in a separate thread, you can add the following to your `getDriver()` method in the `DriverFactory` class: `System.out.println("Current thread: " + Thread.currentThread().getId());`.

This will show the current thread ID so that you can see that the `FirefoxDriver` instances are running in different threads.

Only seeing one browser start up? In `maven-failsafe-plugin`, configuration defaults to searching for all files that end with `IT.java`. If you use filenames that start or end with `Test`, they will be picked up by the `maven-surefire` plugin, and the threading configuration will be ignored. Double-check to make sure that your `failsafe` configuration is correct.

As you may have noticed, with two very small tests such as the ones we are using in our example, you will not see a massive decrease in the time taken to run the complete suite. This is because most of the time is spent compiling the code and loading up browsers, but as you add more tests the decrease in time taken to run the tests becomes more and more apparent.

This is probably a good time to tweak your `BasicIT.java` and start adding some more tests that look for different search terms, play about with the number of threads, and see how many concurrent browsers you can get up and running at the same time. Make sure that you note down execution times to see what speed gains you are actually getting (they will also be useful later on in this chapter). There will come a point where you reach the limits of your computer's hardware, and adding more threads will actually slow things down rather than making them faster. Tuning your tests to your hardware environment is an important part of running your tests in multiple threads.

So, how can we speed things up even more? Well, starting up a web browser is a computationally intensive task, so we could choose to not close the browser after every test. This obviously has some side effects. You may not be at the usual entry page to your application, and you may have some session information that is not wanted.

If there is a risk of side effects, why are we contemplating it? The reason for doing this is, quite simply, speed. Let's imagine we have a suite of fifty tests. If you are spending 10 seconds loading up and shutting down a browser for each test that you run, reusing browsers will dramatically reduce the amount of time it takes. If we can only spend 10 seconds starting up and shutting down a browser for all fifty tests, we have shaved eight minutes and 10 seconds off our total test time.

Let's try it and see how it works for us. First, we will try and deal with our session problem. `WebDriver` has a command that will allow you to clear out your cookies, so we will trigger this after every test. We will then add a new `@AfterSuite` annotation to close the browser once all of the tests have finished. Take a look at the following code:

```java
package com.masteringselenium;

import com.masteringselenium.config.DriverFactory;
import org.openqa.selenium.remote.RemoteWebDriver;
import org.testng.annotations.AfterMethod;
import org.testng.annotations.AfterSuite;
import org.testng.annotations.BeforeSuite;

import java.util.ArrayList;
import java.util.Collections;
import java.util.List;

public class DriverBase {

    private static List<DriverFactory> webDriverThreadPool =
    Collections.synchronizedList(new ArrayList<DriverFactory>());
    private static ThreadLocal<DriverFactory> driverThread;

    @BeforeSuite(alwaysRun = true)
    public static void instantiateDriverObject() {
        driverThread = new ThreadLocal<DriverFactory>() {
            @Override
            protected DriverFactory initialValue() {
                DriverFactory webDriverThread = new DriverFactory();
                webDriverThreadPool.add(webDriverThread);
                return webDriverThread;
            }
        };
    }

    public static RemoteWebDriver getDriver() {
        return driverThread.get().getDriver();
    }
```

```
@AfterMethod(alwaysRun = true)
public static void clearCookies() {
    try {
        getDriver().manage().deleteAllCookies();
    } catch (Exception ex) {
        System.err.println("Unable to delete cookies: " + ex);
    }
}

@AfterSuite(alwaysRun = true)
public static void closeDriverObjects() {
    for (DriverFactory webDriverThread : webDriverThreadPool) {
        webDriverThread.quitDriver();
    }
}
}
```

The first addition to our code is a synchronized list where we can store all our instances of `WebDriverThread`. We have then modified our `initialValue()` method to add each instance of `WebDriverThread` that we create to this new synchronized list. We have done this to enable us to keep track of our threads.

Next, we have renamed our @AfterSuite method to ensure that the method names stay as descriptive as possible. It is now called `closeDriverObjects()`. This method does not just close down the instance of `WebDriver` that we are using as it did previously. Instead, it iterates through our `webDriverThreadPool` list, closing every threaded instance that we are keeping track of.

We don't actually know how many threads we are going to have run since this will be controlled by Maven. This is not an issue though, as this code has been written to make sure that we don't have to know. What we do know is that when our tests are finished, each `WebDriver` instance will be closed down cleanly and without errors, all thanks to the use of the `webDriverThreadPool` list.

Finally, we have added @AfterMethod called `clearCookies()` that will clear down the browser's cookies after each test. This should reset the browser to a neutral state without closing it so that we can start another test safely.

Have a go at tweaking your `BasicIT.java` again by adding some more tests that look for different search terms. Based on your previous experimentation, you will probably have a rough idea of what the sweet spot for your hardware is. Time how long it takes to execute your tests again when you only close all the browsers down when all the tests have finished executing; how much time did you shave off your execution time?

There are no silver bullets

As with everything, keeping your browser windows open while you run all of your tests will not work in every instance.

Sometimes, you may have a site that sets server-side cookies that Selenium is unaware of. In this case, clearing out your cookies may have no effect and you may find that closing down the browser is the only way to ensure a clean environment for each test.

If you use `InternetExplorerDriver`, you will probably find that when you use slightly older versions of Internet Explorer (for example, Internet Explorer 8 and Internet Explorer 9), your tests will get slower and slower until they grind to a halt. Unfortunately, older versions of IE are not perfect and they do have some memory leak issues.

Using `InternetExplorerDriver` does exacerbate these issues because it is really stressing the browser. As a result, it does get a lot of unfair press. It's an excellent bit of code that deals with an awful lot of crap that gets thrown at it.

This is not to say that you can't use this method; you may not see any issues with the application that you are testing. You can of course use a mix of strategies; you can have multiple phases of testing. You can put tests that are able to reuse the browser in the first phase. You can then put tests that need a browser restart in your second phase.

Removing the browser shutdown and startup time after each test really does make a massive difference to the speed of your test runs. From personal experience, I would suggest that you should always try to keep the browser open whenever realistically possible to keep your test times down.

At the end of the day, the only way to be sure if it will work for you is experimentation and hard data. Just remember to do that investigation first. Once you are done, you should then tailor your thread usage to each browser/machine combination or, you should set a baseline that works with everything in your environment.

Multiple browser support

So far, we have parallelized our tests so that we can run multiple browser instances at the same time. However, we are still using only one type of driver, the good old `FirefoxDriver`. I mentioned problems with Internet Explorer in the previous section, but right now we have no obvious way to run our tests using Internet Explorer. Let's have a look at how we can fix this.

To start with, we will need to create a new Maven property called `browser` and a new configuration setting inside our Failsafe Plugin configuration called `systemPropertyVariables`. This is pretty much what is says on the tin; everything defined inside `systemPropertyValues` will become a system property that is available to your Selenium tests. We are going to use a Maven variable to reference a Maven property so that we can dynamically change this value on the command line.

The following code contains the changes you need to make to your POM:

```
<properties>
    <project.build.sourceEncoding>UTF-
    8</project.build.sourceEncoding>
    <project.reporting.outputEncoding>UTF-
    8</project.reporting.outputEncoding>
    <java.version>1.8</java.version>
    <!-- Dependency versions -->
    <selenium.version>3.12.0</selenium.version>
    <testng.version>6.14.3</testng.version>
    <!-- Plugin versions -->
    <maven-compiler-plugin.version>3.7.0
    </maven-compiler-plugin.version>
    <maven-failsafe-plugin.version>2.21.0
    </maven-failsafe-plugin.version>
    <!-- Configurable variables -->
    <threads>1</threads>
    <browser>firefox</browser>
</properties>

<build>
    <plugins>
        <plugin>
            <groupId>org.apache.maven.plugins</groupId>
            <artifactId>maven-compiler-plugin</artifactId>
            <configuration>
                <source>${java.version}</source>
                <target>${java.version}</target>
            </configuration>
```

```
            <version>${maven-compiler-plugin.version}</version>
        </plugin>
        <plugin>
            <groupId>org.apache.maven.plugins</groupId>
            <artifactId>maven-failsafe-plugin</artifactId>
            <version>${maven-failsafe-plugin.version}</version>
            <configuration>
                <parallel>methods</parallel>
                <threadCount>${threads}</threadCount>
                <systemPropertyVariables>
                    <browser>${browser}</browser>
                </systemPropertyVariables>
            </configuration>
            <executions>
                <execution>
                    <goals>
                        <goal>integration-test</goal>
                        <goal>verify</goal>
                    </goals>
                </execution>
            </executions>
        </plugin>
    </plugins>
</build>
```

We now need to create a package where we are going to store our driver configuration code. Into this package, we are going to add a new interface and a new enum. We are also going to move our `DriverFactory` class into this package to keep things nice and clean. Take a look at the following screenshot:

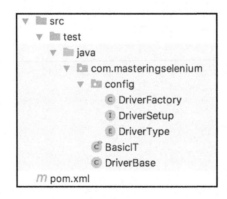

`DriverSetup` is a very simple interface that the `DriverType` class will implement, as shown in the following code:

```
package com.masteringselenium.config;

import org.openqa.selenium.remote.DesiredCapabilities;
import org.openqa.selenium.remote.RemoteWebDriver;

public interface DriverSetup {
    RemoteWebDriver getWebDriverObject(DesiredCapabilities capabilities);
}
```

`DriverType` is where all the work is done, as shown in the following code:

```
package com.masteringselenium.config;

import org.openqa.selenium.chrome.ChromeDriver;
import org.openqa.selenium.chrome.ChromeOptions;
import org.openqa.selenium.edge.EdgeDriver;
import org.openqa.selenium.edge.EdgeOptions;
import org.openqa.selenium.firefox.FirefoxDriver;
import org.openqa.selenium.firefox.FirefoxOptions;
import org.openqa.selenium.ie.InternetExplorerDriver;
import org.openqa.selenium.ie.InternetExplorerOptions;
import org.openqa.selenium.opera.OperaDriver;
import org.openqa.selenium.opera.OperaOptions;
import org.openqa.selenium.remote.CapabilityType;
import org.openqa.selenium.remote.DesiredCapabilities;
import org.openqa.selenium.remote.RemoteWebDriver;
import org.openqa.selenium.safari.SafariDriver;
import org.openqa.selenium.safari.SafariOptions;

import java.util.HashMap;

public enum DriverType implements DriverSetup {


    FIREFOX {
        public RemoteWebDriver
        getWebDriverObject(DesiredCapabilities
        capabilities) {
            FirefoxOptions options = new FirefoxOptions();
            options.merge(capabilities);

            return new FirefoxDriver(options);
        }
    },
```

```
CHROME {
    public RemoteWebDriver
    getWebDriverObject(DesiredCapabilities
    capabilities) {
        HashMap<String, Object> chromePreferences = new
        HashMap<>
        ();
        chromePreferences.put("profile.password_manager_enabled"
        ,false);

        ChromeOptions options = new ChromeOptions();
        options.merge(capabilities);
        options.addArguments("--no-default-browser-check");
        options.setExperimentalOption("prefs",
        chromePreferences);

        return new ChromeDriver(options);
    }
},
IE {
    public RemoteWebDriver
    getWebDriverObject(DesiredCapabilities
    capabilities) {
        InternetExplorerOptions options = new
        InternetExplorerOptions();
        options.merge(capabilities);
        options.setCapability(CapabilityType.ForSeleniumServer.
        ENSURING_CLEAN_SESSION, true);
        options.setCapability(InternetExplorerDriver.
        ENABLE_PERSISTENT_HOVERING, true);
        options.setCapability(InternetExplorerDriver.
        REQUIRE_WINDOW_FOCUS, true);

        return new InternetExplorerDriver(options);
    }
},
EDGE {
    public RemoteWebDriver
    getWebDriverObject(DesiredCapabilities
    capabilities) {
        EdgeOptions options = new EdgeOptions();
        options.merge(capabilities);

        return new EdgeDriver(options);
    }
},
SAFARI {
    public RemoteWebDriver
```

```
            getWebDriverObject(DesiredCapabilities
            capabilities) {
                SafariOptions options = new SafariOptions();
                options.merge(capabilities);

                return new SafariDriver(options);
            }
        },
        OPERA {
            public RemoteWebDriver
            getWebDriverObject(DesiredCapabilities
            capabilities) {
                OperaOptions options = new OperaOptions();
                options.merge(capabilities);

                return new OperaDriver(options);
            }
        }
    }
}
```

As you can see, our basic enum allows us to choose one of the default browsers supported by Selenium. Each enum entry implements the `getWebDriverObject()` method. This allows us to pass in a `DesiredCapabilities` object that we then merge into an `Options` object of the relevant driver type. This is then used to instantiate the `WebDriver` object and return it.

> Instantiating a `<DriverType>Driver` object with a `DeisredCapabilities` object is now deprecated. The new way of doing things is to use a `<DriverType>Options` object. `DesiredCapabilities` is still used in various places right now (for example, if you are instantiating a `RemoteWebDriver` object to connect to a Selenium-Grid, it's still supported), so it hasn't been fully removed.

Let's have a look at the default options that we have set for each driver to help things run smoothly:

- **Chrome**: We have a couple of options here to try and keep things running smoothly. Chrome has various command-line switches that can be used when starting Chrome up with `ChromeDriver`. When we load up Chrome to run our tests, we don't want it asking us whether it can be made the default browser every time it starts, so we have disabled that check. We have also turned off the password manager so that it does not ask if you would like to save your login details every time you have a test that performs a login action.

- **Internet Explorer**: `InternetExplorerDriver` has a lot of challenges; it attempts to work with many different versions of Internet Explorer and generally does a very good job. These options are used to try to ensure that sessions are properly cleaned out when reloading the browser (IE8 is particularly bad at clearing its cache), and then trying to fix some issues with hovering. If you have ever tested an application that needs you to hover over an element to trigger some sort of popup, you have probably seen the popup flickering lots, and had intermittent failures when trying to interact with it. Setting `ENABLE_PERSISTENT_HOVERING` and `requireWindowFocus` should work around these issues.
- **Others**: The other drivers are relatively new (by comparison), and I haven't really come across any problems with the default set of options, so these are just placeholders that return a default options object.

You don't need to use any of the preceding desired capabilities, but I have found them to be useful in the past. If you don't want to use them, just remove the bits you aren't interested in and set each `getWebDriverObject()` method up like the `FirefoxDriver` one. Remember, this is just a starting point for your test framework. You can add in any specific options that you find useful in your tests. This is going to be the place that instantiates a driver object so it's the best place to do it.

Now that everything is in place, we need to rewrite our `DriverFactory` method. Take a look at the following code:

```
package com.masteringselenium.config;

import org.openqa.selenium.remote.DesiredCapabilities;
import org.openqa.selenium.remote.RemoteWebDriver;

import static com.masteringselenium.config.DriverType.FIREFOX;
import static com.masteringselenium.config.DriverType.valueOf;

public class DriverFactory {

    private RemoteWebDriver webDriver;
    private DriverType selectedDriverType;

    private final String operatingSystem =
    System.getProperty("os.name").toUpperCase();
    private final String systemArchitecture =
    System.getProperty("os.arch");

    public DriverFactory() {
        DriverType driverType = FIREFOX;
        String browser = System.getProperty("browser",
```

```
        driverType.toString()).toUpperCase();
        try {
            driverType = valueOf(browser);
        } catch (IllegalArgumentException ignored) {
            System.err.println("Unknown driver specified,
          defaulting to '" + driverType + "'...");
        } catch (NullPointerException ignored) {
            System.err.println("No driver specified,
            defaulting to '" + driverType + "'...");
        }
        selectedDriverType = driverType;
    }

    public RemoteWebDriver getDriver() {
        if (null == webDriver) {
            instantiateWebDriver(selectedDriverType);
        }

        return webDriver;
    }

    public void quitDriver() {
        if (null != webDriver) {
            webDriver.quit();
            webDriver = null;
        }
    }

    private void instantiateWebDriver(DriverType driverType) {
        System.out.println(" ");
        System.out.println("Local Operating System: " +
        operatingSystem);
        System.out.println("Local Architecture: " +
        systemArchitecture);
        System.out.println("Selected Browser: " +
        selectedDriverType);
        System.out.println(" ");
        DesiredCapabilities desiredCapabilities = new
        DesiredCapabilities();
        webDriver =
        driverType.getWebDriverObject(desiredCapabilities);
    }
}
```

There is quite a lot going on here. First, we have added a new variable called `selectedDriverType`. We are going to use this to store the type of driver that we want to use to run tests. We have then added a constructor that will determine what `selectedDriverType` should be when we instantiate the class. The constructor looks for a system property called `browser` to work out what sort of `DriverType` is desired. There is some error handling that will make sure that if we can't identify the requested driver type we always fall back to a default, in this case `FirefoxDriver`. You can remove this error handling if you would prefer to error every time an invalid driver string is passed in.

We have then added a new method called `instantiateWebDriver()`, which is very similar to the code that was previously inside `getDriver()`. The only real difference is that we can now pass a `DriverType` object to specify which sort of `WebDriver` object we want. We also now create a `DesiredCapabilities` object inside this new method because that needs to be passed into the `getWebDriverObject()` method.

Finally, the `getDriver()` method has been tweaked to call the new `instantiateDriver()` method. One other thing that is important to note is that we are no longer passing around a `WebDriver` object; we are instead passing around a `RemoteWebDriver` object. This is because all the drivers now extend `RemoteWebDriver` by default.

Let's try it out. First of all, let's check that everything still works like it used to by using the following code:

```
mvn clean verify -Dthreads=2 -
Dwebdriver.gecko.driver=<PATH_TO_GECKODRIVER_BINARY>
```

This time, you should have seen no difference to the last time you ran it. Let's check the error handling next:

```
mvn clean verify -Dthreads=2 -Dbrowser=iJustMadeThisUp -
Dwebdriver.gecko.driver=<PATH_TO_GECKODRIVER_BINARY>
```

Again, it should have looked exactly the same as the previous run. We couldn't find an enum entry called `IJUSTMADETHISUP`, so we defaulted to the `FirefoxDriver`.

Finally, let's try a new browser:

```
mvn clean verify -Dthreads=2 -Dbrowser=chrome
```

You have probably had mixed success with this one; you will see that it tried to start up `ChromeDriver`, but if you don't have the Chrome Driver executable installed on your system that is in your default `$PATH`, it most likely threw an error saying that it couldn't find the Chrome Driver executable.

You can fix this by downloading the Chrome Driver binary and then providing the path to the binary using `-Dwebdriver.chrome.driver=<PATH_TO_CHROMEDRIVER_BINARY>`, as we did previously with geckodriver. This isn't really making our tests easy to run out of the box for developers, though. It looks as if we have more work to do.

Downloading WebDriver binaries automatically

I came across this problem a few years ago, and at the time there wasn't an easy way to get hold of the binaries using Maven. I didn't find an elegant solution to this problem, so I did what anybody who is into open source software would do: I wrote a plugin to do it for me.

This plugin allows you to specify a series of driver binaries to automatically download and remove the manual setup steps. It also means that you can enforce the version of driver binaries that are used, which removes lots of intermittent issues caused by people using different versions of the binaries that can behave differently on different machines.

We are now going to enhance our project to use this plugin; the new project structure will look like this:

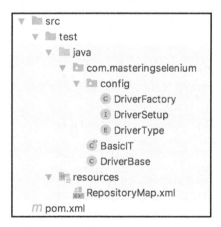

Let's start by tweaking our POM; we will use the following code to create a new property that we will call `overwrite.binaries` and a new property to set the version of the plugin:

```
<properties>
    <project.build.sourceEncoding>UTF-
    8</project.build.sourceEncoding>
    <project.reporting.outputEncoding>UTF-
    8</project.reporting.outputEncoding>
    <java.version>1.8</java.version>
    <!-- Dependency versions -->
    <selenium.version>3.12.0</selenium.version>
    <testng.version>6.14.3</testng.version>
    <!-- Plugin versions -->
    <driver-binary-downloader-maven-plugin.version>1.0.17
    </driver-binary-downloader-maven-plugin.version>
    <maven-compiler-plugin.version>3.7.0
    </maven-compiler-plugin.version>
    <maven-failsafe-plugin.version>2.21.0
    </maven-failsafe-plugin.version>
    <!-- Configurable variables -->
    <threads>1</threads>
    <browser>firefox</browser>
    <overwrite.binaries>false</overwrite.binaries>
</properties>
```

We then need to add the `driver-binary-downloader` plugin by using the following code:

```
<plugin>
    <groupId>com.lazerycode.selenium</groupId>
    <artifactId>driver-binary-downloader-maven-plugin</artifactId>
    <version>${driver-binary-downloader-maven-plugin.version}
    </version>
    <configuration>
        <rootStandaloneServerDirectory>${project.basedir}
        /src/test/resources/selenium_standalone_binaries
      </rootStandaloneServerDirectory>
        <downloadedZipFileDirectory>${project.basedir}
        /src/test/resources/selenium_standalone_zips
        </downloadedZipFileDirectory>
        <customRepositoryMap>${project.basedir}
        /src/test/resources/RepositoryMap.xml
        </customRepositoryMap>
        <overwriteFilesThatExist>${overwrite.binaries}
        </overwriteFilesThatExist>
    </configuration>
    <executions>
```

```
    <execution>
        <goals>
            <goal>selenium</goal>
        </goals>
    </execution>
</executions>
</plugin>
```

Finally, we need to add some new system properties to our `maven-failsafe-plugin` configuration by using the following code:

```
<plugin>
    <groupId>org.apache.maven.plugins</groupId>
    <artifactId>maven-failsafe-plugin</artifactId>
    <version>${maven-failsafe-plugin.version}</version>
    <configuration>
        <parallel>methods</parallel>
        <threadCount>${threads}</threadCount>
        <systemPropertyVariables>
            <browser>${browser}</browser>
            <!--Set properties passed in by the driver binary
            downloader-->
            <webdriver.chrome.driver>${webdriver.chrome.driver}
            </webdriver.chrome.driver>
            <webdriver.ie.driver>${webdriver.ie.driver}
             </webdriver.ie.driver>
            <webdriver.opera.driver>${webdriver.opera.driver}
            </webdriver.opera.driver>
            <webdriver.gecko.driver>${webdriver.gecko.driver}
            </webdriver.gecko.driver>
            <webdriver.edge.driver>${webdriver.edge.driver}
            </webdriver.edge.driver>
        </systemPropertyVariables>
    </configuration>
    <executions>
        <execution>
            <goals>
                <goal>integration-test</goal>
                <goal>verify</goal>
            </goals>
        </execution>
    </executions>
</plugin>
```

The plugin runs in the TEST_COMPILE phase by default. The order it is placed in the POM should not matter, as there shouldn't be any tests actually running in this phase. The new overwite.binaries property that we have added allows us to set the overwriteFilesThatExist configuration setting of the driver-binary-downloader-maven-plugin. By default, it will not overwrite files that already exist. This gives us an option to force the plugin to overwrite existing files if we want to download a new binary version or just refresh our existing binaries.

We have two more configuration settings that are just specifying file paths. The downloadedZipFileDirectory setting is used to specify the file path that will be used to download the binary ZIP files. The rootStandaloneServerDirectory setting is the file path where we extract the driver binaries.

Next, we will use customRepositoryMap to point at a customRepositoryMap.xml. This customRepositoryMap.xml is where download locations for all the binaries we want to download are stored.

Finally, we have added some system properties variables to maven-failsafe-plugin to expose the locations of the binaries when they have been downloaded. driver-binary-downloader-maven-plugin will set a Maven variable that will point to the location of the downloaded binaries. Even though it looks like the variables we are using to set our system properties don't exist, it will be fine.

This is where we have been slightly clever; we have set system properties that Selenium will use automatically to find the location of the driver binaries. This means that we don't need to add any additional code to make things work.

We now need to create RepositoryMap.xml to define the download locations for our binaries; we will probably also need to create the src/test/resources folder since we haven't used it before. The following code has a basic RepositoryMap.xml using the default download locations for the binaries:

```xml
<?xml version="1.0" encoding="utf-8" standalone="yes"?>
<root>
    <windows>
        <driver id="internetexplorer">
            <version id="3.9.0">
                <bitrate sixtyfourbit="true">
                    <filelocation>http://selenium-
                    release.storage.googleapis.com/3.9/
                    IEDriverServer_x64_3.9.0.zip</filelocation>
                    <hash>c9f885b6a339f3f0039d670a23f998868f539e65
                    </hash>
```

```xml
                <hashtype>sha1</hashtype>
            </bitrate>
            <bitrate thirtytwobit="true">
                <filelocation>http://selenium-
                release.storage.googleapis.com/3.9/
                IEDriverServer_Win32_3.9.0.zip</filelocation>
                <hash>dab42d7419599dd311d4fba424398fba2f20e883
                </hash>
                <hashtype>sha1</hashtype>
            </bitrate>
        </version>
    </driver>
    <driver id="edge">
        <version id="5.16299">
            <bitrate sixtyfourbit="true" thirtytwobit="true">
                <filelocation>https://download.microsoft.com/
                download/D/4/1/D417998A-58EE-4EFE-A7CC-
                39EF9E020768/MicrosoftWebDriver.exe
                </filelocation>
                <hash>60c4b6d859ee868ba5aa29c1e5bfa892358e3f96
                </hash>
                <hashtype>sha1</hashtype>
            </bitrate>
        </version>
    </driver>
    <driver id="googlechrome">
        <version id="2.37">
            <bitrate thirtytwobit="true" sixtyfourbit="true">
                <filelocation>
                https://chromedriver.storage.googleapis.com/
                2.37/chromedriver_win32.zip</filelocation>
                <hash>fe708aac4eeb919a4ce26cf4aa52a2dacc666a2f
                </hash>
                <hashtype>sha1</hashtype>
            </bitrate>
        </version>
    </driver>
    <driver id="operachromium">
        <version id="2.35">
            <bitrate sixtyfourbit="true">
                <filelocation>https://github.com/operasoftware
                /operachromiumdriver/releases/download/v.2.35
                /operadriver_win64.zip</filelocation>
                <hash>180a876f40dbc9734ebb81a3b6f2be35cadaf0cc
                </hash>
                <hashtype>sha1</hashtype>
            </bitrate>
            <bitrate thirtytwobit="true">
```

```xml
            <filelocation>https://github.com/operasoftware/
            operachromiumdriver/releases/download/v.2.35/
            operadriver_win32.zip</filelocation>
            <hash>55d43156716d7d1021733c2825e99896fea73815
            </hash>
            <hashtype>sha1</hashtype>
        </bitrate>
    </version>
</driver>
<driver id="marionette">
    <version id="0.20.0">
        <bitrate sixtyfourbit="true">
            <filelocation>
            https://github.com/mozilla/geckodriver/
            releases/download/v0.20.0/
            geckodriver-v0.20.0-win64.zip</filelocation>
            <hash>e96a24cf4147d6571449bdd279be65a5e773ba4c
            </hash>
            <hashtype>sha1</hashtype>
        </bitrate>
        <bitrate thirtytwobit="true">
            <filelocation>
            https://github.com/mozilla/geckodriver
            /releases/download/v0.20.0/
            geckodriver-v0.20.0-win32.zip</filelocation>
            <hash>9aa5bbdc68acc93c244a7ba5111a3858d8cbc41d
            </hash>
            <hashtype>sha1</hashtype>
        </bitrate>
    </version>
</driver>
</windows>
<linux>
    <driver id="googlechrome">
        <version id="2.37">
            <bitrate sixtyfourbit="true">
                <filelocation>https://chromedriver.storage.
                googleapis.com/2.37/
                chromedriver_linux64.zip</filelocation>
                <hash>b8515d09bb2d533ca3b85174c85cac1e062d04c6
                </hash>
                <hashtype>sha1</hashtype>
            </bitrate>
        </version>
    </driver>
    <driver id="operachromium">
        <version id="2.35">
            <bitrate sixtyfourbit="true">
```

```
                <filelocation>
                https://github.com/operasoftware/
                operachromiumdriver/releases/download/
                v.2.35/operadriver_linux64.zip</filelocation>
                <hash>
                f75845a7e37e4c1a58c61677a2d6766477a4ced2
                </hash>
                <hashtype>sha1</hashtype>
            </bitrate>
        </version>
    </driver>
    <driver id="marionette">
        <version id="0.20.0">
            <bitrate sixtyfourbit="true">
                <filelocation>
                https://github.com/mozilla/geckodriver/
                releases/download/v0.20.0/geckodriver-v0.20.0-
                linux64.tar.gz</filelocation>
                <hash>
                e23a6ae18bec896afe00e445e0152fba9ed92007
                </hash>
                <hashtype>sha1</hashtype>
            </bitrate>
            <bitrate thirtytwobit="true">
                <filelocation>
                https://github.com/mozilla/geckodriver/
                releases/download/v0.20.0/geckodriver-v0.20.0-
                linux32.tar.gz</filelocation>
                <hash>
                c80eb7a07ae3fe6eef2f52855007939c4b655a4c
                </hash>
                <hashtype>sha1</hashtype>
            </bitrate>
            <bitrate arm="true">
                <filelocation>
                https://github.com/mozilla/geckodriver/
                releases/download/v0.20.0/geckodriver-v0.20.0-
                arm7hf.tar.gz</filelocation>
                <hash>
                2776db97a330c38bb426034d414a01c7bf19cc94
                </hash>
                <hashtype>sha1</hashtype>
            </bitrate>
        </version>
    </driver>
</linux>
<osx>
    <driver id="googlechrome">
```

```
                <version id="2.37">
                    <bitrate sixtyfourbit="true">
                        <filelocation>
                        https://chromedriver.storage.googleapis.com/
                        2.37/chromedriver_mac64.zip</filelocation>
                        <hash>
                        714e7abb1a7aeea9a8997b64a356a44fb48f5ef4
                        </hash>
                        <hashtype>sha1</hashtype>
                    </bitrate>
                </version>
            </driver>
            <driver id="operachromium">
                <version id="2.35">
                    <bitrate sixtyfourbit="true">
                        <filelocation>
                        https://github.com/operasoftware/
                        operachromiumdriver/releases/download/v.2.35/
                        operadriver_mac64.zip</filelocation>
                        <hash>
                        66a88c856b55f6c89ff5d125760d920e0d4db6ff
                        </hash>
                        <hashtype>sha1</hashtype>
                    </bitrate>
                </version>
            </driver>
            <driver id="marionette">
                <version id="0.20.0">
                    <bitrate thirtytwobit="true" sixtyfourbit="true">
                        <filelocation>
                        https://github.com/mozilla/geckodriver/
                        releases/download/v0.20.0/geckodriver-v0.20.0-
                        macos.tar.gz</filelocation>
                        <hash>
                        87a63f8adc2767332f2eadb24dedff982ac4f902
                      </hash>
                        <hashtype>sha1</hashtype>
                    </bitrate>
                </version>
            </driver>
        </osx>
    </root>
```

This is a big file; it may be easier to copy and paste the latest revision in the driver-binary-downloader README.md on **GitHub:** https://github. com/Ardesco/selenium-standalone-server-plugin/blob/master/ README.md.

If you are on a corporate network that does not allow you to access the outside world, you can of course download the binaries and put them on a local file server. You can then update your RepositoryMap.xml to point at this local file server instead of the internet. This gives you a great deal of flexibility.

Right, let's run our project again to check that everything works; first of all use this code:

```
mvn clean verify -Dthreads=2
```

You will notice that everything worked as normal, despite the fact that we are no longer setting the webdriver.gecko.driver system property on the command line. Next, let's see whether we can now select chrome and have everything still just work by using the following code:

```
mvn clean verify -Dthreads=2 -Dbrowser=chrome
```

This time, you should see two Chrome browsers open up instead of Firefox ones. You may have noticed that the first time you ran this it downloaded a series of binaries, which may have slowed down the first run. This time around though, it had already downloaded them, so it just checked they were there and the test run completed a lot quicker. We no longer have to worry about setting any system properties because this is automatically being done by the plugin modifications we made in our POM file.

We can now give anybody access to our code, and when they check it and run it, things should just work.

Going headless

Going headless seems to be all the rage these days, so let's have a look at how we can add support a headless browser to our burgeoning framework.

It's actually a relatively simple change; first, we are going to use this code to modify our POM to add a <headless> property (we are going to set it to true because you are always going to want to start of running things in headless mode, right?):

```
<properties>
    <project.build.sourceEncoding>UTF-
```

```
        8</project.build.sourceEncoding>
        <project.reporting.outputEncoding>UTF-
        8</project.reporting.outputEncoding>
        <java.version>1.8</java.version>
        <!-- Dependency versions -->
        <selenium.version>3.12.0</selenium.version>
        <testng.version>6.14.3</testng.version>
        <!-- Plugin versions -->
        <driver-binary-downloader-maven-plugin.version>1.0.17
        </driver-binary-downloader-maven-plugin.version>
        <maven-compiler-plugin.version>3.7.0
        </maven-compiler-plugin.version>
        <maven-failsafe-plugin.version>2.21.0
        </maven-failsafe-plugin.version>
        <!-- Configurable variables -->
        <threads>1</threads>
        <browser>firefox</browser>
        <overwrite.binaries>false</overwrite.binaries>
        <headless>true</headless>
    </properties>
```

Then, we need to pass that in through `maven-failsafe-plugin`:

```
<plugin>
    <groupId>org.apache.maven.plugins</groupId>
    <artifactId>maven-failsafe-plugin</artifactId>
    <version>${maven-failsafe-plugin.version}</version>
    <configuration>
        <parallel>methods</parallel>
        <threadCount>${threads}</threadCount>
        <systemPropertyVariables>
            <browser>${browser}</browser>
            <headless>${headless}</headless>
            <!--Set properties passed in by the driver binary
            downloader-->
            <webdriver.chrome.driver>${webdriver.chrome.driver}
            </webdriver.chrome.driver>
            <webdriver.ie.driver>${webdriver.ie.driver}
            </webdriver.ie.driver>
            <webdriver.opera.driver>${webdriver.opera.driver}
            </webdriver.opera.driver>
            <webdriver.gecko.driver>${webdriver.gecko.driver}
            </webdriver.gecko.driver>
            <webdriver.edge.driver>${webdriver.edge.driver}
            </webdriver.edge.driver>
        </systemPropertyVariables>
    </configuration>
    <executions>
```

```
            <execution>
                <goals>
                    <goal>integration-test</goal>
                    <goal>verify</goal>
                </goals>
            </execution>
        </executions>
    </plugin>
```

Finally, we will use this code to update our `DriverType` enum to read in the new headless system property and apply it to the `CHROME` and `FIREFOX` entries:

```
package com.masteringselenium.config;

import org.openqa.selenium.chrome.ChromeDriver;
import org.openqa.selenium.chrome.ChromeOptions;
import org.openqa.selenium.edge.EdgeDriver;
import org.openqa.selenium.edge.EdgeOptions;
import org.openqa.selenium.firefox.FirefoxDriver;
import org.openqa.selenium.firefox.FirefoxOptions;
import org.openqa.selenium.ie.InternetExplorerDriver;
import org.openqa.selenium.ie.InternetExplorerOptions;
import org.openqa.selenium.opera.OperaDriver;
import org.openqa.selenium.opera.OperaOptions;
import org.openqa.selenium.remote.CapabilityType;
import org.openqa.selenium.remote.DesiredCapabilities;
import org.openqa.selenium.remote.RemoteWebDriver;
import org.openqa.selenium.safari.SafariDriver;
import org.openqa.selenium.safari.SafariOptions;

import java.util.HashMap;

public enum DriverType implements DriverSetup {


    FIREFOX {
        public RemoteWebDriver getWebDriverObject
        (DesiredCapabilities capabilities) {
            FirefoxOptions options = new FirefoxOptions();
            options.merge(capabilities);
            options.setHeadless(HEADLESS);

            return new FirefoxDriver(options);
        }
    },
    CHROME {
        public RemoteWebDriver getWebDriverObject
```

```
        (DesiredCapabilities capabilities) {
            HashMap<String, Object> chromePreferences =
            new HashMap<>();
            chromePreferences.put("profile.password_manager_enabled"
            , false);

            ChromeOptions options = new ChromeOptions();
            options.merge(capabilities);
            options.setHeadless(HEADLESS);
            options.addArguments("--no-default-browser-check");
            options.setExperimentalOption("prefs",
            chromePreferences);

            return new ChromeDriver(options);
        }
    },
    IE {
        public RemoteWebDriver getWebDriverObject
        (DesiredCapabilities capabilities) {
            InternetExplorerOptions options = new
            InternetExplorerOptions();
            options.merge(capabilities);
            options.setCapability(CapabilityType.ForSeleniumServer.
            ENSURING_CLEAN_SESSION, true);
            options.setCapability(InternetExplorerDriver.
            ENABLE_PERSISTENT_HOVERING, true);
            options.setCapability(InternetExplorerDriver.
            REQUIRE_WINDOW_FOCUS, true);

            return new InternetExplorerDriver(options);
        }
    },
    EDGE {
        public RemoteWebDriver
        getWebDriverObject(DesiredCapabilities
        capabilities) {
            EdgeOptions options = new EdgeOptions();
            options.merge(capabilities);

            return new EdgeDriver(options);
        }
    },
    SAFARI {
        public RemoteWebDriver getWebDriverObject
        (DesiredCapabilities capabilities) {
            SafariOptions options = new SafariOptions();
            options.merge(capabilities);
```

```
            return new SafariDriver(options);
        }
    },
    OPERA {
        public RemoteWebDriver getWebDriverObject
        (DesiredCapabilities capabilities) {
            OperaOptions options = new OperaOptions();
            options.merge(capabilities);

            return new OperaDriver(options);
        }
    };

    public final static boolean HEADLESS =
    Boolean.getBoolean("headless");
}
```

We can now run our project again exactly the same way as before:

```
mvn clean verify -Dthreads=2
```

You will see the test start up again, but this time you won't see a browser window pop up. Everything should work exactly as before and the tests should pass as expected. If you want to see the browser window pop up again, you can just set headless to `false`:

```
mvn clean verify -Dthreads=2 -Dheadless=false
```

What happened to GhostDriver?

You may have noticed that I haven't mentioned GhostDriver or PhantomJS at all in the headless section. That's because PhatomJS is no longer under active development and GhostDriver no longer has a core maintainer. PhantomJS is still available and it's possible to get GhostDriver up and running. However, you are then testing with these issues:

- An out-of-date rendering engine (an old version of QTWebkit)
- A JavaScript engine that is not used in any of the major browsers
- A tool that is not completely thread safe

With the release of headless modes from ChromeDriver and FirefoxDriver, it just doesn't make sense to keep using PhantomJS. It was great in its heyday, but it just not a useful tool to use with Selenium any more.

Summary

This chapter should have taught you about how to set up a basic project using Maven to download your dependencies, configure your classpath, and build your code. You will be able to run your tests in parallel with multiple instances of the same browser in TestNG, as well as automatically downloading driver binaries using a Maven plugin to make your test code very portable. You should know how to determine the correct number of threads to use in your tests, as well as overriding this if required. Finally you will have learned how to run Firefox and Chrome in headless mode so that you can run your tests without interruption locally, and without a desktop environment on CI servers.

In the next chapter, we are going to have a look at how to cope when things go wrong. We will also examine how we can keep track of things, now that we have lots of tests all running at the same time.

Producing the Right Feedback When Failing

2

In this chapter, we are going to have a look at how you can make life easier for yourself when tests start failing. We will do the following:

- Discuss where our tests should live and examine why
- Have a look at test reliability
- Have a look at ways we can force our tests to be run regularly
- Talk about continuous integration and continuous delivery
- Extend the project we started in the previous chapter so that it can run against a Selenium-Grid
- Have a look at ways to diagnose problems with our tests

Location, location, location

Many companies still have discrete test and development teams. This is obviously not an ideal situation, as the test team is usually not completely aware of what the development team is building. This also provides us with additional challenges if the test team is tasked with writing automated functional tests using the web frontend.

The usual problem is that the test team is behind the development team, and how far behind depends upon how frequent development releases are. The thing is, it doesn't really matter how far behind the development team you are. If you are behind the team, you will always be playing catch up. When you are playing catch up, you are constantly updating your scripts to make them work with a new release of software.

Some people may call "fixing their scripts to work with new functionality" refactoring; they are wrong! *Refactoring* is rewriting your code to make it cleaner and more efficient. The actual code, or, in our case test script, functionality does not change. If you are changing the way your code works, you are not refactoring.

While constantly updating your scripts is not necessarily a bad thing, having your tests break every time when there is a new release of code is a bad thing. If your tests continually stop working for no good reason, people are going to stop trusting them. When they see a failing build, they will assume that it's another problem with the tests, and not an issue with the web application you are testing.

We need to find a way to stop our tests from failing all of the time for no good reason. Let's start off with something easy that shouldn't be too controversial; let's make sure that the test code always lives in the same code repository as the application code.

How does this help?

Well, if the test code lives in the same repository as the application code, it is accessible to all the developers. In the previous chapter, we had a look at how we could make it really easy for developers to just check our tests and run them. If we make sure that our test code is in the same code base as the application code, we have also ensured that any developers who are working on the application will automatically have a copy of our tests. This means that all you have to do now is give your developers a command to run and then they can run the tests themselves against their local copy of code and see if any break.

Another advantage of having your test code in the same repository as the application code is that developers have full access to it. They can see how things work, and they can change the tests as they change the functionality of the application. The ideal scenario is that every change made to the system by developers also results in a change to the tests to keep them in sync. This way, the tests don't start failing for no real reason when the next application release happens and your tests become something more than an automated regression check; they become living documentation. This living documentation is owned by the whole team, can be updated by the whole team, and always describes how the current revision of the application works.

Tests are living documentation

What do I mean by **living documentation**? As the application is built, automated tests are continually being written to ensure that specific criteria are met. These tests come in many different shapes and sizes, ranging from unit tests to integration tests, and leading up to end-to-end functional tests and beyond. All of these tests describe, in some way, how the application works. You have to admit that this sounds just like documentation.

This documentation may not be perfect, but that doesn't stop it from being documentation. Think of an application that has some unit tests, and maybe one badly written end-to-end test. I would equate that to the sort of documentation that you would get with a cheap electrical product, from somewhere such as China. It comes with a manual, which will undoubtedly have a small badly written English bit that doesn't really tell you very much, most likely because it was originally manufactured for the domestic market and never intended to be sent abroad. It will also have lots of documentation in a language that you probably don't understand, in this case Chinese, which is very useful for somebody who speaks that language. This doesn't mean that the product is bad; it's just hard to work out what to do with it. Most of the time, you can work out what to do without the manual. If it's really complex, you will probably go and find somebody who either speaks Chinese, or knows how the product works, and get them to explain it to you.

When I talk about tests as documentation, I usually think of different test phases as being documentation for different people. Let's take the unit tests; these are highly technical in nature and explain how tiny bits of the system work in extreme detail. If you compared this to the manual of an electrical product, these would probably be the tech specs in the appendix that provide lots of in-depth information that most consumers don't care about. Integration tests would probably be the part of the manual that explains how to connect your electrical appliance to other electrical appliances. This is very useful if you are going to connect to another electrical appliance, but you probably don't care about it that much if you aren't. Lastly, the functional end-to-end tests are the bit of the documentation that actually tells you how to use the appliance. This is the bit of the manual that will be read the most by the average user (they probably don't care about the technical nitty gritty).

I think one of the most important things that you can do when writing automated tests is make sure that they are good documentation. This means make sure that you describe how all the parts of the application you are testing works. Or, to put it another way, have a high level of test coverage. The hardest part, though, is making the tests understandable for people who are not technical. This is where **domain-specific language (DSL)** comes in, where you can hide the inner workings of the tests behind human-readable language. Good tests are like good documentation; if they are really good, they will use plain English and describe things so well that the person reading them will not need to go anywhere else to ask for help; bad tests, on the other hand, are the sort of instructions that look as though they have been translated from another language—they almost make sense.

So why is it living documentation, rather than just normal documentation? Well, it's living because every time the application you are testing changes, the automated tests change as well. They evolve with the product and continue to explain how it works in its current state. If our build is passing, our documentation is describing how the system currently works.

Do not think of automated tests as regression tests, which are there to detect changes in behavior. Think of them as living documentation that describes how the product works. If somebody comes and asks you how something works, you should ideally be able to show them a test that can answer their question. If you can't, you probably have some missing documentation.

So where does regression testing come into this? Well, it doesn't. We don't need a regression-testing phase. Our test documentation tells us how the product works. When the functionality of our product changes, the tests are updated to tell us how the new functionality works. Our existing documentation for the old functionality doesn't change unless the functionality changes.

Our test documentation covers regression and new functionality.

Reliability

When it comes to automation, the reliability of tests is the key. If your tests are not reliable, they will not be trusted, which can have far-reaching consequences. I'm sure you have all worked in environments where test reliability has been hard for one of many reasons; let's have a look at a couple of scenarios.

The test automation team that works in isolation

One of the more common reasons that tests are not reliable is having a dedicated test automation team that works in isolation from the team that develops the application. This should really be avoided if possible, as the test automation team is always playing catch up. The development team rolls out new features that the test automation teams have to automate, but they are never sure what is coming next. They usually find out that existing features have changed when their tests break. As well as fixing their tests, they need to work out what the new functionality is and whether this new functionality is behaving as expected.

Something that normally happens in situations like this is that the test manager realizes that they don't have enough time to do everything and they look for ways to reduce the workload. Here are some things that need to be considered:

- Do you fix the existing failing tests instead of automating new tests, and then write some manual regression scripts to cover the gap?
- Do you split your effort and spend some time fixing old tests, and some time writing new tests (never really getting either task completed)?
- Do you continue automating the new functionality and accept that some of your old tests will now be failing?

This is where you usually start to hear suggestions that it is time to lower the bar for the automated tests. "It should be fine as long as 95% of the automated tests pass; we know we have high coverage and those failing 5% are probably due to changes to the system that we haven't yet had the time to deal with." Everybody is happy at first; they continue to automate things and make sure that 95% of tests are always passing, but soon though the pass mark starts to dip below 95%. A couple of weeks later, a pragmatic decision is taken to lower the bar to 90%, then 85%, then 80%. Before you know it, tests are failing all over the place. You have no idea which failures are legitimate problems with the application, which ones are expected failures, and which ones are intermittent failures.

When tests go red, nobody really pays attention any more; they just talk about that magic 80% line; it's a high number, so we must have a decent product if that many tests are still passing, right? If things dip below that line, we massage a few failing tests and make them pass, usually the low-hanging fruit because we don't have time to spend trying to tackle the really thorny issues.

I hate to break it to you, but if you are in this situation, your automation experiment has failed and nobody trusts your tests. Instead of looking at that 80% number, you need to look at the other side of the coin: 20% of the functionality of your site is not working as expected and you don't know why! You need to stop the developers from writing any new code and work out how to fix the massive mess that you are currently in. How did you get here? You didn't think test reliability mattered, and that mistake came back to bite you.

Oh, that test always flickers – don't worry about it

This scenario is one that can occur in both isolated automation teams and integrated teams where everybody works together. You have probably seen automated tests that are not totally reliable: you know, that one flickering test that occasionally fails for no obvious reason. Somebody once had a look at it and said that there was no reason for it to fail so it got ignored, and now whenever it fails again somebody says "Oh, it's that flickering test again—don't worry about it. It will be green again soon."

 A **flickering test** is one that intermittently fails for no obvious reason and then passes when you run it again. There are various phrases used to describe tests such as this; you may have heard of them described as **flaky tests**, **random failures**, **unstable tests**, or some other name unique to your company.

The thing is that we now have a problem: tests do not flicker for no reason. This test is desperately trying to tell you something and you are ignoring it. What is it trying to tell you? Well, you can't be sure until you have found out why it is flickering; it could be one of many things. Among the many possibilities, a few are the following:

- The test is not actually checking what you think it is checking
- The test may be badly written
- There may be an intermittent fault in the application that is under test (for example, there may be a race condition nobody has identified yet)
- Maybe you have some problems with a date/time implementation and it's only going red at specific times when the date implementation goes wrong (date/time implementations are something that are notoriously hard to get right and the cause of many bugs in many systems)
- There are network problems; is there a proxy getting in the way?

The point is that, while your test is flickering, we don't know what the problem is; but don't fool yourself—there is a problem. It's a problem that will, at some point, come back and bite you if you don't fix it.

Let's imagine for a moment that the software you are testing is something that buys and sells shares, and you are pushing new releases out daily because your company has to stay ahead of the game. You have a test that has been flickering for as long as you can remember. Somebody once had a look at it, said they couldn't find any problems with the code, and said that the test is just unreliable; this has been accepted and now everybody just does a quick manual check if it goes red. A new cut of code goes in and that test that keeps flickering goes red again. You are used to that test flickering and everything seems to work normally when you perform a quick manual test, so you ignore it. The release goes ahead, but there is a problem: suddenly your trading software starts selling when it should be buying, and buying when it should be selling. It isn't picked up instantly because the software has been through testing and must be good, so no problems are expected. An hour later all hell has broken loose; the software has sold all the wrong stock and bought a load of rubbish. In the space of an hour, the company has lost half its value and there is nothing that can be done to rectify the situation. There is an investigation and it's found that the flickering test wasn't actually flickering this time; it failed for a good reason, one that wasn't instantly obvious when performing a quick manual check. All eyes turn to you; it was you who validated the code that should never have been released and they need somebody to blame; if only that stupid test hadn't been flickering for as long as you can remember.

The preceding scenario is an extreme example, but hopefully you get the point: flickering tests are dangerous and something that should not be tolerated.

We ideally want to be in a state where every test failure means that there is an undocumented change to the system. What do we do about undocumented changes? Well, that depends; if we didn't mean to make the change, we revert it. If we did mean to make the change, we update the documentation (our automated tests) to support it.

Baking in reliability

How can we try to enforce reliability and make sure that these changes are picked up early?

We could ask our developers to run the tests before every push, but sometimes people forget. Maybe they didn't forget, but it's a small change and it doesn't seem worth going through a full test run for something so minor (have you ever heard somebody say, "It's only a CSS change...?"). Making sure that the tests are run, and pass before every push to the centralized source code repository, takes discipline.

What do we do if our team lacks discipline? What if we still keep getting failures that should have been easily caught, even after we have asked people to run the tests before they push code to the central repository? If nothing else works, we could have a discussion with the developers about enforcing this rule.

This is actually surprisingly easy; most **Source Code Management** (**SCM**) systems support hooks. These are actions that are automatically triggered when you use a specific SCM function. Let's have a look at how we can implement hooks in some of the most widely used SCM systems.

Git

First of all, we need to clone a project. Anything will do; you can create a brand new one on GitHub all by yourself if you want. It may be a good idea to place the code that we wrote in Chapter 1, *Creating a Fast Feedback Loop* in that repository.

Once we have cloned a project from GitHub, the next step is to go to the SCM root folder. Git creates a hidden folder called `.git` that holds all the information about your project that Git needs to do its job. We are going to go into this folder, and then into the `hooks` subfolder by using this code:

```
cd .git/hooks
```

Git has a series of predefined hook names. Whenever you perform a Git command, Git will have a look in the `hooks` folder to see whether there are any files that match any predefined hook names that would be triggered as a result of the command. If there are matches, Git will run them. We want to make sure that our project can be built, and all of our tests are run, before we push any code to Git. To make this happen, we are going to add a file called `pre-push`. When that file is added, we are going to populate it with the following code:

```
#!/usr/bin/env bash
mvn clean install
```

This hook will now be triggered every time we use the `git push` command.

 One thing to note about Git hooks is that they are individual for every user; they are not controlled by the repository you push to or pull from. If you want them automatically installed for developers who uses your code base, you need to think outside the box. You could, for example, write a script that copies them into the `.git/hooks` folder as part of your build.

We could have added a pre-commit hook, but we don't really care if the code doesn't work on the developer's local machine (they may be halfway through a big change and committing code to make sure they don't lose anything). What we do care about is that the code works when it is pushed to the central source code repository.

> If you are a Windows user, you may be looking at the preceding code and thinking that it looks very much like something that you would put on a *nix system. Don't worry—Git for windows installs Git bash, which it will use to interpret this script, so it will work on Windows as well.

Subversion

Subversion (SVN) hooks are a little bit more complicated; they will depend upon how your system is configured to a degree. The hooks are stored in your svn repository in a subfolder called hooks. As with Git, they need to have specific names (a full list of which is available in the SVN manual). For our purposes, we are only interested in the pre-commit hook so let's start off with a *nix-based environment. First of all, we need to create a file called pre-commit, and then we will populate it with this code:

```
#!/usr/bin/env bash
mvn clean verify
```

As you can see, it looks identical to the Git hook script, but there may be problems. SVN hooks are run against an empty environment, so if you are using an environment variable to make mvn a recognized command, things may not work. If there is a symlink in /usr/bin or /usr/local/bin/, you should be fine; if not, you will probably need to specify the absolute filepath location to the mvn command.

Now, we need to also make this hook work for people using Windows; it will be very similar, but this time the file needs to be called pre-commit.bat because SVN looks for different files in different operating systems:

```
mvn clean verify
```

The contents of the file are pretty similar to the *nix implementation; we just don't need to have a bash shebang. Windows suffers from the same empty environment problems, so, again, you will probably have to supply an absolute file path to your Maven install. Let's hope that everybody developing in Windows has installed Maven to the same place.

It is worth bearing in mind that hooks such as this are not infallible. If you have forgotten to commit some local changes on your machine, the tests may pass, but when you push the code to the central code repository some changes will be missing. If anybody else tries to run the latest revision of code at this point, they will probably get a build failure. As with all things, this is not a silver bullet, but it can certainly help.

We have now made sure that our tests run before the code is pushed to our central code repository so we should have caught the vast majority of errors, but things are still not perfect. It's possible that one of the developers made a code change that they forgot to commit. In this case, the tests would run on their local machine and pass, but an important file that makes this change work would be missing from source control. This is one of the causes of "works on my machine" problems.

It's also possible that all files have been committed and the tests pass, but the environment that is on the developer's machines is nothing like the production environment where the code will be deployed. This is the main cause of "works on my machine" problems.

What do we do to mitigate these risks and ensure that we quickly find out when things do go wrong, despite everybody doing their best to ensure everything works?

Continuous integration is key

Continuous integration is a way to try and mitigate the issues that we come across by only building and testing code on our development machines. Our continuous integration server will monitor our source code repository and then every time it detects a change, it will trigger a series of actions. The first action will be to build the code, running any tests that it can as it builds the code (usually unit tests), and then creating a deployable artifact. This artifact would then usually be deployed to a server that is a replica of the live environment. Once this code has been deployed to a server, the rest of our tests will be run against that server to ensure that everything is working as expected. If things do not work as expected, the build fails and the development team is notified so that they can fix the problems. It's important to note that we only build the artifact once; if we rebuild it multiple times, we would be testing artifacts that are potentially different at every step (maybe it was built with a different version of Java; maybe it had different properties applied to it, and so on).

With continuous integration, we are looking for a workflow such as this:

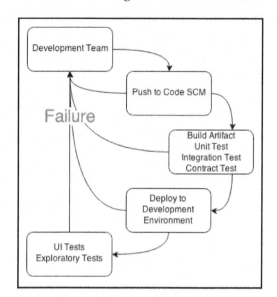

Most continuous integration systems also have big visible dashboards to let people know the status of the build at all times; if your screen ever goes red, people should stop what they are doing and fix the problem as soon as possible.

Let's have a look at how easily we can get our tests running on a continuous integration server. This is not going to be a fully-featured continuous integration setup, just enough for you to run the tests we have built so far.

The first thing we are going to do is configure a Maven profile. This will enable us to isolate our Selenium tests from the rest of the build if desired, so that we can turn them in a separate UI block of tests on our continuous integration server. This is a very simple change to our POM; we are simply going to wrap our `<build>` and `<dependencies>` blocks with a `profile` block. the code will look like this:

```
<profiles>
    <profile>
        <id>selenium</id>
        <activation>
            <activeByDefault>true</activeByDefault>
        </activation>
        <build>
            <plugins>
                <plugin>
                    <groupId>com.lazerycode.selenium</groupId>
```

```xml
        <artifactId>driver-binary-downloader-maven-
        plugin</artifactId>
        <version>${driver-binary-downloader-maven-
        plugin.version}</version>
        <configuration>
            <rootStandaloneServerDirectory>
            ${project.basedir}/src/test/
            resources/selenium_standalone_binaries
            </rootStandaloneServerDirectory>
            <downloadedZipFileDirectory>
            ${project.basedir}/src/test/
            resources/selenium_standalone_zips
            </downloadedZipFileDirectory>
            <customRepositoryMap>${project.basedir}
            /src/test/resources/RepositoryMap.xml
            </customRepositoryMap>
            <overwriteFilesThatExist>
            ${overwrite.binaries}
            </overwriteFilesThatExist>
        </configuration>
        <executions>
            <execution>
                <goals>
                    <goal>selenium</goal>
                </goals>
            </execution>
        </executions>
    </plugin>
    <plugin>
        <groupId>org.apache.maven.plugins</groupId>
        <artifactId>maven-failsafe-plugin</artifactId>
        <version>${maven-failsafe-plugin.version}
        </version>
        <configuration>
            <parallel>methods</parallel>
            <threadCount>${threads}</threadCount>
            <systemPropertyVariables>
                <browser>${browser}</browser>
                <headless>${headless}</headless>
                <!--Set properties passed in by the
                driver binary downloader-->
                <webdriver.chrome.driver>
                ${webdriver.chrome.driver}
                </webdriver.chrome.driver>
                <webdriver.ie.driver>
                ${webdriver.ie.driver}
                </webdriver.ie.driver>
                <webdriver.opera.driver>
```

```
                    ${webdriver.opera.driver}
                    </webdriver.opera.driver>
                    <webdriver.gecko.driver>
                    ${webdriver.gecko.driver}
                    </webdriver.gecko.driver>
                    <webdriver.edge.driver>
                    ${webdriver.edge.driver}
                    </webdriver.edge.driver>
                </systemPropertyVariables>
            </configuration>
            <executions>
                <execution>
                    <goals>
                        <goal>integration-test</goal>
                        <goal>verify</goal>
                    </goals>
                </execution>
            </executions>
        </plugin>
    </plugins>
</build>
    </profile>
</profiles>
```

As you can see, we have created a profile called `selenium`. This will give us the ability to toggle the execution of our Selenium tests as part of the build. If you specifically activate the `selenium` profile now, it will only execute your Selenium tests:

mvn clean verify -Pselenium

You can also specifically prevent Selenium tests from running with this:

mvn clean verify -P-selenium

You will also notice that we have added `<activeByDefault>true</activeByDefault>`; this will ensure that this profile is active if no profiles are specified on the command line, so you will find the following command:

mvn clean verify

The preceding command will run our Selenium tests as part of a normal build, and the SCM hooks that we set up previously still do their job.

Next, we are going to look at two popular continuous integration servers, **TeamCity** and **Jenkins.** TeamCity is popular in a lot of corporate environments, so it's useful to have a basic understanding of it. Jenkins is prolific; you will probably see a Jenkins install at some point in your career if you haven't already.

So, why are we going into such detail on this subject? What has it got to do with Selenium?

- First, I want to show you how easy it is to set up a Maven project on a CI server. It shows just how useful using a build/dependency management tool such as Maven is.
- Secondly, it is good to get some experience setting something up on a couple of CI servers; it's probably something you will be asked to do at some point.
- Finally, CI servers will have some limitations out of the box. We are going to have a look at how we can get around these problems with minimal effort.

Setting up TeamCity

TeamCity (`https://www.jetbrains.com/teamcity/`) is an enterprise-level continuous integration server. It supports a lot of technologies out of the box and is very reliable and capable. One of my favorite features is the ability to spin up **Amazon Web Services (AWS;** `http://aws.amazon.com`) cloud build agents. You will need to create the build agent **Amazon Machines Image (AMI)**, but once you have done this, your TeamCity server can start up however many build agents are required, and then shut them down again when the build has finished.

We are going to need a basic install of TeamCity on our local machine to work through this section; you can either download the WAR file and run it up in an application server such as Tomcat, or if you have Docker installed on your machine, you can just run the following command (you will need to create the `~/teamcity/data` and `~/teamcity/logs` directories on your local machine):

```
docker run -it --name teamcity-server-instance \
    -v ~/teamcity/data:/data/teamcity_server/datadir \
    -v ~/teamcity/logs:/opt/teamcity/logs \
    -p 8111:8111 \
    jetbrains/teamcity-server
```

To get to your TeamCity instance, navigate to the following URL in your browser:

```
http://localhost:8111
```

The first time that you start up TeamCity, it will go through the standard setup process; just click on **Proceed** until you get to the create an administrator account screen. Generate an admin account for yourself (for example, username admin, password admin; this is after all temporary) and then click on the **Projects** button on the top left. You should then see the following screen:

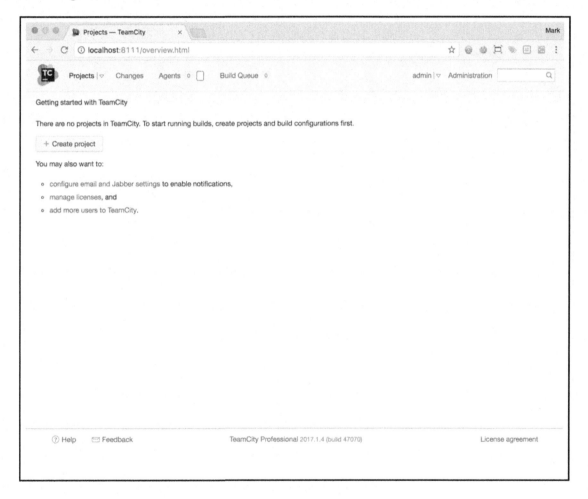

1. Let's start by clicking the **Create project** button.

2. We then need to provide a name for our project and we can add a description to let people know what the project does. Bear in mind that this is not an actual build we are creating yet; it is something that will hold all of our builds for this project. `Selenium Tests` is probably not a great name for a project, but that's all we have at the moment:

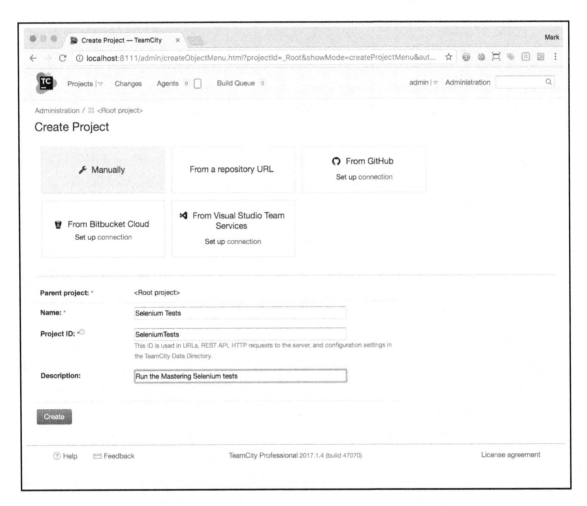

3. Click on **Create** and you will see your project created.

4. We then need to scroll down to the **Build Configurations** section:

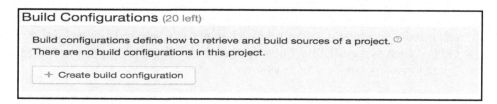

5. When you get there, click on the **Create build configuration** button.

This is where we are going to create our build. I've simply called it `Webdriver` because it is going to run WebDriver tests; I'm sure you can come up with a better name for your build configuration take a look at the following screenshot:

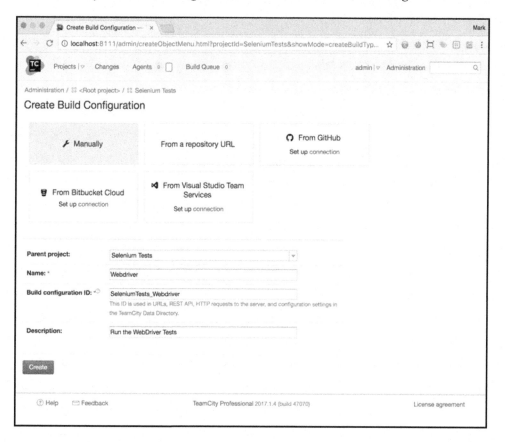

6. When you are happy with the name for your configuration, click on the **Create** button.

7. Now we will be asked to configure our source control system so that TeamCity can monitor your source control for changes. I've selected Git and put in some valid values as a guideline, but you will obviously need to put in values that relate to your source-control system:

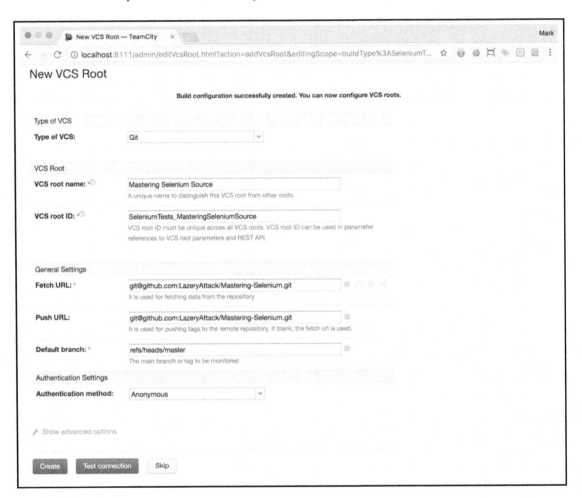

8. Once you have entered your details and clicked on **Create**, you will need to add a build step, as shown in the following screenshot:

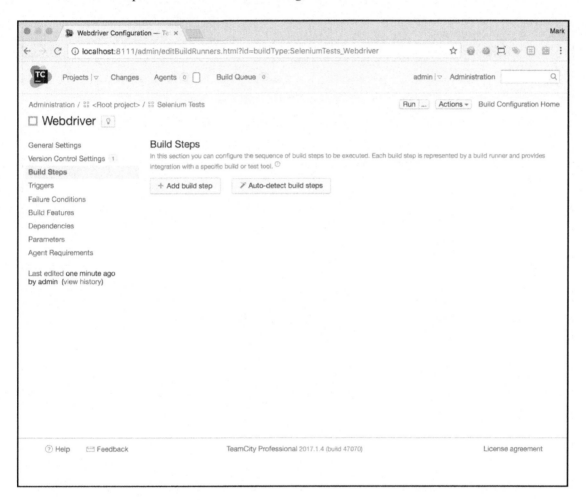

9. This is where we get into the meat of our build; click on **Add build step** to get started:

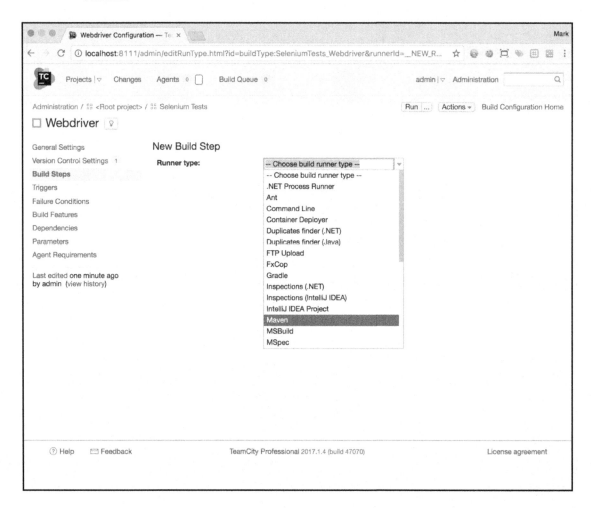

10. First of all, we need to select the type of build; in our case, we have a Maven project, so select **Maven**:

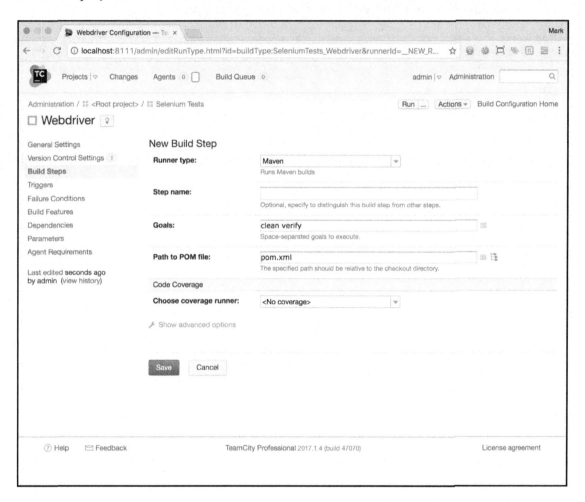

11. Finally, we just need to put in the details of our Maven build; this is simply `clean verify`. We have already made sure that our Selenium profile is run by default, so we don't need to look at the **Advanced options**:

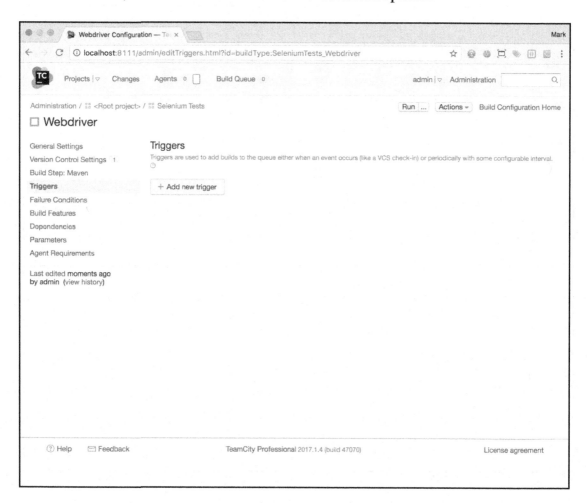

12. Next, scroll down and click on **Save** and your TeamCity build is all ready to go. We now just need to make sure that it will trigger every time that you check code into your source code repository. Click on **Triggers**, as shown in the following screenshot:

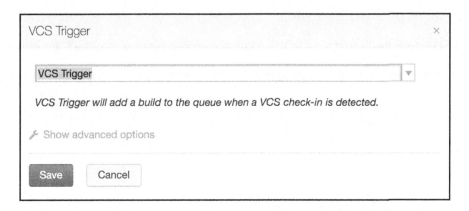

13. This is where you set up a list of actions that will result in a build being performed. Click on **Add new trigger** and select **VCS Trigger**.

14. If you click on **Save** now, a trigger will be set up that will trigger a build every time you push code to your central source code repository.

Setting up Jenkins

Jenkins (http://jenkins-ci.org) is a firm favorite in the CI world and is the basis for some cloud services (for example, cloudbees; https://www.cloudbees.com). It is very widely used and no section about continuous integration would be complete without mentioning it.

We are going to need a basic install of Jenkins on our local machine to work through this section. Let's follow these steps:

1. If you have already installed an application server such as Tomcat for the previous section, you'll just need to download the WAR file and drop it into the webapps directory of your application server. If you decide to go the Docker route, you can run the following command (you will need to create the ~/jenkins directory on your local machine):

```
docker run -it --name jenkins-instance \
    -p 8080:8080 \
```

```
-p 50000:50000 \
-v ~/jenkins:/var/jenkins_home \
Jenkins
```

2. To get to your Jenkins instance, navigate to the following URL in your browser:

   `http://localhost:8080`

3. The first thing that you will see is a screen asking you to unlock Jenkins:

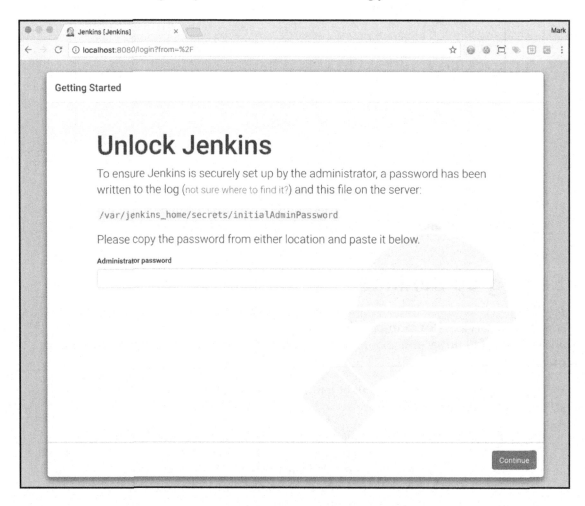

4. Have a look in your Terminal window (assuming you are using Docker) and you will see something that looks like this:

```
fyre — docker run -it --name jenkins-instance -p 8080:8080 -p 50000:50000 -v ~/jenkins:/var/jenkins_home jenkins — 128×38
INFO: Bean factory for application context [org.springframework.web.context.support.StaticWebApplicationContext@6fc4eb2f]: org.s
pringframework.beans.factory.support.DefaultListableBeanFactory@488815ce
Sep 17, 2017 4:40:36 PM org.springframework.beans.factory.support.DefaultListableBeanFactory preInstantiateSingletons
INFO: Pre-instantiating singletons in org.springframework.beans.factory.support.DefaultListableBeanFactory@488815ce: defining be
ans [filter,legacy]; root of factory hierarchy
Sep 17, 2017 4:40:36 PM jenkins.install.SetupWizard init
INFO:

*************************************************************
*************************************************************
*************************************************************

Jenkins initial setup is required. An admin user has been created and a password generated.
Please use the following password to proceed to installation:

0bfdd97c602742b9a27177d4c5961a30

This may also be found at: /var/jenkins_home/secrets/initialAdminPassword

*************************************************************
*************************************************************
*************************************************************

Sep 17, 2017 4:40:37 PM hudson.model.UpdateSite updateData
INFO: Obtained the latest update center data file for UpdateSource default
Sep 17, 2017 4:40:37 PM hudson.model.DownloadService$Downloadable load
INFO: Obtained the updated data file for hudson.tasks.Maven.MavenInstaller
Sep 17, 2017 4:40:38 PM hudson.model.DownloadService$Downloadable load
INFO: Obtained the updated data file for hudson.tools.JDKInstaller
Sep 17, 2017 4:40:38 PM hudson.model.AsyncPeriodicWork$1 run
INFO: Finished Download metadata. 6,287 ms
Sep 17, 2017 4:40:40 PM hudson.model.UpdateSite updateData
INFO: Obtained the latest update center data file for UpdateSource default
Sep 17, 2017 4:40:40 PM hudson.WebAppMain$3 run
INFO: Jenkins is fully up and running
--> setting agent port for jnlp
--> setting agent port for jnlp... done
```

5. Copy the password from the Terminal, enter it, and then click on **Continue**. You will then be asked which plugins you would like to install. Just use the default Jenkins recommendations for now. Jenkins will then download the required plugins and set itself up ready for initial use. The final setup step is to create yourself an admin account (you can use username `admin` and password `admin` again; this is another temporary account).

6. Now that Jenkins is ready to go, you will see the **Welcome to Jenkins** screen:

Let's have a look at how we can set up a build in Jenkins that will enable us to run our tests:

1. The first thing to do is to click on the **create new jobs** link:

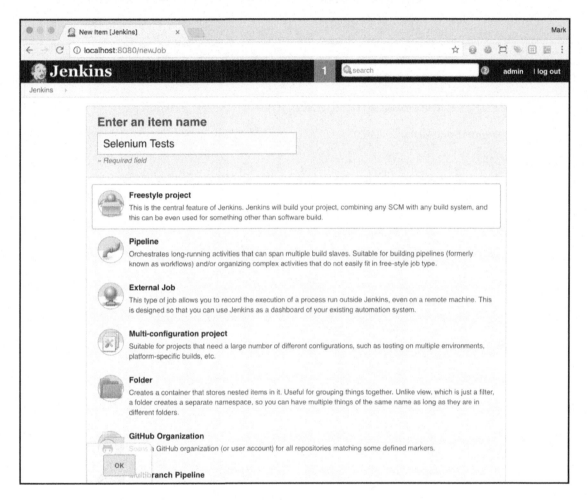

2. Put in the name of your build and then select the **Freestyle project** option.
3. Next, click on **OK** and you will be taken to the build configuration screen. Click on the tab that says **Source Code Management**, and select **Git** and fill in your details:

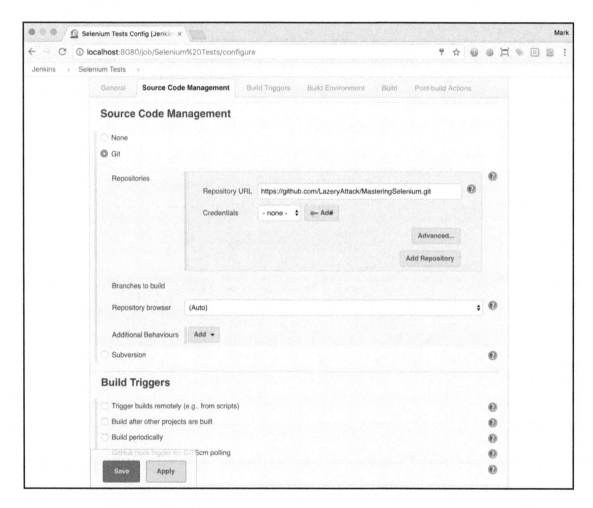

You can of course use any source code management system you would like to use. Git is very popular, but Jenkins does support a variety of others as well.

4. Next, we can set up our build triggers and our build environment. It's normally a good idea to have a Git hook set up to trigger builds every time a change is committed to source control:

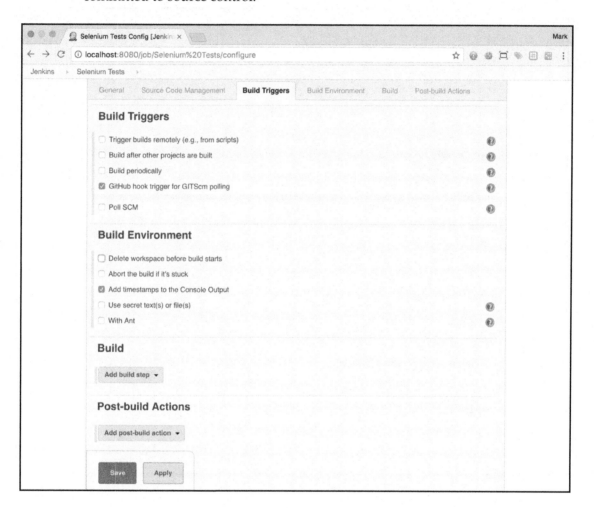

5. Then, we need to set up our Maven job. Click on the **Add build step** button and then select **Invoke top-level Maven targets**. Refer to the following screenshot:

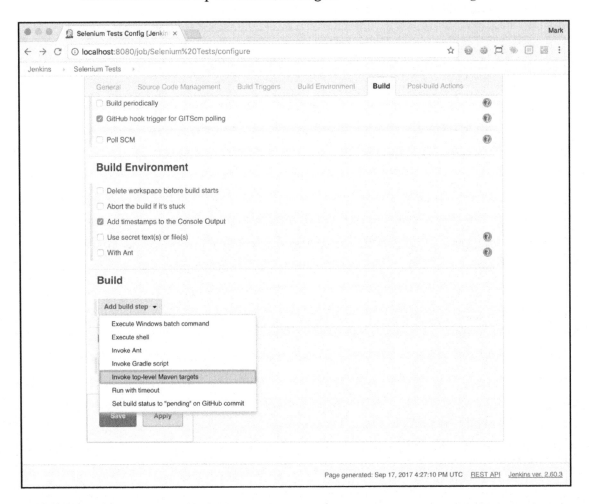

6. Now you just need to enter your default Maven goal, and we are ready to go. Refer to the following screenshot:

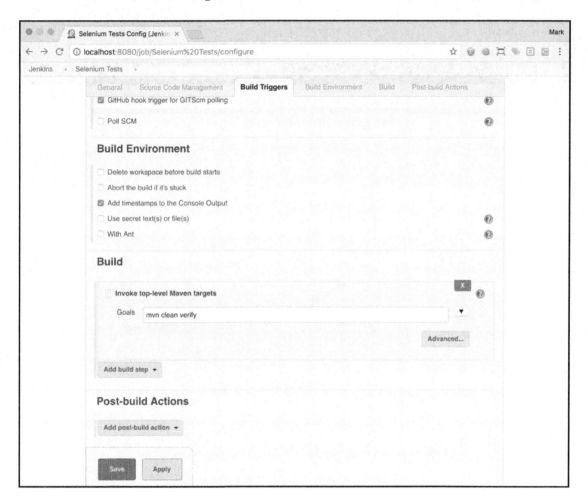

7. Click on **Save** and you will be sent to your newly created project; that's all! Refer to the following screenshot:

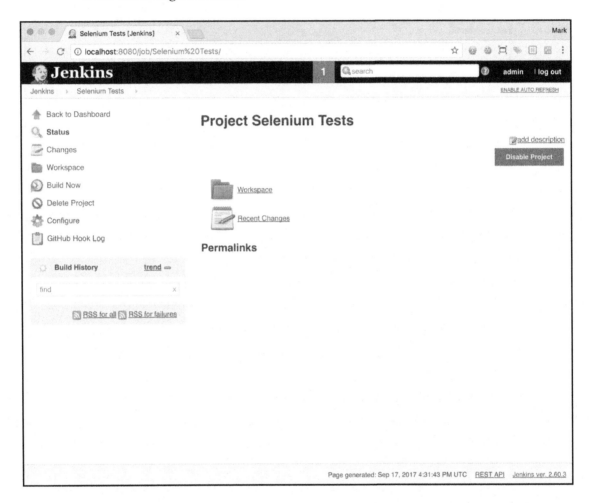

You should now be able to run your Jenkins build and it will download all the dependencies and run everything for you.

So far, we have looked at how we can set up a very simple continuous integration service, but this is only the tip of the iceberg. We have used continuous integration to give us a fast feedback loop so that we are notified of, and can react to, problems quickly. What if we could extend this to tell us not just whether there are any problems, but whether something is ready to be deployed into production instead? This is the goal of continuous delivery. Refer to the following diagram:

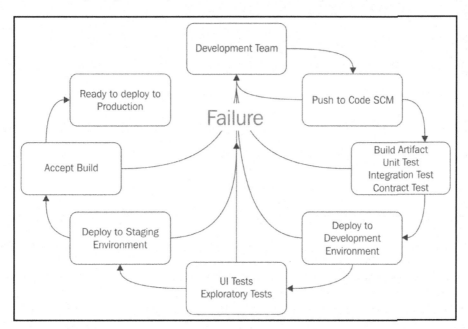

What's next after continuous delivery? How about continuous deployment? This is where we get to the point that we are so confident in our pipeline that as soon as every continuous delivery phase has been marked as passed, the code will automatically be deployed to live. Just imagine a new feature being completed and within a matter of hours we have performed enough testing on that functionality that we can automatically release it to live.

From code complete to being in the hand of your customers on the same day! Refer to the following diagram:

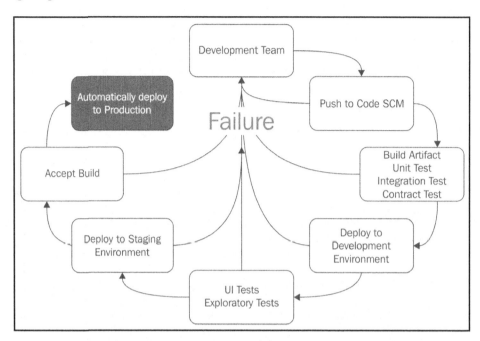

We haven't got quite that far yet. We now have a basic CI setup that we can use to run our tests on CI, but we still have some pretty big gaps. The basic CI setup that you have so far is running on one operating system and cannot run our tests against all browser/operating system combinations. We can deal with this issue by setting up various build agents that connect to our CI server and run different versions of operating systems/browsers. This does however take time to configure and can be quite fiddly. You could also extend the capabilities of your CI server by setting up a Selenium-Grid that your CI server can connect to and run various Selenium test jobs. This can be very powerful, but it also does have setup costs. This is where third-party services such as **SauceLabs** (https://saucelabs.com) can be used. Most third-party grid services have free tiers, which can be very useful when you are getting started and working out what works for you. Remember that getting set up with the one third-party service does not lock you into them. One Selenium-Grid is pretty much the same as another, so even though you start off using a third-party service, there is nothing to stop you building up your own grid, or configuring your own build agents and moving away from the third-party service in the future.

Extending our capabilities by using a Selenium-Grid

Since we already have a working Maven implementation, let's enhance it so that it can connect to Selenium-Grid. These enhancements will enable you to connect to any Selenium-Grid, but we are going to specifically look at connecting to a third-party service provided by SauceLabs, since they offer a free tier. Let's have a look at the modifications we need to make to our TestNG code.

We will start off with the modifications to our POM; initially, we are going to add some properties that we can configure on the command line by using this code:

```
<properties>
    <project.build.sourceEncoding>UTF-
    8</project.build.sourceEncoding>
    <project.reporting.outputEncoding>UTF-
    8</project.reporting.outputEncoding>
    <!-- Dependency versions -->
    <phantomjsdriver.version>1.4.3</phantomjsdriver.version>
    <selenium.version>3.5.3</selenium.version>
    <testng.version>6.11</testng.version>
    <!-- Plugin versions -->
    <driver-binary-downloader-maven-plugin.version>1.0.14</driver-
    binary-downloader-maven-plugin.version>
    <maven-failsafe-plugin.version>2.20</maven-failsafe-
    plugin.version>
    <!-- Configurable variables -->
    <threads>1</threads>
    <browser>firefox</browser>
    <overwrite.binaries>false</overwrite.binaries>
    <remote>false</remote>
    <seleniumGridURL/>
    <platform/>
    <browserVersion/>
</properties>
```

I've left the `seleniumGridURL` blank because I don't know your Selenium-Grid URL, but you can give this a default value if you want. The same applies to the `platform` and `browserVersion` properties. Next, we need to make sure that these properties are set by the `maven-failsafe-plugin` as system properties in our test JVM. To do this, we need to modify our `maven-failsafe-plugin` configuration by using this code:

```
<plugin>
    <groupId>org.apache.maven.plugins</groupId>
```

```xml
            <artifactId>maven-failsafe-plugin</artifactId>
            <version>${maven-failsafe-plugin.version}</version>
            <configuration>
                <parallel>methods</parallel>
                <threadCount>${threads}</threadCount>
                <systemProperties>
                    <browser>${browser}</browser>
                    <remoteDriver>${remote}</remoteDriver>
                    <gridURL>${seleniumGridURL}</gridURL>
                    <desiredPlatform>${platform}</desiredPlatform>
                    <desiredBrowserVersion>
                    ${browserVersion}
                    </desiredBrowserVersion>
                    <!--Set properties passed in by the driver
                    binary downloader-->
                    <phantomjs.binary.path>${phantomjs.binary.path}
                    </phantomjs.binary.path>
                    <webdriver.chrome.driver>${webdriver.chrome.driver}
                    </webdriver.chrome.driver>
                    <webdriver.ie.driver>${webdriver.ie.driver}
                    </webdriver.ie.driver>
                    <webdriver.opera.driver>${webdriver.opera.driver}
                    </webdriver.opera.driver>
                    <webdriver.gecko.driver>${webdriver.gecko.driver}
                    </webdriver.gecko.driver>
                    <webdriver.edge.driver>${webdriver.edge.driver}
                    </webdriver.edge.driver>
                </systemProperties>
            </configuration>
            <executions>
                <execution>
                    <goals>
                        <goal>integration-test</goal>
                        <goal>verify</goal>
                    </goals>
                </execution>
            </executions>
        </plugin>
```

These properties will now be available to our test code using `System.getProperty()`. Now, we need to make some modifications to our `DriverFactory` class. First, we are going to add a new class variable called `useRemoteWebdriver` by using this code:

```java
private static final DriverType DEFAULT_DRIVER_TYPE = FIREFOX;
 private final String browser = System.getProperty("browser",
DEFAULT_DRIVER_TYPE.name()).toUpperCase();
 private final String operatingSystem =
```

```
System.getProperty("os.name").toUpperCase();
private final String systemArchitecture =
System.getProperty("os.arch");
private final boolean useRemoteWebDriver =
Boolean.getBoolean("remoteDriver");
```

This variable is going to read in the system property that we set in our POM and work out whether we want to use a `RemoteWebDriver` instance. Now that we know whether we want a `RemoteWebDriver` instance, we need to update our `instantiateWebDriver` method to actually create one if required by using this code:

```
private void instantiateWebDriver(DesiredCapabilities  desiredCapabilities)
throws MalformedURLException {
    System.out.println(" ");
    System.out.println("Current Operating System: " +
    operatingSystem);
    System.out.println("Current Architecture: " +
    systemArchitecture);
    System.out.println("Current Browser Selection: " +
    selectedDriverType);
    System.out.println(" ");
    if (useRemoteWebDriver) {
        URL seleniumGridURL = new
        URL(System.getProperty("gridURL"));
        String desiredBrowserVersion =
        System.getProperty("desiredBrowserVersion");
        String desiredPlatform =
        System.getProperty("desiredPlatform");

        if (null != desiredPlatform && !desiredPlatform.isEmpty())
        {
            desiredCapabilities.setPlatform
            (Platform.valueOf(desiredPlatform.toUpperCase()));
        }

        if (null != desiredBrowserVersion &&
        !desiredBrowserVersion.isEmpty()) {
            desiredCapabilities.setVersion(desiredBrowserVersion);
        }

        webdriver = new RemoteWebDriver(seleniumGridURL,
        desiredCapabilities);
    } else {
        webdriver = selectedDriverType.getWebDriverObject
        (desiredCapabilities);
    }
}
```

This is where all of the hard work is done. We are using our `useRemoteWebDriver` variable to work out whether we want to instantiate a normal `WebDriver` object or a `RemoteWebDriver` object. If we want to instantiate a `RemoteWebDriver` object, we start off by reading in the system properties that we set in our POM. The most important bit of information is the `seleniumGridURL`. If we don't have this, we don't know where to go to connect to the grid. We are reading in the system property and trying to generate a URL from it. If the URL is not valid, `InvalidURLException` will be thrown; this is fine because we won't be able to connect to the grid anyway at this point, so we may as well end our test run at that point and throw a useful error. The other two bits of information are optional. If we supply `desiredPlatform` and `desiredBrowserVersion`, the Selenium-Grid will use an agent matching these criteria. If we don't supply this information, the Selenium-Grid will just grab any free agent and run our test on it.

Looking at this code, it's not instantly obvious what browser we are requesting, but don't worry; it's covered. Each `DesiredCapabilities` object will set a browser type by default. So, if we create `DesiredCapabilities.firefox()`, we will be asking the Selenium-Grid to run our test against Firefox. This is one of the reasons we originally kept the `getDesiredCapabilities()` method separate from the `instantiateWebDriver()` method.

Now that we have changed out code, we will need to test that it works; the easiest way to test this is to set up a free account with a Selenium-Grid provider such as SauceLabs (`https://saucelabs.com`) and run your tests against them. To do that, put the following into your command line (obviously you'll need to supply your own SauceLabs username and access key for this to work):

```
mvn clean install \
    -Dremote=true \
    -DseleniumGridURL=http://{username}:
{accessKey}@ondemand.saucelabs.com:80/wd/hub \
    -Dplatform=win10 \
    -Dbrowser=firefox \
    -DbrowserVersion=55
```

It's great to be able to connect to a third-party grid and see all your tests running without having to do the hard setup work. This gives us the ability to run our tests remotely on our working CI.

However, this does give us some new challenges. When you are running your tests remotely, it's a lot harder to work out what the problem is when things go wrong, especially if they appear to work locally. We now need to find a way to make it easier to diagnose problems with our tests when we run them remotely.

A picture paints a thousand words

Even if you have made your tests totally reliable, they will fail occasionally. When this happens, it is often very hard to describe the problem with words alone. If one of your tests failed, wouldn't it be easier to explain what went wrong if you had a picture of what was happening in the browser when things went wrong? I know that when any of my Selenium tests fail, the first thing I want to know is what was on the screen at the time of failure. If I knew what was on the screen at the time of failure, I would be able to diagnose the vast majority of issues without having to hunt through a stack trace for a specific line number, and then go and look at the associated code to try and work out what went wrong. Wouldn't it be nice if we got a screenshot showing what was on the screen every time a test failed? Let's take the project that we built in Chapter 1, *Creating a Fast Feedback Loop*, and extend it a bit to take a screenshot every time there is a test failure. Let's have a look at how we can implement this with TestNG:

1. First of all, we are going to create a package called listeners. Refer to the following screenshot:

2. Then, we are going to implement a custom listener for TestNG that will detect a test failure and then capture a screenshot for us by using the following code:

```
package com.masteringselenium.listeners;

import org.openqa.selenium.OutputType;
import org.openqa.selenium.TakesScreenshot;
import org.openqa.selenium.WebDriver;
import org.openqa.selenium.remote.Augmenter;
import org.testng.ITestResult;
import org.testng.TestListenerAdapter;

import java.io.File;
import java.io.FileOutputStream;
import java.io.IOException;

import static com.masteringselenium.DriverBase.getDriver;


public class ScreenshotListener extends TestListenerAdapter {

    private boolean createFile(File screenshot) {
        boolean fileCreated = false;

        if (screenshot.exists()) {
            fileCreated = true;
        } else {
            File parentDirectory = new
            File(screenshot.getParent());
            if (parentDirectory.exists() ||
            parentDirectory.mkdirs()) {
                try {
                    fileCreated = screenshot.createNewFile();
                } catch (IOException errorCreatingScreenshot) {
                    errorCreatingScreenshot.printStackTrace();
                }
            }
        }

        return fileCreated;
    }

    private void writeScreenshotToFile(WebDriver driver,
    File screenshot) {
        try {
            FileOutputStream screenshotStream = new
            FileOutputStream(screenshot);
```

```
            screenshotStream.write(((TakesScreenshot)
            driver).getScreenshotAs(OutputType.BYTES));
            screenshotStream.close();
        } catch (IOException unableToWriteScreenshot) {
            System.err.println("Unable to write " +
            screenshot.getAbsolutePath());
            unableToWriteScreenshot.printStackTrace();
        }
    }
    @Override
    public void onTestFailure(ITestResult failingTest) {
        try {
            WebDriver driver = getDriver();
            String screenshotDirectory =
            System.getProperty("screenshotDirectory",
            "target/screenshots");
            String screenshotAbsolutePath =
            screenshotDirectory +
            File.separator + System.currentTimeMillis() + "_" +
            failingTest.getName() + ".png";
            File screenshot = new File(screenshotAbsolutePath);
            if (createFile(screenshot)) {
                try {
                    writeScreenshotToFile(driver, screenshot);
                } catch (ClassCastException
                weNeedToAugmentOurDriverObject) {
                    writeScreenshotToFile(new
                    Augmenter().augment(driver), screenshot);
                }
                System.out.println("Written screenshot to " +
                screenshotAbsolutePath);
            } else {
                System.err.println("Unable to create " +
                screenshotAbsolutePath);
            }
        } catch (Exception ex) {
            System.err.println("Unable to capture
            screenshot...");
            ex.printStackTrace();
        }
    }
}
```

First, we have the rather imaginatively named `createFile` method, which will try to create a file. Next, we have the equally imaginatively named `writeScreenShotToFile` method. This will try to write the screenshot to a file. Notice that we aren't catching any exceptions in these methods, because we will do that in the listener.

 TestNG can get itself in a twist if exceptions are thrown in listeners. It will generally trap them so that your test run doesn't stop, but it doesn't fail the test when it does this. If your tests are passing but you have failures and stack traces, check to see if it's the listener at fault.

The last block of code is the actual listener. The first thing that you will notice is that it has a `try...catch` wrapping the whole method, which initially looks wrong. While we do want a screenshot to show us what has gone wrong, we probably don't want to kill our test run if we are unable to capture or write a screenshot to disk for some reason. To make sure that we don't disrupt the test run, we catch the error and log it out to the console for future reference. We then carry on with what we were doing before.

You cannot cast all driver implementations in Selenium into a `TakesScreenshot` object. As a result, we capture the `ClassCastException` for driver implementations that cannot be cast into a `TakesScreenshot` object and augment them instead. We don't just augment everything, because a driver object that doesn't need to be augmented will throw an error if you try. It is usually `RemoteWebDriver` instances that need to be augmented. Apart from augmenting the driver object when required, the main job of this function is to generate a filename for the screenshot. We want to make sure that the filename is unique so that we don't accidentally overwrite any screenshots. To do this, we use the current timestamp and the name of the current test. We could use a randomly generated **Globally Unique Identifier** (**GUID**), but timestamps make it easier to track what happened at what time.

Finally, we want to log the absolute path to the screenshot out to console. This will make it much easier to find any screenshots that have been created.

As you may have noticed in the preceding code, we are using a system property to get the directory that we save our screenshots in. This will allow you to redirect your error screenshots to any location you desire. We have set a default location of target/screenshots; if you want to override this, we will need to set this system property in our POM.

To give us that ability, we will need to modify the `maven-failsafe-plugin` section to add an additional property by using this code:

```
<plugin>
        <groupId>org.apache.maven.plugins</groupId>
        <artifactId>maven-failsafe-plugin</artifactId>
        <version>${maven-failsafe-plugin.version}</version>
```

```xml
    <configuration>
        <parallel>methods</parallel>
        <threadCount>${threads}</threadCount>
        <systemProperties>
            <browser>${browser}</browser>
            <screenshotDirectory>${screenshotDirectory}
            </screenshotDirectory>
            <remoteDriver>${remote}</remoteDriver>
            <gridURL>${seleniumGridURL}</gridURL>
            <desiredPlatform>${platform}</desiredPlatform>
            <desiredBrowserVersion>${browserVersion}
            </desiredBrowserVersion>
            <!--Set properties passed in by the driver binary
            downloader-->
            <phantomjs.binary.path>${phantomjs.binary.path}
            </phantomjs.binary.path>
            <webdriver.chrome.driver>${webdriver.chrome.driver}
            </webdriver.chrome.driver>
            <webdriver.ie.driver>${webdriver.ie.driver}
            </webdriver.ie.driver>
            <webdriver.opera.driver>${webdriver.opera.driver}
            </webdriver.opera.driver>
            <webdriver.gecko.driver>${webdriver.gecko.driver}
            </webdriver.gecko.driver>
            <webdriver.edge.driver>${webdriver.edge.driver}
            </webdriver.edge.driver>
        </systemProperties>
    </configuration>
    <executions>
        <execution>
            <goals>
                <goal>integration-test</goal>
                <goal>verify</goal>
            </goals>
        </execution>
    </executions>
</plugin>
```

Since we have used a Maven variable to make this property configurable, we will then need to set it in the `properties` section of our POM:

```xml
<properties>
    <project.build.sourceEncoding>UTF-
    8</project.build.sourceEncoding>
    <project.reporting.outputEncoding>UTF-
    8</project.reporting.outputEncoding>
    <!-- Dependency versions -->
```

```xml
        <phantomjsdriver.version>1.4.3</phantomjsdriver.version>
        <selenium.version>3.5.3</selenium.version>
        <testng.version>6.11</testng.version>
        <!-- Plugin versions -->
        <driver-binary-downloader-maven-plugin.version>1.0.14</driver-
        binary-downloader-maven-plugin.version>
        <maven-failsafe-plugin.version>2.20</maven-failsafe-
        plugin.version>
        <!-- Configurable variables -->
        <threads>1</threads>
        <browser>firefox</browser>
        <overwrite.binaries>false</overwrite.binaries>
        <remote>false</remote>
        <seleniumGridURL/>
        <platform/>
        <browserVersion/>
        <screenshotDirectory>${project.build.directory}
        /screenshots</screenshotDirectory>
    </properties>
```

You can see that in our Maven variable definition, we have used a Maven variable that we have not defined before. Maven has a series of predefined variables that you can use; `${project.build.directory}` will provide you the location of your target directory. Whenever Maven builds your project, it will compile all of the files into a temporary directory called `target`; it will then run all of your tests and store the results in this directory. This directory is basically a little sandbox for Maven to play in while it's doing its stuff.

When performing Maven builds, it is generally good practice to use the `clean` command:

```
mvn clean verify
```

The `clean` command deletes the target directory to make sure that when you build your project, you don't have anything left over from the previous build that may cause problems. This does mean that you will delete screenshots from previous runs if you have not copied them anywhere else before kicking off another run of your tests.

Generally speaking, when we run tests we are only going to be interested in the result of the current test run (any previous results should have been archived for future reference), so deleting old screenshots should really not be a problem. To keep things clean and easy to find, we are generating a screenshot subdirectory that we will store our screenshots in.

Now that our screenshot listener is ready, we just have to tell our tests to use it. This is surprisingly simple; all of our tests extend `DriverBase`, so we just add a `@Listeners` annotation to it by using this code:

```
import com.masteringselenium.listeners.ScreenshotListener;
import org.testng.annotations.Listeners;

@Listeners(ScreenshotListener.class)
public class DriverBase
```

From this point onwards, if any of our tests fail, a screenshot will automatically be taken.

 Why don't you give it a go? Try changing your test to make it fail so that screenshots are generated. Try putting some windows or OS dialogs in front of your browser while the tests are running and taking screenshots. Does this affect what you see on the screen?

Screenshots are a very useful aid when it comes to diagnosing problems with your tests, but sometimes things go wrong on a page that looks completely normal. How do we go about diagnosing these sorts of problems?

Don't be afraid of the big bad stack trace

It's surprising how many people are intimidated by stack traces. A reaction that I regularly see when a stack trace appears on screen is panic!

"Oh my god! Something has gone wrong! There are hundreds of lines of text talking about code I don't recognize and I can't take it all in; what do I do?"

The first thing to do is to relax; stack traces have a lot of information but they are actually really friendly and helpful things. Let's modify our project to produce a stack trace and work through it. We are going to make a small change to the `getDriver()` method in `DriverFactory` to force it to always return `null` by using this code:

```
public static WebDriver getDriver() {
    return null;
}
```

This is going to make sure that we never return a driver object, something that we would expect to cause errors. Let's run our tests again, but make sure that Maven displays a stack trace by using the `-e` switch:

```
mvn clean verify -e
```

This time, you should see a couple of stack traces output to the Terminal; the first one should look like this:

```
● ● ●                           ⬛ Part 2 — -bash — 142×38
[INFO] Failsafe report directory: /Users/fyre/Programming/Mastering-Selenium/Chapter 2/Part 2/target/failsafe-reports
[INFO]
[INFO] -------------------------------------------------------
[INFO]  T E S T S
[INFO] -------------------------------------------------------
[INFO] Running com.masteringselenium.BasicIT
Configuring TestNG with: TestNG60Configurator
Unable to capture screenshot...
java.lang.NullPointerException
        at com.masteringselenium.listeners.ScreenshotListener.writeScreenshotToFile(ScreenshotListener.java:41)
        at com.masteringselenium.listeners.ScreenshotListener.onTestFailure(ScreenshotListener.java:58)
        at org.testng.internal.Invoker.runTestListeners(Invoker.java:1731)
        at org.testng.internal.Invoker.runTestListeners(Invoker.java:1714)
        at org.testng.internal.Invoker.invokeMethod(Invoker.java:714)
        at org.testng.internal.Invoker.invokeTestMethod(Invoker.java:869)
        at org.testng.internal.Invoker.invokeTestMethods(Invoker.java:1193)
        at org.testng.internal.TestMethodWorker.invokeTestMethods(TestMethodWorker.java:126)
        at org.testng.internal.TestMethodWorker.run(TestMethodWorker.java:109)
        at java.util.concurrent.ThreadPoolExecutor.runWorker(ThreadPoolExecutor.java:1149)
        at java.util.concurrent.ThreadPoolExecutor$Worker.run(ThreadPoolExecutor.java:624)
        at java.lang.Thread.run(Thread.java:748)
[ERROR] Tests run: 3, Failures: 2, Errors: 0, Skipped: 1, Time elapsed: 0.333 s <<< FAILURE! – in com.masteringselenium.BasicIT
[ERROR] googleCheeseExample(com.masteringselenium.BasicIT)  Time elapsed: 0.009 s  <<< FAILURE!
java.lang.NullPointerException
        at com.masteringselenium.BasicIT.googleExampleThatSearchesFor(BasicIT.java:16)
        at com.masteringselenium.BasicIT.googleCheeseExample(BasicIT.java:38)

[ERROR] clearCookies(com.masteringselenium.BasicIT)  Time elapsed: 0.009 s  <<< FAILURE!
java.lang.NullPointerException

[INFO]
[INFO] Results:
[INFO]
[ERROR] Failures:
[ERROR]   BasicIT>DriverBase.clearCookies:39 » NullPointer
[ERROR]   BasicIT.googleCheeseExample:38->googleExampleThatSearchesFor:16 NullPointer
[INFO]
[ERROR] Tests run: 3, Failures: 2, Errors: 0, Skipped: 1
```

It's not too big, so let's have a look at it in more detail. The first line tells you the root cause of our problem: we have got a `NullPointerException`. You have probably seen these before. Our code is complaining because it was expecting to have some sort of object at some point and we didn't give it one. Next, we have a series of lines of text that tell us where in the application the problem occurred.

We have quite a few lines of code that are referred to in this stack trace, most of them unfamiliar, as we didn't write them. Let's start at the bottom and work our way up. We first of all have the line of code that was running when our test failed; this is `Thread.java` line 748. This thread is using a `run` method (on `ThreadPoolExecutor.java` line 624) that is using a `runWorker` method (on `ThreadPoolExecutor.java` line 1,149), and this carries on up the stack trace. What we are seeing is a hierarchy of code with all the various methods that are being used. We are also being told which line of code in that method caused a problem.

We are specifically interested in the lines that relate to the code that we have written, in this case, the second and third lines of the stack trace. You can see that it is giving us two very useful bits of information, it's telling us where in our code the problem has occurred. If we have a look at our code, we can see what it was trying to do when the failure occurred so that we can try and work out what the problem is. Let's start with the second line. First of all, it tells us which method is causing the problem. In this case, it is `com.masteringselenium.listeners.ScreenshotListener.onTestFailure`. It then tells us which line of this method is causing us a problem, in this case `ScreenshotListener.java:58`. This is where our `onTestFailure()` method tries to pass a `WebDriver` instance into our `writeScreenshotToFile()` method. If you look at the next line up, you will see that `writeScreenshotToFile()` is failing on line 41 where it tries to use the driver instance to get a screenshot and it's throwing a null pointer error.

Now, if you remember, we modified `getDriver()` to return a null instead of a valid driver object, and obviously we cannot call `.getScreenshotAs()` on a null, hence the null pointer error.

So why didn't it fail in `WebDriverThread`? After all, that's where the problem is. Passing `null` around is quite valid. It's trying to do something with `null` that causes the problem. This is why it also didn't fail on line 34 of `DriverBase`. The `getDriver()` method just passes on a variable, it doesn't actually try to do anything with it. The first time that we tried to do anything with `null` is when it failed, which was at line 41 of the `ScreenshotListener` class.

Now if you look closely, you'll notice that although we got a stack trace showing us an error in the `ScreenshotListener` class, we didn't actually get an error there. This is because we have a `try...catch` block around the screenshot code; it will report the stack trace so that you can work out why a screenshot wasn't taken, but it doesn't actually fail the test. The errors we actually got were slightly lower down.

If you look a bit further down, you will see that an error was triggered on line 16 of `BasicIT.java`. This is also a null pointer error, and this line of code is where we first try to use our driver object to do something. This again makes sense.

Finally, we have got yet another null pointer error. This one is in our `clearCookies()` method, but it's not clear where this has gone wrong, as there is no line number. This is because we have made a mistake: when we wrote our bit of code to clear down cookies between tests to avoid stopping and starting the browser all the time, we didn't take into account the possibility that something may have gone wrong and there may not be a driver object available at this point. This mistake has also resulted in us not attempting to run any of the other tests and we have also got a strange message that three tests were run.

Let's clean this up and stop it causing an error when this happens by using this code:

```
@AfterMethod(alwaysRun = true)
 public static void clearCookies() throws Exception {
     try {
         getDriver().manage().deleteAllCookies();
     } catch (Exception ex) {
         System.err.println("Unable to clear cookies: "
         + ex.getCause());
     }
 }
```

We have now modified our `clearCookies` method so that it's surrounded by `try...catch`. This means that it will capture the error and carry on with the rest of the test run. We are printing some information out to the console so that we can work out what happened, but we have gone for something that's not quite as verbose this time. Rather than print the whole stack trace, we are just going to print the cause. This way, we can still work out what has gone wrong, but we won't have a big stack trace catching our eye and distracting us from stack traces that have actually caused real errors. Let's tweak our `ScreenshotListener` as well to make the stack trace a little less verbose by using this code:

```
@Override
 public void onTestFailure(ITestResult failingTest) {
     try {
         WebDriver driver = getDriver();
         String screenshotDirectory =
         System.getProperty("screenshotDirectory",
         "target/screenshots");
         String screenshotAbsolutePath = screenshotDirectory +
         File.separator + System.currentTimeMillis() + "_" +
         failingTest.getName() + ".png";
         File screenshot = new File(screenshotAbsolutePath);
         if (createFile(screenshot)) {
             try {
                 writeScreenshotToFile(driver, screenshot);
             } catch (ClassCastException
             weNeedToAugmentOurDriverObject) {
                 writeScreenshotToFile(new Augmenter()
                 .augment(driver), screenshot);
             }
             System.out.println("Written screenshot to " +
             screenshotAbsolutePath);
         } else {
             System.err.println("Unable to create " +
             screenshotAbsolutePath);
```

```
        }
    } catch (Exception ex) {
        System.err.println("Unable to capture screenshot: "
        + ex.getCause());
    }

}
```

Again, we are now just logging the cause, so let's rerun our tests and see what the output looks like this time. Take a look at this screenshot:

```
                                          Part 2 — -bash — 142×38
[INFO] ------------------------------------------------------------
[INFO]
[INFO]
[INFO] --- maven-surefire-plugin:2.12.4:test (default-test) @ mastering-selenium-testng ---
[INFO]
[INFO] --- maven-jar-plugin:2.4:jar (default-jar) @ mastering-selenium-testng ---
[WARNING] JAR will be empty - no content was marked for inclusion!
[INFO] Building jar: /Users/fyre/Programming/Mastering-Selenium/Chapter 2/Part 2/target/mastering-selenium-testng-DEV-SNAPSHOT.jar
[INFO]
[INFO] --- maven-failsafe-plugin:2.20:integration-test (default) @ mastering-selenium-testng ---
[INFO]
[INFO] ------------------------------------------------------------
[INFO]  T E S T S
[INFO] ------------------------------------------------------------
[INFO] Running com.masteringselenium.BasicIT
Unable to capture screenshot: null
Unable to clear cookies: null
Unable to capture screenshot: null
Unable to clear cookies: null
[ERROR] Tests run: 2, Failures: 2, Errors: 0, Skipped: 0, Time elapsed: 0.268 s <<< FAILURE! - in com.masteringselenium.BasicIT
[ERROR] googleCheeseExample(com.masteringselenium.BasicIT)  Time elapsed: 0.007 s  <<< FAILURE!
java.lang.NullPointerException
        at com.masteringselenium.BasicIT.googleExampleThatSearchesFor(BasicIT.java:16)
        at com.masteringselenium.BasicIT.googleCheeseExample(BasicIT.java:38)

[ERROR] googleMilkExample(com.masteringselenium.BasicIT)  Time elapsed: 0 s  <<< FAILURE!
java.lang.NullPointerException
        at com.masteringselenium.BasicIT.googleExampleThatSearchesFor(BasicIT.java:16)
        at com.masteringselenium.BasicIT.googleMilkExample(BasicIT.java:43)

[INFO]
[INFO] Results:
[INFO]
[ERROR] Failures:
[ERROR]   BasicIT.googleCheeseExample:38->googleExampleThatSearchesFor:16 NullPointer
[ERROR]   BasicIT.googleMilkExample:43->googleExampleThatSearchesFor:16 NullPointer
[INFO]
[ERROR] Tests run: 2, Failures: 2, Errors: 0, Skipped: 0
```

This time, we can see the same errors, but it's a lot easier to understand now that we have cleaned up our code. This time, it's very clear that the problem is on line 16 of our BasicIT.java. If we look at that line of code, we will see that this is the first time that we try to do something with the driver object that we got using the getDriver() method. The error is NullPointerException and this makes perfect sense due to the change that we put in to the cause errors in the first place.

Stack traces can seem scary, but when they are explained, they normally end up being quite obvious. It does however takes a while to get used to reading stack traces and using the information they give you to work back to the core problem. The important thing to remember with stack traces is to read them in full. Don't be scared of them, or skim through them and guess at the problem. Stack traces provide a lot of useful information to help you diagnose problems. They may not take you directly to the problematic bit of code, but they give you a great place to start.

 Try causing some more errors in your code and then run your tests again. See whether you can work your way back to the problem you put in your code by reading the stack trace.

Summary

After reading this chapter, you will hopefully no longer think of automated checks as regression tests; instead you should think of them as living documentation that continues to grow and flourish as the code they are validating changes. When things go wrong you will be able to take screenshots to aid diagnosis, as well as being able to fluently read stack traces. You will know how to connect your tests to a Selenium-Grid to provide additional flexibility. Finally, you will also have a good understanding of why reliability matters and how this feeds into successful continuous integration, continuous delivery, and continuous deployment.

In the next chapter, we are going to have a look at exceptions generated by Selenium. We will work through various exceptions that you may see and what they mean.

3
Exceptions Are Actually Oracles

Let's start by asking, what is an oracle? An oracle was traditionally seen as a portal that Gods used to talk to people; as with anything, there are various definitions in use. To be clear about what an oracle is in the context of this book, we are going to use the following definition:

"A statement believed to be infallible and authoritative."

Why is an exception an oracle? Like an oracle, an exception is an infallible statement; it will always tell you why something has gone wrong in your code. It may not always be easy to understand, but it does always tell the truth. In this chapter, let's have a look at some exceptions that we often see while writing and running Selenium tests and see what they are trying to tell us.

In this chapter, we will do the following:

- Have a look at some of the more common exceptions that you may see when working with Selenium
- Provide some reasons why you may see these exceptions and give you some pointers to help you use them to fix your code

NoSuchElementException

This is probably the most straightforward exception that you will come across. The element you are trying to find does not exist. There are three common causes for this exception:

- The locator you are using to find the element is incorrect
- Something has gone wrong and the element has not been rendered
- You tried to find the element before it was rendered

The first one is pretty easy to check. You can use the Google Chrome development tools to test your locator. To do this follow these steps:

1. Open the Chrome development tools (*cmd + Alt + I* or *Ctrl + Alt + I*)
2. If your site has multiple frames, or iframes, make sure you select the correct frame
3. Type `$(<myCSSLocator>)` or `$x(<myXPathLocator>)` into the console

If the locator finds an element, or multiple elements that match the locator, it will display it in the console. You will then be able to examine the element(s) and reveal them in the markup to check that it is the element you think you are finding.

You don't have to use Google Chrome to do this. Most browsers have their own development console. There are also other tools available to you. If you use Firebug, there is an additional extension called **Firepath**, which is very useful for this sort of thing as well.

The second one is a little harder to diagnose, as you will need to walk through your code and see what happens to cause the failure. Is it a bug in the application you are testing, or is the previous step failing (that is, did you use valid login credentials)?

Screenshots can be a big help in diagnosing `NoSuchElementException` issues, as they give a good view of the state of the application you are testing when the error failed. They are, however, not infallible. If the cause of the problem is that the element has not yet been rendered, it is possible that the element was not rendered when the error occurred but it was rendered when the screenshot was taken. In this case, the screenshot will appear to show the element was there, when in actual fact it was missing when Selenium tried to find it. These are normally a little bit awkward to diagnose, but if you watch the test running in a browser, you will normally catch it eventually.

This brings us nicely to the third potential problem. Lots of modern websites use technologies such as jQuery or AngularJS, which use JavaScript to manipulate the DOM. Selenium is fast; in many cases it's ready to start interacting with your website before all of the JavaScript has finished doing its job. When this happens, things may seem to be missing when in reality they just haven't been created yet. There are some tricks that you can use to wait for JavaScript to finish rendering the page, but the real solution is to know the application that you are automating. You should know what is required for the page to be ready to use and write your code to be aware of these conditions. A good question to ask in many situations is: *What would I do if I were testing this manually?*

Normally, you would wait for the page to load before starting your testing; you have to write your code so that it can do the same thing. Explicit waits are usually your best friend in this scenario. You should never use `Thread.sleep()` to wait for the page to load. If you do this, you are tailoring the test to work on your machine, and your machine alone. If the test is run on a slower machine, the sleep that you have added will most likely not be long enough and the test will fail. If the test is run on a faster machine, it may work, but it will make the test slower than it needs to be.

Remember, good testing is all about having a **fast** and **reliable** feedback loop.

NoSuchFrameException

It is worth remembering that this exception will be thrown for both errors with frames and errors with iFrames. Frames are not so common in modern web applications, but iFrames are becoming ubiquitous. This exception has a lot in common with `NoSuchElementException`, in that it is usually thrown because the frame doesn't exist when you try to find it. If this is the case the solutions for `NoSuchElementException` should also work for `NoSuchFrameException`. However, working with frames can also have its own unique problems. Let's imagine a scenario where you have a page with multiple frames; we will call them frame A and frame B. We will assume that we first switched to frame B to check something in that frame. If we then try to find frame A, we will get stuck.

This is because frame A does not exist in the context of frame B. The way to work around this issue is to always go back to the parent frame before trying to switch to another frame (unless we are trying to switch to a frame that lives inside another frame). Selenium provides a simple way to do this; you just need to use the following code:

```
driver.switchTo().defaultContent();
```

Don't try to switch to `relative=top`. If you have a very complex frame structure, things can go wrong and it can be really frustrating to diagnose the cause of the problem as everything will look like it should work.

NoSuchWindowException

This exception is caused because the list of windows that you currently have is not up to date. One of the windows that previously existed no longer exists and you can't switch to it. The first thing to do is to check your code and make sure that you are not closing a window without refreshing the available list of windows using:

```
driver.getWindowHandles();
```

The other reason you may get this exception is by trying to switch to a window before calling `driver.getWindowHandles()`. It's not instantly obvious which window handle relates to which window. The best way to track things is to get the handle of the current window before opening up any new windows, using:

```
String currentWindowHandle = driver.getWindowHandle();
```

When you then open a new window and get a list of window handles, you can iterate through the list and ignore the handles for currently open windows. By a process of elimination, you can work out which handle is associated with the new window that was just opened.

This can be tricky if your code opens up multiple windows at the same time. If you do this, you will need to switch to each window in turn and search for something in the DOM that will identify the window so that you can keep track of it. That being said, if your site is continually opening up lots of new windows, you will probably want to have a chat with the developers to find out why. It may well be the case that it shouldn't do that.

ElementNotVisibleException

This is a very useful exception that you will probably come across on a regular basis. It tells you that the `WebElement` that you are trying to interact with is not visible to the user. It's amazing how many people don't realize how important this exception is. Remember, if the element is not visible to the user, they are not going to be able to interact with it.

Please don't ignore or try to work around this exception. You will probably come across lots of so-called "solutions" to this problem that are really nasty hacks; they usually involve some custom JavaScript to perform the desired action and totally ignore the fact that you really have a legitimate problem.

The Selenium development team has spent a lot of time trying to work out if something is visible to the user and, they have done a very good job. There is code to work out if the element is actually on the screen, or if it is a size that is too small to be seen by a person. There is even code in Selenium to try and work out whether it is covered by other elements (this is a lot harder than it sounds, as CSS can make things extremely hard).

If you see this exception, there is a problem that needs to be fixed with your code. Selenium is very fast and will often try and interact with an element before it has had a chance to render on the screen. Your code should be aware of what needs to happen for the element to be displayed to the end user. You will need to wait for the page rendering (or at least the part of the page you are interested in) to complete before trying to interact with the element.

When you see this exception, the best thing to do is walk through the code manually and check whether you can see things that load slowly. The usual fix is to then add an explicit wait to wait for the correct conditions to be met before trying to interact with the element in question.

StaleElementReferenceException

This is an exception that you will quite often see if you work with AJAX or JavaScript-heavy websites where the DOM is continuously being manipulated.

You are probably used to seeing code like this:

```
WebElement googleSearchBar = driver.findElement(By.name("q"));
```

The `WebElement` object that you have created is actually a reference to a specific element in the DOM; think of it as a phone number that you call to talk to that element:

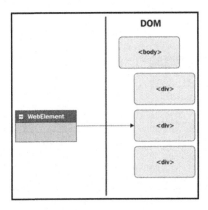

When the DOM is manipulated and the old element is destroyed, that reference no longer links to an element in the DOM and it becomes stale. Using our phone number analogy, this is where the phone line is disconnected. You can keep calling that number, but it will not ring anymore; you'll just get a message telling you that the phone number is not valid:

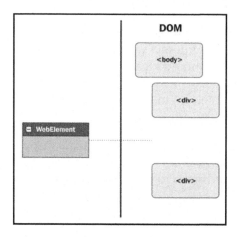

This can get very confusing when the element we have a reference to has been destroyed, and then another identical looking element has replaced it. On the face of it, everything looks identical, but for some reason it just doesn't work. To finish off with our phone analogy, think of a situation where one of your friends switches mobile phone networks and gets a new number. Their phone looks the same and they can still make calls on it, but if you try to call them on their old number, you get that message telling you that the phone number is not valid:

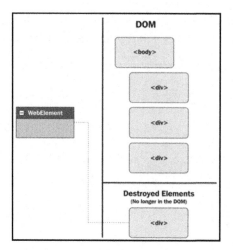

Using the phone analogy, the solution is simple: you ask your friend for their new number, and you can call them again and everything is back to normal. The Selenium solution is just as simple, you ask Selenium to find that element again:

```
googleSearchBar = driver.findElement(By.name("q"));
```

The reference is updated and you can carry on interacting with that `WebElement`.

It is easy to say that it is simple to fix this problem, but how did we get there in the first place?

Well, we did not know what our application was going to do. We did not expect the DOM to be rebuilt and that the original element that we created a reference to would be destroyed.

We now need to start asking questions: does it matter that the original element was destroyed and then recreated?

If it doesn't matter, maybe we should just find the element every time we want to use it to ensure that we don't get `StaleElementReferenceException`.

Maybe we were expecting the element to be destroyed and recreated and we want to check for that. If so, we could use a conditional wait to wait for the element to become stale before continuing with our test. Let's have a look at some code that will do that for us:

```
WebDriverWait wait = new WebDriverWait(driver, 10);
wait.until(ExpectedConditions.stalenessOf(googleSearchBar));
```

It's actually pretty easy to do; Selenium's Java bindings have some predefined expected conditions that we can use without having to write our own explicit wait condition.

Finally, maybe we're not expecting this to happen. If that is the case, good news, your test may have found a bug that needs to be fixed.

InvalidElementStateException

This is an exception that you probably won't see that often, but when it does pop up it is not always instantly clear what it means. `InvalidElementStateException` is thrown when the `WebElement` that you are trying to interact with is not in a state that would allow you to perform the action that you would like to perform.

Think of a <select> element that gives you a list of countries to select when filling in an address form; this element will allow you to select the country associated with your address.

Now, what if the developers have added some validation that will not let you enter a postcode (or ZIP code) until you have selected a country, so that they can trigger the correct postcode validation routine? In this case, the <input> element where you enter your postcode may be disabled until you have selected your country.

If you try to enter a postcode into this disabled <input> element, you will get InvalidElementStateException.

The fix is to do whatever a user manually testing the site would do to enable the <input> element; in this case, select a country from the <select> element.

UnsupportedCommandException

This is one of those exceptions that you may never see or, depending upon the driver implementation you use, one you may see all the time. You will find UnsupportedCommandException getting thrown when the WebDriver implementation you are running does not support one of the core WebDriver API commands.

There are quite a few third-party WebDriver bindings, and these bindings are in various states of completeness. Not all third-party projects have managed to implement the entire WebDriver API yet. When a driver binding that you are using does not support a command that is part of the WebDriver API, it will throw UnsupportedCommandException.

If this happens to you, there is really not a lot you can do about it. Your choices are:

- Code around the problem by using a different command
- Switch to a different WebDriver binding
- Write the code required to support that command yourself (and raise a pull request!)

UnreachableBrowserException

To understand UnreachableBrowserException, we should first understand how Selenium works. To most people, Selenium is simply an API that you use to write code to drive a browser. Notice that I said code, not tests. The Selenium API is designed to be a browser automation tool, not just a test tool. It is commonly used for testing, but it can be used for any purpose that would require browser automation.

The current API that is in use is the WebDriver API; the old Selenium RC API has been deprecated since Selenium 2 came out and should not be actively used by anybody creating a new project.

Selenium is a bit more than just an API though. It is also a series of plugins, or binaries, or native implementations that enable you to talk to the browser. The Selenium API talks to all of these implementation methods using the common wire protocol. This wire protocol is a RESTful web service using JSON over HTTP. When we talk about the bit of Selenium that commands are sent to using the wire protocol, we call it the **RemoteWebDriver**.

All browser-specific driver implementations are extensions of the core RemoteWebDriver class. The implementation method differs from driver to driver; some use client mode and some use server mode.

Client mode is where the RemoteWebDriver implementation is either loaded as a browser plugin or natively supported by the browser. The language bindings connect directly to the remote instance and tell it what to do. An example of this implementation method would be the old FirefoxDriver bindings (since Selenium 3, the FirefoxDriver implementation has switched from client mode to server mode and is on par with the ChromeDriver implementation):

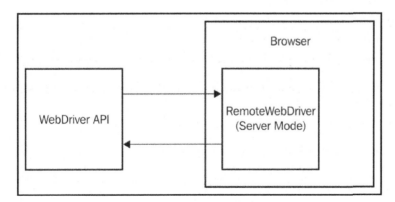

Server mode is where the language binding sets up a server, which acts as a go-between for the language binding and the browser. It basically translates the commands sent by your code into something the browser can understand. An example of this implementation method would be ChromeDriver:

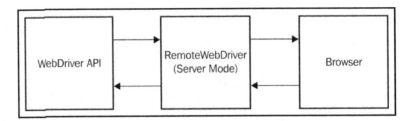

As you can see from the preceding diagram, the code you wrote using the WebDriver API is sent over to the browser via the `RemoteWebDriver` instance, using the wire protocol. As you can imagine, this process is problematic if there is no browser available for us to talk to.

If we send commands out but cannot get a response, we get `UnreachableBrowserException`; it means that you cannot connect to the RemoteWebDriver instance. There are various problems that could cause this error:

- The browser didn't start
- The browser crashed
- The version of the RemoteWebDriver instance you are using is incompatible with the version of the browser you are using
- Network issues
- Are you connecting to another machine?
- Is a firewall involved?
- Are you connecting to the correct port?
- The browser you are trying to use has not been installed
- The browser is not installed in the default location and Selenium can't find it

Debugging the issue can be frustrating, and you will probably kick yourself when you find out what the root cause was.

SessionNotFoundException

Occasionally, when you are running your tests, things will go wrong and you will lose connection with the browser instance you are driving. When you lose connection to the browser instance, `SessionNotFoundException` will be thrown.

This is a similar error to `UnreachableBrowserException` but in this case, you have a much smaller list of things to check since you know you were successfully talking to the `RemoteWebDriver` instance for a while.

The following problems usually cause this error:

- You inadvertently quit the driver instance
- The browser crashed

WebDriverException – element is not clickable at point

This is an exception that you will generally only see in ChromeDriver. What has happened is that when Selenium has tried to click on an element, ChromeDriver has detected that the element that you tried to click will not actually get the click event because something else is in the way. There are a few possible causes of this:

- Another element is layered on top of the element that you are trying to click
- The screen has not finished rendering yet, and in this semi-rendered state something has temporarily covered the element you are trying to click on

The solution is to put in an explicit wait that waits for the element to become clickable:

```
By locator = By.id("someElement");
WebDriverWait wait = new WebDriverWait(driver, 10);
wait.until(ExpectedConditions.elementToBeClickable(locator));
```

Once you know that the element is clickable, you shouldn't get any errors trying to click on it.

NoAlertPresentException

This one is pretty straightforward, but questions still come up about it. This is caused by Selenium expecting an alert to appear, but one not being there. Say you have the following code:

```
driver.switchTo().alert().accept();
```

But the alert never appears; this is the exception that will be thrown. This is the same for any alert interaction; it doesn't just have to be `accept()`.

Summary

In this chapter, we have had a look at the common, and some not so common exceptions that you are likely to see on your automation journey. This should have helped you to see that exceptions are actually really useful, and can provide a great deal of insight as to what has gone wrong with your automated checks.

After reading through this chapter you should have understood that exceptions are actually trying to tell you something. When you look at commonly thrown exceptions you should now be able to quickly diagnose the root cause of the issue. You should have an understanding of the basic architecture of Selenium and how it send commands over to the browser. You will also understand how `WebElement` is a reference to a specific element in the DOM, and how it can become stale.

In the next chapter, we will have a look at the various wait solutions in Selenium. We will discuss which ones are good and which ones are bad, and include detailed explanations.

4
The Waiting Game

In the previous chapter, we had a look at various exceptions and some of the possible causes of them. In this chapter, we will do the following:

- Look at implicit and explicit waits
- Find out about the `ExpectedConditions` class in the Selenium support package
- Examine how we can extend `ExpectedConditions` by adding our own customized waits
- Have a look at the core fluent wait functionality built into Selenium, and the use of functions and predicates

Are we nearly ready yet?

How do we know that the page we are interested in has loaded and is ready for us to start running our scripts against?

It sounds like a simple question; however, it is one of the things that always catches people out. If you are ever asked why a script doesn't work when the code seems sensible, your usual reply should probably be, *It's a wait problem!*

Wait problems are probably the most common error in Selenium scripts; shockingly, most of the time, people don't even know they have them. JavaScript-heavy sites are especially prone to wait problems, but you can run into them with sites that don't use much JavaScript as well.

Why are wait problems so prevalent? It's largely due to people not thinking about the consequences of external variables when they write their scripts.

Let's take a made-up scenario. We have a page that waits until it is loaded to make an AJAX request to a server. This page is not ready to be used until the AJAX request is complete, but Selenium thinks it is ready after the initial page load. How do we let Selenium know that the page has loaded and is ready for us to start our automated script?

I've timed it, and I know it takes 5 seconds for the page to load

You would be surprised how often people say this. They then tend to add something like this to their scripts:

```
Thread.sleep(5000);
```

Code like this will never work reliably. It doesn't take into account any external variables, and it will slow your tests down. What do we mean by external variables? Well, we have the following.

Machine specification

Different machines have different specifications. It sounds obvious, yet it is something that many people who write automation scripts do not take into account. A slow machine with very little memory will run your scripts much slower than a fast machine. It will probably take it longer to render the page that you are testing. This means that the web element that has been rendered instantly on a fast machine may not actually be there for a few hundred milliseconds on a slow machine. This is long enough to cause an error in your test, but not long enough for it to be instantly obvious to the human eye.

Server specification

First of all, let's be clear by what we mean when we say server specification. We mean the machine (virtual or physical) that is hosting the website that you are attempting to test. The effect of the server specification can have varying effects on the site you are testing that in large part, is dependent upon the design of the site. If your site depends upon a lot of server-side processing, it could slow down significantly when under load. If you have a high number of concurrent users, the server may have problems servicing the requests, and the responses coming back to the client may take longer than expected. Maybe the site that you are visiting allows the user to download lots of files, but the hard drives in the server are not up to the task, and your request to read data from the disk is being queued up.

There are hundreds of possible reasons why a server may not always respond to your request promptly; don't expect it to be prompt when you write your tests.

JavaScript engine performance

This can make a massive difference when testing modern JavaScript-heavy sites. Something that is rendered instantly in the latest version of Google Chrome could take seconds to render in Internet Explorer 8. If you are interested in how much variance there is in the various JavaScript engines, have a look at the SunSpider JavaScript benchmark (`http://www.webkit.org/perf/sunspider/sunspider.html`). Try running the test in various browsers. It's amazing how slow some of the older browsers are.

Networks

If you are testing an AJAX-heavy site, network performance will matter. If your AJAX requests take a long time to resolve, the site you are testing will take longer to rerender the frontend as a result of the AJAX calls. Something that works fine on your local machine can suddenly start failing all over the place when you run the same tests on a real server.

If you start looking at all of these potential problems, it soon becomes clear that an arbitrary wait of 5 seconds is never going to be reliable. The reaction some people have when they are faced with this problem is that they extend their waits. Before you know it, you have 10-second waits littered around your test code, then 15-second waits. Before you know it, your simple test case that wants to load up a page and click on a couple of buttons is taking two minutes to run.

Simply telling people not to use `Thread.sleep()` is not going to fix the problem either. You need to explain why people should not use `Thread.sleep()`. I worked on a project where we had one member of our team who kept putting `Thread.sleep()` into our code base. We told him not to, but he persisted. Eventually, we added a commit rule to SVN that would reject any code that had `Thread.sleep()` in it. This didn't fix our problem; instead, he changed his code to use `Object.wait()`!

The real problem was that we had not sat him down and explained why we didn't want him to use `Thread.sleep()`. We had just said that it was something we didn't do. Our assumption was that he would know why it was a bad code pattern. The problem was that he didn't.

So, what do we do?

Let's face it: working out whether something is ready for you to interact with is actually quite a complex process. What would you do if you were testing the site manually?

That's simple: if you were manually testing the site, you would wait for it to be ready before you start testing. The problem is, what does ready mean?

Well, to me, it means that the page has downloaded, the site has had a chance to render everything that looks like it needs to be rendered, and it appears ready to use. Sometimes, I may start using it before it has downloaded all of the images, but I'll usually wait for the main scaffolding to be in a state that looks ready. Unless I'm looking at the network traffic, I won't know that AJAX requests have resolved, but this is where my experience of what the site should look like comes in.

You may have noticed that I used the phrase "looks ready" a couple of times here. So how do we code "looks ready"? Well, the problem is that you can't; there is a lot of processing that goes on in our brains to come up with "looks ready".

It's like asking a computer to tell you if some cream that has been left in the fridge has gone off. How do you define gone off? Is it a look, or a smell? If there is some mold on the top and we remove it, has it still gone off?

I suspect that, for the last question, some people will have said yes because once it has gone moldy they throw it out, whereas others would quite happily remove the mold and continue using it. So, who is right? What should the computer do?

Obviously, building up a mental model in a computer and asking it to interpret the status of "looks right" is generally not realistic. So, what can we do?

Well, we can programmatically make sure that specific actions have happened before we start trying to do things, or in other words, we can define what "looks right" means in the context of our test. Different tests may have different definitions of "looks right," or they may share a common understanding of "looks right."

We are going to use various types of wait to help us define "looks right."

I just want Selenium to do it for me

Well, you do have some options available if you just want Selenium to try to do it for you. Selenium has three built-in waiting mechanisms that you can configure universally by configuring the `Timeouts()` object that is set on your driver object when you instantiate it. The available mechanisms are these:

- Page load timeout
- Script timeout
- Implicitly wait timeout

Let's have a look at them in some more detail.

Page load timeout

This defines the amount of time that Selenium will wait for a page to load. By default, it is set to 0 (which equates to an infinite time out). If you want to ensure that an error is thrown if your page takes longer than expected to load, you can modify this by using this line of code:

```
driver.manage().timeouts().pageLoadTimeout(15, TimeUnit.SECONDS);
```

If your page does not load within 15 seconds, `WebDriverException` will be thrown.

You should of course be aware that, while Selenium does its best to ensure that the page is loaded, you should not rely on it. With a simple website with no JavaScript manipulation of the DOM or AJAX requests firing away in the background, Selenium will be pretty accurate. With modern websites, it isn't that easy, and as a result Selenium doesn't always get it right.

Selenium will do a variety of things to try to ensure that the page has loaded. A couple of examples of this are these:

- Wait for the onload event to trigger
- See whether new elements are still being added to the DOM

The exact mechanisms used can differ from driver to driver, and it is constantly under review to try to make it as accurate and as stable as possible. However, modern websites are a moving target, so the current revision of code in Selenium may not work for the site you are testing.

It is also worth noting that there are a plethora of JavaScript frameworks that don't actually start doing their DOM manipulation until the onload event has triggered.

With this in mind, you should always treat the fact that Selenium thinks the page has loaded as a guess. You are going to have to work out whether the JavaScript manipulation of the DOM or any pending AJAX requests have completed by yourself (we will have a look at ways in which we can do this later on in this chapter).

Script timeout

This one is pretty simple really: it sets the amount of time that Selenium will wait for a bit of JavaScript to execute when you use the `executeAsyncScript()` method.

Errors in this area are normally due to callbacks not being invoked or, very occasionally, the script timeout being set to a negative number. It's normally pretty easy to diagnose these problems, as you will see an exception that looks like this:

```
org.openqa.selenium.TimeoutException: Script execution failed.
```

Implicitly wait timeout

Implicit waits were not originally part of the `WebDriver` API; they are actually a hangover from the old Selenium 1 API. They were not going to be put into the `WebDriver` API, because they encourage people to write tests without thinking, something like this:

Why is my test failing when the element should be there? Oh, let's just slap in an arbitrary wait; if it goes green, it must be fine.

The only reason it made it into the `WebDriver` API was the massive outcry from the community who had got used to the Selenium 1 API and wanted it back.

This is probably the timeout that causes the most confusion, even though, on the face of it, it seems very simple. What it does is add a grace period when trying to find an element. If you set your `implicitlyWait` timeout as shown in the following code, Selenium will wait for up to 15 seconds for an element to appear in the DOM when trying to find it:

```
driver.manage().timeouts().implicitlyWait(15, TimeUnit.SECONDS);
```

A lot of people will have been told not to use implicit waits because they are bad form, but they don't really know why. You may come across code patterns that look something like this:

```
private static final int DEFAULT_TIMEOUT_IN_SECONDS = 10;

public WebElement reliableFindElement(final WebDriver driver,
final By selector) {
    WebElement element;
    long endTime = System.currentTimeMillis() +
    Duration.ofSeconds(DEFAULT_TIMEOUT_IN_SECONDS).toMillis();
    while (System.currentTimeMillis() < endTime) {
        try {
            element = driver.findElement(selector);
            return element;
        } catch (NoSuchElementException ignored) {
            System.out.println("Not found, trying again...");
        }
    }
    throw new NoSuchElementException("Could not find " + selector);
}
```

What this is actually doing is re-implementing an implicit wait. That's a lot of code to write and maintain that provides no real benefit!

What makes things worse is that once code such as this has been written; it's usually used across the project, which means that the problems it might have fixed will still exist.

So, what are the problems with implicit waits? They are as follows:

- If you want to check that an element does not exist, it increases the time for that check to be performed, slowing your tests down
- They can break explicit waits

It can slow my tests down?

This is something that seems very obvious when you stop and think about it, but it is surprising how many people don't.

Something that we all do from time to time in our tests is check that something doesn't exist. For example, you may have a phone book application, and you want to check that clicking on the delete link removes a contact from your phone book and no longer displays that contact on the screen.

The obvious thing to do is delete the contact and then try to find the elements on the screen that were used to display the contact. Let's say that, in our example, we have four elements that we display for a contact:

- Name
- Number
- Type of number
- Address

When we delete a contact, we want to make sure that all four elements are removed from the screen, so we check them one after the other. The problem is that we have set an implicit wait of 15 seconds. This means that each time we try to find an element, Selenium waits for 15 seconds to allow the element to appear, before reporting back that it cannot be found. We have inadvertently added a minute to our test's run time, when these checks could have been performed in under a second.

As you can see, the more times we check that something is not there, the slower our tests get, until, before you know it, we have a 2-hour-long test run that nobody bothers to run anymore because it takes so long and it's just quicker to check it manually.

Now, there are ways around this: we could change the implicit wait timeout before each test that checks for the non-existence of an element, and then change it back again afterward. The problem is that it doesn't take long for somebody to slip up and forget to do this. Before you know it, your test execution time has started increasing, and you have to go hunting through the code to find out what is wrong. The worst-case scenario is that it happens slowly over a period of time, so you don't notice the odd 15-second increase in the time it takes to run your tests. By the time you do realize, the code is riddled with excessive waits.

It can break explicit waits?

This is the other side effect that people don't always pick up on. Once you have set an implicit wait, it lives for the life of the driver object. This means that when you create your explicit waits, they will use the driver object that already has an implicit wait set on it.

Let's have a look at a couple of scenarios to illustrate the problem.

The explicit wait that never finds an element

You have just started working with a development team that already has a Selenium test framework and a series of tests. The tests are reasonably well factored, and there is a decent `DriverFactory` class that deals with all the driver setup for various browsers. You have been working with this framework for a couple of months and are quite confident with it, but you've never really needed to dig into the internal workings of how the driver object is set up because it has always worked for you.

You now have a requirement to write a test for a new bit of functionality. This functionality is the same as when you log into your site, there should now be an animated GIF displayed while your account details are loaded. When all the information is ready to show you your homepage, the animated GIF will disappear. Your UX team has spent some time investigating this area of the site, and it has found that if it takes longer than 10 seconds to load your home page, most customers will give up and close the browser, so we have a hard requirement that this page must load within 10 seconds.

You start writing your test and decide that this is a good candidate for an explicit wait, and write some code that looks like this:

```
WebDriverWait wait = new WebDriverWait(getDriver(), 10, 500);
wait.until(not(presenceOfElementLocated(By.id("loading_image"))));
```

It all looks good, so you run your test and it fails. You manually check the functionality and it looks as if it should work. Looking at it, there is a delay of about 2 seconds before the loading image disappears, but your explicit wait is waiting for 10 seconds, and it is rechecking the page every 500 milliseconds. Why isn't it working?

You decide to go through it step by step and debug it. It all looks fine until you get to your explicit wait. When you go through it step by step, you see it perform the initial check; the animated GIF is still there, so it loops around. You see it keep looping around in your explicit wait while the animated GIF is displayed. The animated GIF disappears, and you don't see your breakpoint in your explicit wait hit again, but after 10 seconds the test fails with `TimeoutException`.

How did that happen? You double-check your code, and you do indeed have a 500-millisecond interval set for your explicit wait. What is going on? The element is there! Time to raise a bug on Selenium, perhaps, or complain on a mailing list?

Wait! It's a trap!

What has actually happened is that you have been tricked. In the `DriverFactory` code, somebody has helpfully set a 15-second implicit wait. This means that when the code drops into your explicit wait, a `findElement()` call is made, and that call goes off and tries to find the `<image>` element that holds our GIF. If the `<image>` element is not there, this call will wait for up to 15 seconds for the element to appear. However, your explicit wait is going to timeout after only 10 seconds. So, what happens is the following sequence:

1. We keep checking for the existence of the `<image>` element every 500 milliseconds; it's there for the first 2 seconds, and this works as expected
2. After 2 seconds, the `<image>` element disappears, so when we next check for it, it's not there
3. The check to see if it's not there takes 15 seconds to respond with the information that the element has gone because of the implicit wait
4. Our expected condition times out after 10 seconds and fails the test because we still haven't had a response about the state of the element, even though it's not there

To fix it, you are either going to have to increase your timeout in your explicit wait, or decrease the timeout set in the implicit wait.

Hang on, I've tried this and it didn't work that way for me!

You have actually just hit on the next problem of mixing implicit and explicit waits: you are in the realms of undefined behavior. Explicit waits and implicit waits were never supposed to be mixed, so the Selenium spec never defined what should happen if you do mix them.

Generally (but not always), explicit waits are code in the client bindings, and implicit waits are code on the remote side. So, does the client binding you are using interrupt a request to the remote server to cause a timeout, or does it wait for the response from the outstanding request before checking to see if it should timeout?

As you can see, we are totally at the mercy of different driver implementations. Different versions of the same implementation also have no predefined expectations of what should happen when you mix implicit and explicit waits. It may work fine, it may not work at all, and it may intermittently work. If it does work, it also may break when you upgrade to a newer version because, yup, you guessed it: There's no guarantee when it comes to how this stuff should be implemented.

The explicit wait that works, but slows your tests down

This scenario is basically the same as the preceding scenario, but this time the UX team has decided that the drop off point is 15 seconds. So, your explicit wait code now looks like this:

```
WebDriverWait wait = new WebDriverWait(getDriver(), 15, 500);
wait.until(not(presenceOfElementLocated(By.id("loading_image"))));
```

However, this time the implicit wait inside the driver factory has helpfully been set to 10 seconds. Everything works, so at the time you don't notice any problems; you run your test and it passes, and everything looks fine. The problem is that the animated GIF actually disappeared after 2 seconds, but your test waited the whole 10 seconds set by the implicit wait before it realized that the animated GIF had gone.

You have inadvertently added a few seconds delay to your test for no good reason. The build is reliably green, so this doesn't get noticed; you are on your first step towards the death of your fast feedback loop by one thousand cuts.

The solution

It is generally safer to not fiddle with the implicit wait timeouts and just deal with the exceptions to the rule (that is, the slow loading elements) on a case-by-case basis.

You can of course use implicit waits and program around the problems highlighted before, but are you sure you want to?

Using explicit waits

The recommended solution for waiting problems is to use explicit waits. There is already a class full of precanned examples called `ExpectedConditions` to make your life easy, and it really is not that hard to use them. You can do the simple things, such as finding an element once it becomes visible in two lines of code:

```
WebDriverWait wait = new WebDriverWait(getDriver(), 15, 100);
```

```
WebElement myElement = wait.until(ExpectedConditions.
visibilityOfElementLocated(By.id("foo")));
```

Bear in mind that the ExpectedConditions class are prime examples. While being helpful, they are really designed to show you how to set explicit waits up so that you can easily create your own. With these examples, it is trivial to create a new class with conditions that you care about in it, which can be reused again and again in your project.

Earlier, we said we would look at a way to work out if your site had finished processing AJAX requests; let's do that now. First of all, we will create a new class that lets you work out whether a website that uses jQuery has finished making AJAX calls, by using this code:

```
package com.masteringselenium;

import org.openqa.selenium.JavascriptExecutor;
import org.openqa.selenium.WebDriver;
import org.openqa.selenium.support.ui.ExpectedCondition;

public class AdditionalConditions {

    public static ExpectedCondition<Boolean>
    jQueryAJAXCallsHaveCompleted() {
        return new ExpectedCondition<Boolean>() {

            @Override
            public Boolean apply(WebDriver driver) {
                return (Boolean) ((JavascriptExecutor)
                driver).executeScript("return
                (window.jQuery != null)    && (jQuery.active === 0);");
            }
        };
    }
}
```

What this will do is use JavascriptExecutor to make a request to the page to find out whether jQuery has any outstanding active AJAX requests. There is also some protection built in to ensure that if the page does not initially have jQuery loaded when ExpectedCondition fires, the JavaScript snippet will not error. The ExpectedCondition class will still obviously throw an exception if it times out.

We can now call this condition anywhere in our code by using the following:

```
WebDriverWait wait = new WebDriverWait(getDriver(), 15, 100);
wait.until(AdditionalConditions.jQueryAJAXCallsHaveCompleted()));
```

We now have an easy way to find out whether jQuery has finished running AJAX calls in the background, before we interact with our jQuery-based site.

Maybe you don't use jQuery; well, how about AngularJS? Take a look at this code:

```
public static ExpectedCondition<Boolean> angularHasFinishedProcessing() {
    return new ExpectedCondition<Boolean>() {
        @Override
        public Boolean apply(WebDriver driver) {
            return Boolean.valueOf(((JavascriptExecutor)
            driver).executeScript("return
            (window.angular !== undefined) &&
            (angular.element(document).injector()
            !== undefined) && (angular.element(document).injector()
            .get('$http').pendingRequests.length === 0)").toString());
        }
    };
}
```

This one is a little more complex on the JavaScript side. We have a chain of conditions to ensure that AngularJS is available, and has had time to bootstrap and generate its services. We then hook into the internal `pendingRequests` array and count the number of AJAX requests that still need to complete. We are using some internal knowledge of Angular for this example, so your mileage may vary, but it should be easy enough to tweak it if Angular does change the way it tracks pending requests.

As with our previous example, this is now trivial to use elsewhere in your code; you just need the following:

```
WebDriverWait wait = new WebDriverWait(getDriver(), 15, 100);
wait.until(AdditionalConditions.angularHasFinishedProcessing());
```

As you can see, it really is quite easy to create new conditions to use in your code. The next question is, how complex can we make these waits?

Fluent waits, the core of explicit waits

At the core of explicit waits is the incredibly powerful fluent wait API. All `WebDriverWait` objects extend `FluentWait`. So, why would we want to use `FluentWait`?

Well, we get more granular control of the `wait` object, and we can easily specify exceptions to ignore. Let's have a look at an example:

```
Wait<WebDriver> wait = new FluentWait<>(driver)
        .withTimeout(Duration.ofSeconds(15))
        .pollingEvery(Duration.ofMillis(500))
        .ignoring(NoSuchElementException.class)
        .withMessage("The message you will see in
        if a TimeoutException is thrown");
```

As you can see, in the preceding code snippet, we have created a `wait` object with a 15-second timeout that polls every 500 milliseconds to see whether a condition is met. We have decided that while waiting for our condition to become true, we want to ignore any instances of `NoSuchElementException`, so we have specified it using the `.ignoring()` command. We also want to return a custom message if we get `TimeoutException`, so we have also added it here.

If you want to ignore multiple exceptions, you have two choices. First of all, you can chain the `ignoring()` method multiple times by using this code:

```
Wait<WebDriver> wait = new FluentWait<WebDriver>(driver)
        .withTimeout(15, TimeUnit.SECONDS)
        .pollingEvery(500, TimeUnit.MILLISECONDS)
        .ignoring(NoSuchElementException.class)
        .ignoring(StaleElementReferenceException.class)
        .withMessage("The message you will see in if a
        TimeoutException is thrown");
```

Or, you can pass multiple types of exception into the `.ignoreAll()` command by using this code:

```
Wait<WebDriver> wait = new FluentWait<>(driver)
        .withTimeout(Duration.ofSeconds(15))
        .pollingEvery(Duration.ofMillis(500))
        .ignoring(NoSuchElementException.class)
        .ignoring(StaleElementReferenceException.class)
        .withMessage("The message you will see in if a
        TimeoutException is thrown");
```

If you prefer, you can even pass a collection of exceptions into the `.ignoreAll()` method by using this code:

```
Wait<WebDriver> wait = new FluentWait<>(driver)
        .withTimeout(Duration.ofSeconds(15))
        .pollingEvery(Duration.ofMillis(500))
        .ignoreAll(Arrays.asList(
```

```
                NoSuchElementException.class,
                StaleElementReferenceException.class
    ))
    .withMessage("The message you will see in if
    a TimeoutException is thrown");
```

We now have a `wait` object that is ready to wait for something to happen. So, how do we make it wait for something? We have two options: a function or a predicate. For more information on functions and predicates, have a look at the Guava Libraries documentation (https://code.google.com/p/guava-libraries/wiki/FunctionalExplained). Selenium uses the Guava libraries for functions and predicates.

Functions

We are going to create a very basic function that will find and return `WebElement`. Take a look at this code:

```
Function<WebDriver, WebElement> weFindElementFoo = new Function<WebDriver,
WebElement>() {
    public WebElement apply(WebDriver driver) {
        return driver.findElement(By.id("foo"));
    }
};
```

The function may look confusing, but it is actually quite simple. It is simply specifying an input and an output. Let's break it down and take the object definition in isolation. Look at this code:

```
Function<WebDriver, WebElement> weFindElementFoo
```

What we are saying is that we are going to create a function named `weFindElementFoo()`. We are going to supply this `function` with an object of type `WebDriver` as the input, and we will get an object of type `WebElement` returned to us as the output.

All functions need to have a single method called `apply`, which takes our input (in this case, a `WebDriver` object) and returns our output (in this case, a `WebElement` object):

```
new Function<WebDriver, WebElement>() {
    public WebElement apply(WebDriver driver) {
        //Do something here
    }
};
```

The code inside the method then just needs to do something with our input to transform it into our output which is, in this case, the following:

```
return driver.findElement(By.id("foo"));
```

Overall, it is very simple once you have broken it down.

The advantage of using a function is that you can pass in an object of any type as the input, and return an object of any type as the output. This gives you a huge amount of flexibility with your waits, as you can return all sorts of useful objects when your waiting criteria have been met. Most functions you come across in Selenium will probably be returning a single `WebElement` or a list of `WebElement` objects. Don't think that functions can only return `WebElement` though. They are also quite capable of returning other object types. Let's have a look at some code that returns a `Boolean`:

```
Function<WebDriver, Boolean> didWeFindElementFoo = new Function<WebDriver,
Boolean>() {
    public Boolean apply(WebDriver driver) {
        return driver.findElements(By.id("foo")).size() > 0;
    }
};
```

Let's break this down in the same way as we broke down our previous function. First of all, we have this line of code:

```
Function<WebDriver, Boolean> didWeFindElementFoo
```

Here, we are saying that we are going to create a function named `didWeFindElementFoo`. We are going to supply this function with an object of type `WebDriver`, and we will get an object of type Boolean returned to us.

We still need to add our single method, called `apply`, which takes your input (in this case, a `WebDriver` object). As this is a predicate, our `apply` method will have to return an output of type Boolean, as shown in this code:

```
new Function<WebDriver, Boolean>() {
    public Boolean apply(WebDriver driver) {
        //TODO - Do something here
    }
};
```

Finally, we need to add the code inside the method that does something to our input to transform it into our output, which of course must be an object of type Boolean:

```
return driver.findElements(By.id("foo")).size() > 0;
```

Once again, it's pretty simple when you break it down.

 Remember, you can return any type of object. It doesn't have to just be a WebElement or Boolean. Why don't you try and create your own functions that return different object types right now? You could try returning an `ArrayList` of a `WebElement` objects, or maybe the location of `WebElement` on screen using `webElement.getCoordinates()`.

Now that we have something to put into our `wait` object, we can use it to wait for something to happen; let's start off with this code:

```
wait.until(weFindElementFoo);
```

So, what happens when we use this? We are ignoring any instance of `NoSuchElementException`, so we will keep trying to find an element with an ID of `foo` for 15 seconds. If we did not successfully find the element, we will pause for 500 milliseconds and then try again. If we have not found our element with an ID of `foo` after 15 seconds, we will then throw `TimeoutException` with the custom message "The message you will see if `TimeoutException` is thrown."

As you can see, we can create nice readable tests that tell us what they are doing. When things go wrong, we can throw exceptions with useful information in the message. Not only do we have a lot of control over timeouts and polling, they are also very clearly readable for anybody else who starts looking at our code. We have given ourselves the ability to do very simple, or complex, things using functions or predicates that can be given really good descriptive names.

Let's have a look at some more code examples.

We will start off with a function that uses jQuery to see whether a specific listener has been registered on an element:

```
public static Function<WebDriver, Boolean>
listenerIsRegisteredOnElement(final String listenerType, final WebElement
element) {
    return new Function<WebDriver, Boolean>() {
        public Boolean apply(WebDriver driver) {
            Map<String, Object> registeredListeners = (Map<String,
            Object>)
            ((JavascriptExecutor) driver).
            executeScript("return (window.jQuery != null) &&
            (jQuery._data(jQuery(arguments[0]).get(0)),
            'events')", element);
            for (Map.Entry<String, Object> listener :
            registeredListeners.entrySet()) {
```

```
            if (listener.getKey().equals(listenerType)) {
                return true;
            }
        }
        return false;
    }
};
}
```

Why is this useful? Well, you may have a requirement that says when you select an input element, an onfocus event is triggered, which adds a blue border around the element that you are currently editing. That is a hard requirement to test, so checking that an onfocus event has been registered on an element may be the easiest way to do it.

Next, we have a function that will check to see whether an element is moving on the screen, as shown in this code:

```
public static Function<WebDriver, Boolean> elementHasStoppedMoving(final
WebElement element) {
    return new Function<WebDriver, Boolean>() {
        public Boolean apply(WebDriver driver) {
            Point initialLocation = ((Locatable)
            element).getCoordinates().inViewPort();
            try {
                Thread.sleep(50);
            } catch (InterruptedException ignored) {
                //ignored
            }
            Point finalLocation = ((Locatable)
            element).getCoordinates().inViewPort();
            return initialLocation.equals(finalLocation);
        }
    };
}
```

This would be useful if you have some objects that move around the screen for a period of time, before stopping so that you can click on them. Trying to click on a moving target is hard, and you will probably get intermittent test failures. This allows you to wait until the object has stopped moving.

You may be asking how this could be useful; type CSS3 games into Google and see what's possible. One that's worth looking at is http://www.cssplay.co.uk/menu/cssplay-whack-a-rat.html.

Java8 lambdas

Since Selenium now requires Java8, we can safely use Java8 language constructs such as lambdas to reduce the amount of boilerplate code in our functions. Lambdas enable you to execute anonymous functions without having to write a load of boilerplate code; they have the following three main parts:

1. The arguments you want to pass into the anonymous function (this can be 1 -n arguments).
2. An assignment operator that lets Java know that something is being passed in: ->.
3. The body of your anonymous function. The lambda will work out the return type, so you don't need to worry about it.

They are really a lot easier to use than many people think; let's convert our `didWeFindElementFoo` method that we wrote earlier into something that uses lambdas to prove it.

> If you are new to lambdas in Java, you will probably want to go and have a look at the quick start guide provided by Oracle. You can find this at http://www.oracle.com/webfolder/technetwork/tutorials/obe/java/Lambda-QuickStart/index.html.

First of all we have the original function:

```
Function<WebDriver, Boolean> didWeFindElementFoo = new Function<WebDriver,
Boolean>() {
    public Boolean apply(WebDriver driver) {
            return driver.findElements(By.id("foo")).size() > 0;
        }
    };
```

We can simply refactor this to our new function using lambdas:

```
Function<WebDriver, Boolean> didWeFindElementFoo =
        driver -> driver.findElements(By.id("foo")).size() > 0;
```

The argument that we pass into the lambda is the driver object. We use the -> operator to let Java know that that's everything we intend to pass in. Finally, we write the code that was in our method exactly the same way as before. The only difference is that we don't need to specify a return; the lambda does this for us. It works in exactly the same way and is much easier to read and has much less boilerplate.

Summary

In this chapter, we spent some time looking at the different sorts of waits and timeouts that are available to you when working with Selenium. We exposed some of the pitfalls of using static waits, such as `Thread.sleep()`, and implicit waits. We then went into some depth with explicit waits, examining how they work, and how you can create your own. As part of this investigation we explored the fluent wait API; then we learnt how to use and extend both fluent and explicit waits with functions and lambdas. Eventually we came to the conclusion that explicit waits are the solution we should always be aspiring to use. We also explored the effects of mixing up different wait strategies, highlighting the various potential errors that could occur.

In the next chapter, we will be looking at page objects and how we can use them effectively without letting them get out of control.

Working with Effective Page Objects

5

In this chapter, we are going to examine page objects and see how we can use them to keep our code both clean and maintainable. Remember that test code is just as important as production code, so we should strive to make sure that it is well written and easy to refactor.

If your test code is not high-quality, how are you ever going to be sure that your production code works as expected? In this chapter, we will:

- Introduce **Don't Repeat Yourself (DRY)** and have a look at how we can apply it to page objects.
- Examine why we should keep our assertions separate from our page objects.
- Have a look at the Java `PageFactory` classes that are available in the Selenium Support package.
- Look at how we can build sensible, extensible page objects that do the hard work of driving your tests.
- Talk about how we can make a readable **Domain-Specific Language (DSL)** using page objects. We don't need Cucumber to write readable tests.

Why do you keep repeating yourself?

After you have been writing automated checks for a while, you tend to see similar patterns emerging. One of the most common bad patterns that you will see is tests that interact with the same page, and the same elements on that page, in different ways.

This normally happens because more than one person has been automating scenarios in the same area, and as with all things, different people have different ways of doing things.

Let's take as an example a couple of basic HTML pages. First of all, we will have our index page. This is the page that everybody is going to see when they navigate to our website:

```html
<!DOCTYPE html>
<html lang="en">
<head>
    <title>Some generic website</title>
    <link href="http://cdnjs.cloudflare.com/ajax/libs/twitter-
    bootstrap/3.3.2/css/bootstrap.min.css" rel="stylesheet">
    <link href="../css/custom.css" rel="stylesheet">
</head>
<body>
<nav class="navbar navbar-inverse navbar-fixed-top"
 role="navigation">
    <div class="container">
        <div class="navbar-header">
            <a class="navbar-brand" href="#">
                <img src="http://placehold.it/150x50&text=Logo"
                 alt="">
            </a>
        </div>
        <div id="navbar-links">
            <ul class="nav navbar-nav">
                <li><a href="services.html">Services</a></li>
                <li><a href="contact.html">Contact</a></li>
            </ul>
        </div>
    </div>
</nav>
<div class="container">
    <div class="row">
        <div class="col-md-8">
            <img class="img-responsive img-rounded"
            src="http://placehold.it/900x350" alt="">
        </div>
        <div class="col-md-4">
            <h1>Lorem ipsum dolor</h1>

            <p>Duis in turpis finibus, eleifend nisl et, accumsan
            dolor. Pellentesque sed ex fringilla,
            gravida tellus in, tempus libero. Maecenas mi urna,
            fermentum et sem vitae, congue pellentesque velit.</p>
            <a class="btn btn-primary btn-lg" href="#">
            Nam mattis</a>
        </div>
    </div>
    <hr>
```

```
    <footer>
        <div class="row">
            <div class="col-lg-12 left-footer">
                <a href="about.html">About</a>
            </div>
            <div class="col-lg-12 right-footer">
                <p>Copyright &copy; Your Website 2015</p>
            </div>
        </div>
    </footer>
</div>
</body>
</html>
```

Our index page will look like this in a browser:

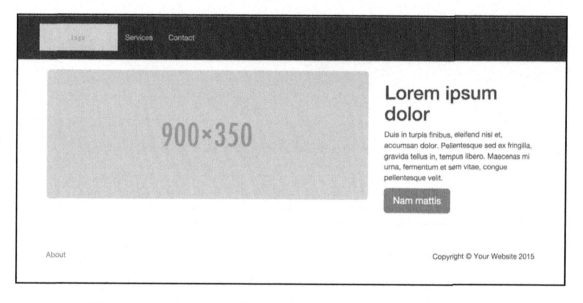

Next, we will have our about page. This page is going to tell the user a bit about the company history because people are interested in that sort of thing:

```
<!DOCTYPE html>
<html lang="en">
<head>
    <title>Some generic website - About us</title>
    <link href="http://cdnjs.cloudflare.com/ajax/libs/twitter-
    bootstrap/3.3.2/css/bootstrap.min.css" rel="stylesheet">
    <link href="../css/custom.css" rel="stylesheet">
</head>
```

```html
<body>
<nav class="navbar navbar-inverse navbar-fixed-top"
 role="navigation">
    <div class="container">
        <div class="navbar-header">
            <a class="navbar-brand" href="#">
                <img src="http://placehold.it/150x50&text=Logo"
                 alt="">
            </a>
        </div>
        <div id="navbar-links">
            <ul class="nav navbar-nav">
                <ul class="nav navbar-nav">
                    <li><a href="services.html">Services</a></li>
                    <li><a href="contact.html">Contact</a></li>
                </ul>
            </ul>
        </div>
    </div>
</nav>
<div class="container">
    <div class="row">
        <div class="col-md-4">
            <h1>About us!</h1>

            <p>Lorem ipsum dolor sit amet, consectetur adipiscing
            elit. In nec elit feugiat, egestas tortor vel,
            pharetra tellus. Mauris auctor purus sed mi finibus,
            at feugiat enim commodo. Nunc sed eros nec libero
            aliquam varius non vel sapien. Cras et nulla non
            purus auctor tincidunt.</p>
        </div>
    </div>
    <hr>
    <footer>
        <div class="row">
            <div class="col-lg-12 left-footer">
                <a href="about.html">About</a>
            </div>
            <div class="col-lg-12 right-footer">
                <p>Copyright &copy; Your Website 2014</p>
            </div>
        </div>
    </footer>
</div>
</body>
</html>
```

Our about page will look like this in a browser:

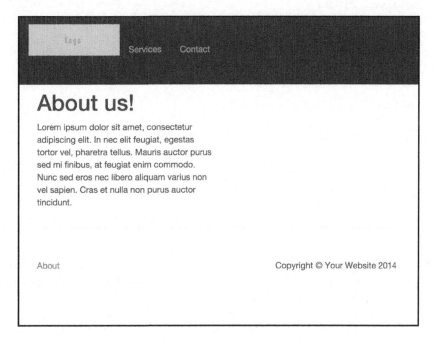

Both of these pages use a common `custom.css` that contains the following code:

```
body {
    padding-top: 70px;
}

.navbar-fixed-top .nav {
    padding: 15px 0;
}

.navbar-fixed-top .navbar-brand {
    padding: 0 15px;
}

footer {
    padding: 30px 0;
}

.left-footer {
    float: left;
    width: 20%;
}
```

```
.right-footer {
    text-align: right;
    float: right;
    width: 50%;
}

@media (min-width: 768px) {
    body {
        padding-top: 100px
    }

    .navbar-fixed-top .navbar-brand {
        padding: 15px 0;
    }
}
```

There are probably many more pages that make up this site, but we are only interested in these two for our example.

We have already put together a basic test framework in Chapter 1, *Creating a Fast Feedback Loop* and Chapter 2, *Producing the Right Feedback When Failing*. To make things easy, we are going to write our tests using that framework.

To make the code look more familiar in the tests below we are going to add a private variable called driver to our test classes which will hold our RemoteWebDriver object. We will then use a @BeforeMethod to assign our RemoteWebDriver object to this private variable. You don't have to do this if you don't want to, you can instead replace all instances of driver with getDriver().

```
private WebDriver driver;

@BeforeMethod
public void setup() throws MalformedURLException {
    driver = getDriver();
}
```

Before we start writing any code, let's modify our POM.xml and add in an assertion library; after all, tests without assertions are not really tests. The assertion library that we are going to use is called AssertJ. It's a fluent assertion library that provides concise feedback in the console when things go wrong. Since it is a fluent API, it's also quite easy to find available assertion methods using your IDE's code autocompletion functionality. If you want to find out a bit more about AssertJ, have a look at the AssertJ web page: http://joel-costigliola.github.io/assertj/. To bring this library in, we need to add the following dependency to our POM file:

```xml
<dependency>
    <groupId>org.assertj</groupId>
    <artifactId>assertj-core</artifactId>
    <version>3.10.0</version>
    <scope>test</scope>
</dependency>
```

Now that we have an assertion library in place, let's go back to the website. We have a couple of test scripts that have already been written for us and use our framework. This task was performed by a team of people in an attempt to get the work done really quickly. As a result, we had two different people working in isolation, on scripts that interact with these pages.

We will call these scripts goToTheAboutPage() and checkThatAboutPageHasText():

```java
@Test
public void goToTheAboutPage() {
    driver.get("http://web.masteringselenium.com/index.html");
    driver.findElement(By.cssSelector(".left-footer > a")).click();
    WebElement element = driver.findElement(By.cssSelector("h1"));

    assertThat(element.getText()).isEqualTo("About us!");
}

@Test
public void checkThatAboutPageHasText() {
    driver.get("http://web.masteringselenium.com/index.html");
    driver.findElement(By.cssSelector("footer div:nth-child(1)
    > a")).click();
    String titleText = driver.findElement(By.cssSelector
    (".container > div h1")).getText();

    assertThat(titleText).isEqualTo("About us!");
}
```

If you look closely, you can see that, while the scripts initially look different, they are actually doing the same thing. Which one is correct? Well, they both are! They are both reasonably sensible; they just use slightly different locator strategies. In fact, the reason that the second one was written is probably because the person writing the second one didn't realize that what they were writing had already been written.

So how could we get around this problem? How about making it clearer to the person reading the code what each locator is by giving it a sensible name?

Let's refactor `goToTheAboutPage()` a bit and see if we can make it easier to read:

```
@Test
public void goToTheAboutPage() {
    driver.get("http://web.masteringselenium.com/index.html");

    WebElement aboutLink = driver.findElement(By.cssSelector
    (".left-footer > a"));

    aboutLink.click();

    WebElement aboutHeading =
    driver.findElement(By.cssSelector("h1"));

    assertThat(aboutHeading.getText()).isEqualTo("About us!");
}
```

We have now made `goToTheAboutPage()` much clearer. Anybody adding scripts will probably be able to look at this script and realize that some of the locators that they want to use have already been defined. You would then hope that they would use the same locators to save time and ensure consistency. This does of course assume that the somebody else who starts writing scripts looks at the old ones, or the somebody who is coming back to this set of tests after a period of time remembers what they did before and checks to see whether they already have something usable.

Wouldn't it be easier if we could make some explicit definitions for the elements we are interested in that everybody knows about in advance? That way people won't have to keep repeating work that has already been done.

Well, we can; we can use the **Don't Repeat Yourself** (DRY) principle. We can take some common code that is regularly reused and put it into a centralized location where it can be repeatedly called. In the Selenium world, these definitions are called **page objects**.

Page objects are badly named; they do **not** specifically refer to a page. They actually refer to any group of related objects. In many cases this will be an entire page, but in other cases it may be a part of a page or a component that is reused across many pages.

Remember: If your page objects are hundreds of lines of code in length, you should break them up into much smaller classes so that they become manageable chunks of code.

When people start using page objects, they often fall into a few traps. Let's have a look at some common pitfalls.

Starting out with page objects

Let's take `goToTheAboutPage()` as an example. We have refactored it to make it nice and clear, but we now want to abstract things away into a page object to encourage other people to use all that hard work finding the correct locators. Let's create two page objects called `IndexPage` and `AboutPage` and move our element definitions across into them. We will start off with the index page:

```
package com.masteringselenium.page_objects;

import org.openqa.selenium.By;

public class IndexPage {

    public static By heading = By.cssSelector("h1");
    public static By mainText = By.cssSelector(".col-md-4 > p");
    public static By button = By.cssSelector(".btn");
    public static By aboutLinkLocator =
    By.cssSelector(".left-footer > a");
}
```

Then, we need to create the page object for the about page:

```
package com.masteringselenium.page_objects;

import org.openqa.selenium.By;

public class AboutPage {

    public static By heading = By.cssSelector("h1");
    public static By aboutUsText = By.cssSelector(".col-md-4 > p");
    public static By aboutHeadingLocator = By.cssSelector("h1");
}
```

You may have noticed that we added a few more locators to the `IndexPage` and `AboutPage` objects. Page objects are a codified representation of a page, so it's fine to add some information about elements that we don't use yet. This information will be used later on in this chapter, but we don't need to worry about this for now. Next, we need to modify the `goToTheAboutPage()` test to use the page objects:

```
@Test
public void goToTheAboutPage() {
    driver.get("http://web.masteringselenium.com/index.html");

    WebElement aboutLink =
    driver.findElement(IndexPage.aboutLinkLocator);
```

```
    aboutLink.click();

    WebElement aboutHeading =
    driver.findElement(AboutPage.aboutHeadingLocator);

    assertThat(aboutHeading.getText()).isEqualTo("About us!");
}
```

Excellent, we are now using our page objects and have a series of element definitions that can be reused, but we still have a couple of issues.

First of all; we have put our page object in with our tests:

It may seem like a good idea at first, but when you have a mature product with quite a few tests, you will find that it will start to become hard to find your page objects. So, what should we do? We will follow good programming practices and keep our page objects separate, to ensure that we have a good separation of concerns.

Let's create a place for our page objects to live that is separate from the tests and has a sensible name that will indicate to people what these pieces of code are:

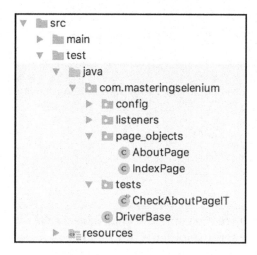

Separation of concerns with page objects

Our second issue is that, while we abstracted away our `WebElement` creation, we didn't abstract away any of the heavy lifting performed by our test script. We are now using a page object, but we are still going to have lots of duplication in our code. Let's illustrate this by looking at a script to perform a login and how we would do that using our new page objects.

Let's start with a basic login page object:

```
package com.masteringselenium.page_objects;

import org.openqa.selenium.By;
import org.openqa.selenium.WebDriver;

public class LoginPage {

    public static By usernameLocator = By.id("username");
    public static By passwordLocator = By.id("password");
    public static By loginButtonLocator = By.id("login");
}
```

Next, we need a test that uses this `LoginPage` object:

```
@Test
public void logInToTheWebsite() {
    driver.get("http://web.masteringselenium.com/index.html");
```

```
        WebElement username =
        driver.findElement(LoginPage.usernameLocator);
        WebElement password =
        driver.findElement(LoginPage.passwordLocator);
        WebElement submitButton =
        driver.findElement(LoginPage.loginButtonLocator);

        username.sendKeys("foo");
        password.sendKeys("bar");
        submitButton.click();

        assertThat(driver.getTitle()).isEqualTo("Logged in");
    }
```

Our script is quite clean and we are using our page object to find the elements that we need to use. However, what if we write another script that needs to use the login process? We will end up reusing the first six lines of code that are in this script. The same will apply for any other script that performs a login; that's a lot of code duplication!

We can make this better! We know that the duplicate lines of code are filling in the form fields to perform a login. Let's abstract this action away into the page object:

```java
package com.masteringselenium.page_objects;

import org.openqa.selenium.By;
import org.openqa.selenium.WebDriver;

public class LoginPage {

    public static By usernameLocator = By.id("username");
    public static By passwordLocator = By.id("password");
    public static By loginButtonLocator = By.id("login");

    public static void logInWithUsernameAndPassword
    (String username, String password, WebDriver driver) {

        driver.findElement(usernameLocator).sendKeys(username);
        driver.findElement(passwordLocator).sendKeys(password);
        driver.findElement(loginButtonLocator).click();
    }
}
```

We can now use the action that is in the page object in our tests:

```
@Test
public void logInToTheWebsiteStep2() {
    driver.get("http://web.masteringselenium.com/index.html");
    LoginPage.logInWithUsernameAndPassword("foo", "bar", driver);

    assertThat(driver.getTitle()).isEqualTo("Logged in");
}
```

Our test is now much cleaner, it has fewer lines of code, and it is nice and descriptive without being overly verbose. We can also reuse this login function in all of the tests that we write, that perform a login.

 Keep your assertions in your tests, **not** in your page objects.

Introducing the Java PageFactory class

Inside the WebDriver support library, the PageFactory class provides a series of annotations that you can use when you create your page objects.

You can use this class to predefine a series of WebElement objects that can be used later in your test. The PageFactory class turns these WebElement objects into proxied objects using a Java Proxy class. When you try to use them, the annotations that you specify are used to transform these proxied objects into real WebElement objects that can be used in your tests. We need to do two things to use the PageFactory class:

- Annotate the variables that we want to proxy
- Initialize the proxied objects before we try to use them

Using PageFactory annotations

We are going to take our existing LoginPage class and convert it to one backed by the Selenium PageFactory class. Let's start with the most common annotation that is in use, the @FindBy annotation. You have a couple of options when it comes to defining them:

```
@FindBy(how = How.ID, using = "username")
private WebElement usernameField;
```

```
@FindBy(id = "username")
private WebElement usernameField;
```

The preceding two examples are functionally equivalent and both are correct; it doesn't matter which one you decide to use.

I personally prefer the first option; I have configured a live template in IntelliJ that creates the annotation and allows me to just press *cmd + J* (or *Ctrl + J* if you are not using OS X) and then . (period) to trigger it. I can then press . (period) again and IntelliJ IDEA then gives me a series of options for the How enum. I don't have to remember all the selector options and it's very quick and easy for me to create annotations.

> The live template I use in IntelliJ IDEA for creating @FindBy annotations is:
>
> ```
> @FindBy(how = How$VAR$, using = "$END$")
> ```
>
> To learn more about live templates, have a look at https://www.jetbrains.com/idea/help/creating-and-editing-live-templates.html.

Other people will prefer the second, less verbose, option. Either option is perfectly fine.

So, what does the @FindBy annotation do? Well, it is a way to pass a By object into a driver.findElement() call to create a WebElement. This driver.findElement() call is completely transparent to you and will be performed in the background whenever you use a WebElement that has this annotation applied to it. This also means that you are much less likely to get StaleElementReferenceException because the element will be found every time you try to interact with it.

A good general rule of thumb to use when writing page objects using the PageFactory implementation is to make all of the WebElement objects that you define private. This forces you to write functions in your page objects that interact with the WebElement objects that you have defined, rather than using the page object as a glorified WebElement store.

Let's convert our LoginPage object into one backed by the PageFactory class:

```
package com.masteringselenium.page_factory_objects;

import org.openqa.selenium.WebElement;
import org.openqa.selenium.support.FindBy;
import org.openqa.selenium.support.How;

public class LoginPage {
```

```
@FindBy(how = How.ID, using = "username")
private WebElement usernameField;

@FindBy(how = How.ID, using = "password")
private WebElement passwordField;

@FindBy(how = How.ID, using = "login")
private WebElement loginButton;

public void logInWithUsernameAndPassword(String username,
String password) throws Exception {
    usernameField.sendKeys(username);
    passwordField.sendKeys(password);
    loginButton.click();
}
}
```

Initializing proxied objects

For the `PageFactory` annotation to work, you must initialize your class. `WebElement` objects will not be proxied and the annotations that you have specified will not be applied if you forget to do this. Initializing your class is one very simple line of code:

```
PageFactory.initElements(DriverBase.getDriver(), LoginPage.class);
```

While this is easy, it is also quite ugly and not instantly obvious to people who don't know about the `PageFactory` class. Let's make this easier and more understandable for any developers who are going to look at our code. What we are going to do is initialize our class in the constructor of our page object:

```
package com.masteringselenium.page_factory_objects;

import org.openqa.selenium.WebDriver;
import org.openqa.selenium.WebElement;
import org.openqa.selenium.support.FindBy;
import org.openqa.selenium.support.How;
import org.openqa.selenium.support.PageFactory;

public class LoginPage {

    @FindBy(how = How.ID, using = "username")
    private WebElement usernameField;

    @FindBy(how = How.ID, using = "password")
    private WebElement passwordField;
```

```
    @FindBy(how = How.ID, using = "login")
    private WebElement loginButton;

    public LoginPage(WebDriver driver) {
        PageFactory.initElements(driver, this);
    }

    public void logInWithUsernameAndPassword(String username,
    String password) {
        usernameField.sendKeys(username);
        passwordField.sendKeys(password);
        loginButton.click();
    }
}
```

Now, our code that creates a new page object instance will look like this:

```
LoginPage loginPage = new LoginPage(getDriver());
```

It's much cleaner and a pattern that all Java developers will instantly recognize. We do still have a code smell here though. We are needlessly passing around a driver object all the time, so how can we go one step further? Well, the getDriver() method that we are using to pass our driver object into the page object is static. This means that anything can use it to get the driver object associated with the current thread. We can use this in our page objects to remove the need to pass around the driver object:

```
package com.masteringselenium.page_factory_objects;

import com.masteringselenium.DriverBase;
import org.openqa.selenium.By;
import org.openqa.selenium.WebElement;
import org.openqa.selenium.support.FindBy;
import org.openqa.selenium.support.How;
import org.openqa.selenium.support.PageFactory;
import org.openqa.selenium.support.ui.ExpectedConditions;
import org.openqa.selenium.support.ui.WebDriverWait;

public class LoginPage {

    @FindBy(how = How.ID, using = "username")
    private WebElement usernameField;

    @FindBy(how = How.ID, using = "password")
    private WebElement passwordField;

    @FindBy(how = How.ID, using = "login")
    private WebElement loginButton;
```

```
    public LoginPage() throws Exception {
        PageFactory.initElements(DriverBase.getDriver(), this);
    }

    public void logInWithUsernameAndPassword(String username,
    String password) throws Exception {
        usernameField.sendKeys(username);
        passwordField.sendKeys(password);
        loginButton.click();

        WebDriverWait wait = new
        WebDriverWait(DriverBase.getDriver(), 15, 100);
        wait.until(ExpectedConditions.visibilityOfElementLocated
        (By.id("username")));
    }
}
```

This now means that all we need to create a new page object instance is:

```
LoginPage loginPage = new LoginPage();
```

Our page objects now look like any other object in Java and the fact that we can just new-up our page object without providing any parameters means that it is easy to start using our page objects as building blocks.

Problems with the Java PageFactory class

The `PageFactory` class is quite useful, but after you have used it a while, you will find that it raises certain questions, and has some limitations. One of the first questions that is usually asked is "How do I get the locator out of the `@FindBy` annotation so that I can use in `WebDriverWait` objects?" You could write a method that takes `WebElement` and converts it into a string, and then try to work out what the various components are. This will not be reliable though, as things will change and the `.toString()` representation of a `WebElement` is not set in stone.

We could try populating the `@FindBy` annotations with variables like this:

```
private static final String USERNAME_LOCATOR = "username";

@FindBy(how = How.ID, using = USERNAME_LOCATOR)
private WebElement usernameField;
```

This will work, but there are some caveats. In Java, annotation processing occurs during compile time. Due to this, you cannot pass a mutable object into an annotation definition. We are working around this in the preceding piece of code by creating an immutable object, and then using that in the annotation definition.

> An **immutable** or **unchangeable** object is an object whose state cannot be modified after it is created. Something marked as static belongs to the class (rather than being an instance variable), so it is the same for every instance of the same class. A variable marked as final can only be assigned a value once. By marking a variable as static and final, we make it immutable.

We now have a WebElement using the PageFactory annotation, which also uses a locator that is defined in a separate variable that could be used elsewhere. So if, for example, we want to wait for this element to become visible before using it, we can now do this:

```
WebDriverWait wait = new WebDriverWait(getDriver(), 15, 100);
wait.until(ExpectedConditions.visibilityOfElementLocated
(By.id(USERNAME_LOCATOR)));
```

This does leave us with another problem though. You may have noticed that the USERNAME_LOCATOR variable is a String type and not a By object. This means that, when we reuse the locator in other places in our code, we have to remember that this locator is an ID, and not an XPath or a CSS locator. Apart from the fact that we now have something to remember, we are also starting to create a lot of code. It looks like we need to look at other options.

Introducing the Query object

To remove the issues we are experiencing here, we are going to start building our page objects using something designed to get around the problems noted earlier: the Query object.

First of all, you will need to add the following dependency to your POM.xml file:

```
<dependency>
    <groupId>com.lazerycode.selenium</groupId>
    <artifactId>query</artifactId>
    <version>1.2.0</version>
    <scope>test</scope>
</dependency>
```

Then we are going to create an abstract class called `BasePage` that all other pages will be able to inherit from. We are doing this because we are going to need to have access to a `RemoteWebDriver` object, and we don't want to add this code to every single page object:

```
package com.masteringselenium.query_page_objects;

import com.masteringselenium.DriverBase;
import org.openqa.selenium.remote.RemoteWebDriver;

import java.net.MalformedURLException;

public abstract class BasePage {

    protected RemoteWebDriver driver;

    public BasePage() {
        try {
            driver = DriverBase.getDriver();
        } catch (MalformedURLException ignored) {
            //This will be be thrown when the test starts
            //if it cannot connect to a RemoteWebDriver Instance
        }
    }
}
```

You will notice that we are ignoring any MalformedURLExceptions that are thrown. This is because those will be thrown when the test initially starts as well so we don't need to worry about them in our page objects. We won't get as far as actually using them if we can't get a valid driver instance to start our test. We now have access to the `Query` object in our tests. Let's convert our `LoginPage` to use it:

```
package com.masteringselenium.query_page_objects;

import com.lazerycode.selenium.util.Query;
import org.openqa.selenium.By;
import org.openqa.selenium.remote.BrowserType;

public class LoginPage extends BasePage {

    private Query usernameField = new Query(By.id("username"),
    driver);
    private Query passwordField = new Query(By.id("password"),
    driver);
    private Query loginButton = new Query(By.id("login"), driver);

    public void logInWithUsernameAndPassword(String username,
```

```
       String password) {
           usernameField.findWebElement().sendKeys(username);
           passwordField.findWebElement().sendKeys(password);
           loginButton.findWebElement().click();
       }
   }
```

You can instantly see that there is much less code, but we have the same level of functionality. Using the object is a little more verbose because we specify that we want to find `WebElement` instead of directly using `WebElement`. With autocomplete in modern IDEs, it's really not noticeable. You may have also noticed that we have removed the constructor. The `Query` object is initialized by passing in a `RemoteWebDriver` object when we declare our `Query` object. Hang on a minute, where did that driver object come from? We haven't defined it in this class! All of our page objects now extend the `BasePage` abstract class so we inherit all of the objects that have been initialized there.

If you have anything else that's reused by your page objects on a regular basis, you can also put them inside the `BasePage` class. I tend to put in an explicit wait object that can be inherited by all page objects so that I don't have to keep defining it again and again. This would also be a good place to start adding some generic utility classes. Make sure your `BasePage` class doesn't grow too large though; you don't want to turn it into a god class by mistake.

Now that we are up-and-running with the `Query` object, let's have a look at what else we can do with it. Remember the `WebDriverWait` example we had with the `PageFactory` class; let's convert it to use our `Query` object:

```
WebDriverWait wait = new WebDriverWait(driver, 15, 100);
wait.until(ExpectedConditions.visibilityOfElementLocated
(usernameField.locator()));
```

You'll see that now, instead of using the `.findWebElement()` command on the `Query` object, we are now using the `.locator()` command. This returns a full `By` object that can be used in our expected condition. We no longer have to try and remember whether that locator was an XPath, an ID, or a CSS locator.

What else can we do? Well, since the `Query` object is holding the locator, it's able to return multiple types for us. As well as returning an individual `WebElement`, we can return a list of `WebElement` objects, or even a `Select` object. We can also return objects of type `MobileElement`, which is useful if you are using Appium. Finally, we can specify different locators for different driver types. So, if we have some strange markup shown in IE that's different from every other modern browser, we could do this:

```
loginButton.addAlternateLocator(BrowserType.IE, By.id("only_in_ie"));
```

If the current `WebDriver` object is detected as having `BrowserType` as IE, any calls to `.findWebElement()` or `.locator()` will automatically use the IE locator instead of the default one.

So, which option should I use?

At the end of the day, it really doesn't matter. Use the option that you find most comfortable and is the best fit for your particular set of problems. The rest of the examples in this book will however be using the `Query` object.

What is more important to remember is that when using page objects, our page objects are going to abstract away all of the heavy work of actually driving the browser. Things that we want to check should be in our tests.

This separation of concerns has two benefits. First of all, it ensures that people do not inadvertently bring assertions into their tests when they don't mean to. Secondly, it means that your tests do not depend upon specific implementations in your page objects. You don't want a test to lose the ability to fail because somebody updated a page object and removed an assertion that shouldn't have been there in the first place.

Remember, a test that cannot fail is worse than no test at all. If there is no test at all, you can see that a specific area of code has no test coverage (or in other words, no documentation) using static analysis tools. Tests that cannot fail are incorrect documentation that may be lying to the user when they describe how the system works. The problem is that we will also never know when they are going to start lying.

We are going to make sure that our page objects provide some nice, clear, and descriptively named functions for our tests to use. We are not going to use our page objects as a glorified `WebElement` store. If we did this, we would not be utilizing the full potential of page objects.

Creating extensible page objects

So far, we have only looked at examples where a page object has been used to describe a whole page. Unfortunately, in the real-world web pages that we want to automate are usually much larger, and more complicated, than the examples you find in a book. So, how are we going to deal with large complicated pages while keeping our test code well factored and readable? We are going to break things down into manageable chunks.

Let's have another look at our HTML page examples we used earlier in this chapter. We will start with the index page.

If you look carefully, you will see that there are two parts that look particularly generic: the header (the area enclosed in the <nav> tag) and the footer (the area enclosed in the <footer> tag). It is probably fair to expect a header and a footer on every page of the website to share a common set of elements.

Let's take these two areas and turn them into reusable components that have their own page objects. First of all, we will create one for the header:

```
package com.masteringselenium.query_page_objects;

import com.lazerycode.selenium.util.Query;
import org.openqa.selenium.By;


public class PageHeader extends BasePage {

    private Query servicesLink = new Query(By.cssSelector(".nav
    li:nth-child(1) > a"), driver);
    private Query contactLink = new Query(By.cssSelector(".nav
    li:nth-child(2) > a"), driver);

    public void goToTheServicesPage() {
        servicesLink.findWebElement().click();
    }

    public void goToTheContactPage() {
        contactLink.findWebElement().click();
    }
}
```

Then, we need to create one for the footer:

```
package com.masteringselenium.query_page_objects;

import com.lazerycode.selenium.util.Query;
import org.openqa.selenium.By;

public class PageFooter extends BasePage {

    private Query aboutUsLink = new Query(By.cssSelector(".left-
    footer > a"), driver);

    public void goToTheAboutUsPage() {
        aboutUsLink.findWebElement().click();
    }
}
```

Now, we need to convert our IndexPage object into one that uses Query objects:

```
package com.masteringselenium.query_page_objects;

import com.lazerycode.selenium.util.Query;
import org.openqa.selenium.By;

public class IndexPage extends BasePage {

    private Query heading = new Query(By.cssSelector("h1"), driver);
    private Query mainText = new Query(By.cssSelector(".col-md-4
    > p"), driver);
    private Query button = new Query(By.cssSelector(".btn"),
    driver);

    public boolean mainTextIsDisplayed() {
        return mainText.findWebElements().size() == 1;
    }

    public boolean mainPageButtonIsDisplayed() {
        return button.findWebElements().size() == 1;

    }
}
```

We now have the reusable components of the page in separate page objects so that we can reuse them when testing other pages that share these reusable components. We have also added a couple of methods that check for the existence of elements on the page. We can use these methods for assertions in our tests.

Now, we have to look back at the HTML markup for the about page. The about page has exactly the same HTML code for the header and the footer as the last page. This is brilliant; we can now reuse our header and footer page objects without having to duplicate code. Let's convert our AboutPage object into one that uses Query objects as well:

```
package com.masteringselenium.query_page_objects;

import com.lazerycode.selenium.util.Query;
import org.openqa.selenium.By;

public class AboutPage extends BasePage {

    private Query heading = new Query(By.cssSelector("h1"),
    driver);
    private Query aboutUsText = new Query(By.cssSelector
    (".col-md-4 > p"));

    public boolean aboutUsTextIsDisplayed() {
        return aboutUsText.findWebElements().size() == 1;
    }
}
```

Again, we have added an additional method that performs a check on the page. Next, we will need to write a quick test that goes to our index page, checks for the existence of some elements, and then goes to the about page and does the same thing.

You may have noticed that the additional methods that I've added to check for the existence of elements are not using Seleniums .isDisplayed() method.

Why haven't I done this?

Well, the .isDisplayed() method will throw NoSuchElementException if the element does not exist. We are using a Query object that tries to find the element every time the .findWebElement() or .findWebElements() command is called. This means that we don't know if the element has been found or not.

We don't want to have exceptions thrown and then have to catch the exceptions, so the easiest thing to do is to return a list of elements and then count them. We know that there should only be one of these elements available, so we check that the size of the list of the WebElements list is equal to 1.

Now that we have added the methods to check for elements in our page objects, we need to create our test:

```
@Test
public void checkThatAboutPageHasText() {
    driver.get("http://web.masteringselenium.com/index.html");
    IndexPage indexPage = new IndexPage();

    assertThat(indexPage.mainTextIsDisplayed()).isEqualTo(true);
    assertThat(indexPage.mainPageButtonIsDisplayed()).isEqualTo(true);

    PageFooter footer = new PageFooter();
    footer.goToTheAboutUsPage();
    AboutPage aboutPage = new AboutPage();

    assertThat(aboutPage.aboutUsTextIsDisplayed()).isEqualTo(true);
}
```

By breaking our HTML pages up into small bite-sized chunks and creating separate page objects for each of these chunks, we have ended up with smaller page objects and less code duplication.

There has been an unfortunate side-effect caused by breaking our page objects up, though. Our tests are now starting to look a bit untidy and they are much harder to read. I know that I'm interacting with a header, but I don't really know which page this header is referring to. If my tests were covering multiple pages, it would probably get quite confusing seeing us switch between the various page objects. It's going to be hard to keep track of what is going on.

What can we do to clean up this mess that we have started to make?

Turning your page objects into a readable DSL

Well it's actually not that hard to make things better. Earlier in this chapter, we moved our page object initialization into the constructor and had a look at a way of initializing page objects without passing in any parameters. Let's use this simplicity to start turning our page objects into a fluent, readable DSL.

We will start off by taking our index page object and creating a reference to the header and footer page objects inside it:

```
package com.masteringselenium.query_page_objects;

import com.lazerycode.selenium.util.Query;
import org.openqa.selenium.By;

public class IndexPage extends BasePage {

    private Query heading = new Query(By.cssSelector("h1"), driver);
    private Query mainText = new Query(By.cssSelector(".col-md-4 >
    p"), driver);
    private Query button = new Query(By.cssSelector(".btn"),
    driver);

    public PageHeader header = new PageHeader();
    public PageFooter footer = new PageFooter();

    public boolean mainTextIsDisplayed() {
        return mainText.findWebElements().size() == 1;
    }

    public boolean mainPageButtonIsDisplayed() {
        return button.findWebElements().size() == 1;

    }
}
```

As you can see, we are now instantiating a page object from a page object. We have made this public so that anyone who creates a new instance of the parent page object automatically gets to use all the subpage objects defined in the parent as well.

We can now refactor our test to make it much cleaner and easier to read:

```
@Test
public void checkThatAboutPageHasText() {
    driver.get("http://web.masteringselenium.com/index.html");
    IndexPage indexPage = new IndexPage();

    assertThat(indexPage.mainTextIsDisplayed()).isEqualTo(true);
    assertThat(indexPage.mainPageButtonIsDisplayed()).isEqualTo(true);

    indexPage.footer.goToTheAboutUsPage();
    AboutPage aboutPage = new AboutPage();

    assertThat(aboutPage.aboutUsTextIsDisplayed()).isEqualTo(true);
}
```

It's starting to look cleaner, but let's not stop there. Rather than instantiating a new page object in the test when we need it, we can make our page objects return what we want. If you are clicking on a link that takes you to the about page, you know where you are going, so why not return the page objects that you are going to use? We can do that; let's tweak our footer page object to make it return an about page object:

```
package com.masteringselenium.query_page_objects;

import com.lazerycode.selenium.util.Query;
import org.openqa.selenium.By;

public class PageFooter extends BasePage {

    private Query aboutUsLink = new Query(By.cssSelector(".left-
    footer > a"), driver);

    public AboutPage goToTheAboutUsPage() {
        aboutUsLink.findWebElement().click();
        return new AboutPage();
    }
}
```

This will turn our test into:

```
@Test
public void checkThatAboutPageHasText() {
    driver.get("http://web.masteringselenium.com/index.html");
    IndexPage indexPage = new IndexPage();

    assertThat(indexPage.mainTextIsDisplayed()).isEqualTo(true);
    assertThat(indexPage.mainPageButtonIsDisplayed()).isEqualTo(true);
```

```
AboutPage aboutPage = indexPage.footer.goToTheAboutUsPage();

assertThat(aboutPage.aboutUsTextIsDisplayed()).isEqualTo(true);
}
```

It's still a bit messy, so let's predefine all of our page object variables in our `DriverBase` class. We don't need to assign anything to the variables, we will be doing this in our tests. In our `DriverBase` class, we will need to add the following:

```
protected IndexPage indexPage;
protected AboutPage aboutPage;
protected LoginPage loginPage;
```

All of our tests extend `DriverBase` so the variables will be available to them since they have been defined as `protected`. We can now make our test look like this:

```
@Test
public void checkThatAboutPageHasText() {
    driver.get("http://web.masteringselenium.com/index.html");
    indexPage = new IndexPage();

    assertThat(indexPage.mainTextIsDisplayed()).isEqualTo(true);
    assertThat(indexPage.mainPageButtonIsDisplayed()).isEqualTo(true);

    aboutPage = indexPage.footer.goToTheAboutUsPage();

    assertThat(aboutPage.aboutUsTextIsDisplayed()).isEqualTo(true);
}
```

Remember, the naming conventions for page objects are completely under your control, as are the names of the functions that do the heavy lifting. There is nothing to stop you from using readable method names for all of the things that you do.

The first two lines of this test still seem quite generic: we use the `driver` object to load up a URL, and then instantiate our `IndexPage` object. Have a think about how you could modify the `IndexPage` object to do this and make your code even more readable.

If you take your time and think about your naming strategies, there is no reason why your tests should not be completely readable by people who are not technical.

In `Chapter 2`, *Producing the Right Feedback When Failing*, I talked about tests being technical documentation that explained how the system that you are testing works. If you gave the preceding test to a business analyst or a product owner, would they be able to understand it without you needing to explain it to them? The preceding example is contrived, but it illustrates the potential that you have to start turning your tests into documentation that describes how the system that you are testing works.

It looks like we are well on our way to creating readable technical documentation that describes how the application under test works, and we haven't had to start pulling in another layer to put on top of our tests such as Cucumber.

Who needs Cucumber to write tests that can be read and understood by non-technical people?

So, is there anything else we can do to make page objects even better? How about making them use a fluent interface?

Fluent page objects

We are going to have a look at how we can turn our existing page objects into fluent page objects to enhance the readability and discoverability of our code. To do that, we are going to design DSL for our page objects that uses chains of commands to describe the action(s) that are being performed. Each chained command will return either a reference to itself, a reference to a new method, or a void.

The `LoginPage` object that we created earlier in this chapter will provide a good base for a fluent page object. It currently looks like this:

```
package com.masteringselenium.query_page_objects;

import com.lazerycode.selenium.util.Query;
import com.masteringselenium.fluent_page_objects.BasePage;
import org.openqa.selenium.By;

public class LoginPage extends BasePage {

    private Query usernameField = new Query(By.id("username"),
    driver);
    private Query passwordField = new Query(By.id("password"),
    driver);
    private Query loginButton = new Query(By.id("login"), driver);

    public void logInWithUsernameAndPassword(String username, String
```

```
password) {
    usernameField.findWebElement().sendKeys(username);
    passwordField.findWebElement().sendKeys(password);
    loginButton.findWebElement().click();
}
}
```

Looking at the preceding code snippet, you will remember that we created the `.logInWithUsernameAndPassword()` method to make it quick and easy to perform a login.

This method is not perfect, however; what if:

- We want to only enter a username? We are stuck with sending a null over to the password field.
- We want to enter a username and a password to trigger some client side validation, but we don't want to click the login button?
- We have already entered the username and password and we just want to click the login button? We will end up re-entering data.

Let's rewrite this page object using a fluent interface so that we can easily do all of these things.

 So what is a fluent interface? Well, it's a way to write your code that makes it understandable. You can chain a series of commands together to create something that is both clear in intent and easily readable for whoever looks at it in the future. The chaining works because each method returns an instance of itself. You, of course, do not have to chain every command, and you can have methods that don't return an instance of themselves if you don't wish to continue chaining. Martin Fowler and Eric Evans came up with the idea. Martin explains it in a bit more detail here: https://martinfowler.com/bliki/FluentInterface.html.

Once we have finished our rewrite, the code will look like this:

```
package com.masteringselenium.fluent_page_objects;

import com.lazerycode.selenium.util.Query;
import org.openqa.selenium.By;

public class LoginPage extends BasePage {

    private Query usernameField = new Query(By.id("username"),
    driver);
```

```
private Query passwordField = new Query(By.id("password"),
driver);
private Query loginButton = new Query(By.id("login"), driver);

public LoginPage enterUsername(String username) {
    usernameField.findWebElement().sendKeys(username);

    return this;
}

public LoginPage enterPassword(String password) {
    passwordField.findWebElement().sendKeys(password);

    return this;
}


public void andLogin() {
    loginButton.findWebElement().click();
}
}
```

We will also need to modify our DriverBase to be aware of the `LoginPage` object:

```
protected LoginPage loginPage;
```

And then we will need to change our test to take advantage of our new fluent page object, so it will now look like this:

```
@Test
public void logInToTheWebsite() {
    driver.get("http://web.masteringselenium.com/index.html");
    loginPage = new LoginPage();

    loginPage.enterUsername("foo")
            .enterPassword("bar")
            .andLogin();

    assertThat(driver.getTitle()).isEqualTo("Logged in");
}
```

As you can see, the test is still readable, but by converting it into a fluent page object and making each action a different method, we have increased the flexibility massively. Let's have a look at a slightly different scenario where we check some client-side validation; how would we do it with this new fluent page object? Well, it would look something like this:

```
@Test
public void logInToTheWebsiteWithClientSideValidationCheck() {
    driver.get("http://web.masteringselenium.com/index.html");
    loginPage = new LoginPage();

    loginPage.enterUsername("foo")
            .enterPassword("bar");

    //TODO Perform client side validation check here

    loginPage.andLogin();

    assertThat(driver.getTitle()).isEqualTo("Logged in");
}
```

As you can see, we have gained lots of flexibility. We now get to set specific values in the username and password fields, and we could perform assertions before we click the button to log in.

Looking at the preceding code snippet, you may have noticed that currently, the `.andLogin()` method does not return anything, whereas earlier we were returning page objects when we clicked on links. This is because a login is not deterministic; there are many places that we could go when we log in. I've selected the easy option, which is to have a terminating context. If you wanted to, you could create multiple methods that expect different outcomes. For example, you could create different login methods that have different outcomes:

```
public void andFailLogin() {
    loginButton.findWebElement().click();
}

public IndexPage andSuccessfullyLogin() {
    loginButton.findWebElement().click();

    return new IndexPage();
}
```

Or, you could make the `.andLogin()` method fluent and create some transitionary methods like so:

```
public LoginPage andLogin() {
    loginButton.findWebElement().click();
    return this;
}

public ChangePasswordPage andGoToChangePasswordPage() {

    return new ChangePasswordPage();
}

public IndexPage successfully() {

    return new IndexPage();
}
```

It is up to you to decide which is the least complex and most understandable implementation for your domain. There is no right or wrong answer; that being said, if you end up having 30 different login commands, you're probably unnecessarily overcomplicating things.

Remember, try to write as little code as possible while still making it readable.

Summary

In this chapter, we had a look at various different ways of creating page objects. It should now be clear that there are many slightly different ways to implement them. One of the key things to remember is to try and use your page objects to reduce duplication, which in turn will make your code concise and your automated checks readable. Another thing to remember is to put your assertions into your tests, not inside your page objects. Page objects are used to control the web page that you are testing. Methods annotated with `@Test` are used to validate that the web page you are testing does what it is expected to do.

By the time you have finished reading this chapter, you will understand that page objects do not need to define actual pages, they can just define collections of related objects. As a result you will be confidently building highly readable fluent page objects, using support libraries like `PageFactory`, or alternative libraries like `Query`.

In the next chapter, we are going to have a look at the advanced user interaction API inside Selenium.

6
Utilizing the Advanced User Interactions API

This chapter is going to teach you about the Advanced User Interactions API, and how to utilize it. The Advanced User Interactions API, more commonly known as the `Actions` object, has been built to enable you to perform complex actions that you may find difficult with the standard Selenium API. The majority of the command set is based around mouse movements and clicks, but it does allow keyboard actions as well. It is a fluent API so it provides you with the ability to chain a series of commands together; as you will see, this tends to make your actions easier to read.

 To get a full list of available actions, you can have a look at the Javadoc for the `Actions` class. It is available at
`http://seleniumhq.github.io/selenium/docs/api/java/org/openqa/selenium/interactions/Actions.html`.

There are three main areas to the API that we will cover in this chapter:

- Simulating moving the mouse to perform hover actions
- Simulating using the mouse to drag and drop
- Simulating a user pressing keys on their keyboard

We are going to work through some examples in this chapter. So, you will need your development IDE set up and ready to start writing some code. You can use the base Selenium implementation that we put together in Chapter 1, *Creating a Fast Feedback Loop*. If you do this, you will probably want to add the following line of code at the beginning of your tests:

```
WebDriver driver = getDriver();
```

This will get a `driver` object that we can seamlessly use with the examples used in this chapter.

Getting started with the API

Let's start off by creating a basic `Actions` object that we can use to perform a series of actions, as follows:

```
Actions advancedActions = new Actions(driver);
```

It's very simple to create. We just pass in a `driver` object, and we now have an `Actions` object available.

Let's start off by performing a couple of basic commands to give you an idea of what can be done:

```
WebElement anElement = driver.findElement(By.id("anElement"));
advancedActions.moveToElement(anElement).contextClick().perform();
```

We have now created a very basic script that will move the mouse cursor to an element and then right-click on it. The `Actions` object allows us to queue up a series of commands that we want to execute and then perform them all at the same time. With long lists of commands, this can soon get confusing if we keep everything on the same line. We could make each command step clearer by reformatting the code to look like this:

```
WebElement anElement = driver.findElement(By.id("anElement"));
advancedActions.moveToElement(anElement)
        .contextClick()
        .perform();
```

We have now put each action on a separate line to make it more readable, which is something that I would highly recommend.

You may have noted that there is an extra command on the final line called `.perform()`. This tells Selenium that we have no more commands that we want to queue up and we should now go and perform all the commands that we have queued up so far.

If you look at the Javadoc for the `Actions` class (or the various tutorials on the internet), you may come across a chained command called `.build()` that I have not used in the preceding example. The `.build()` command is automatically called by `.perform()`, so you don't need to explicitly call it as well. Some people call it anyway for clarity; I don't use it to reduce code clutter.

Using the API to solve difficult problems

So far, we had a quick look at the basic API implementation. Now, let's have a look at some day-to-day problems that you will probably come across and how we can use the `Actions` class to solve them.

Working with hover menus

First of all, we need to create a basic HTML page. We are going to use some CSS to style the HTML into a CSS hover menu. To try and keep it in small, manageable chunks, we will break up the page into a couple of pieces. Let's start by writing the HTML:

```
<!DOCTYPE html>
<html lang="en">
<head>
    <meta charset="utf-8">
    <title>CSS Menu</title>
    <style type="text/css">${TBC}</style>
</head>
<body>
<ul>
    <li id="home">Home</li>
    <li id="about">About</li>
    <li id="services">
        Services
        <ul>
            <li>Web Design</li>
            <li>Web Development</li>
            <li>Illustrations</li>
        </ul>
    </li>
</ul>
</body>
</html>
```

As you can see, it's just a very simple ordered list; you may have also noted that I have added a `<style>` tag, but I've not put anything in it yet. The contents of the `<style>` tag is what make this page work. You can either put the styling inline or put it in a separate file and reference it. The styling that needs to be used to turn this list into a CSS menu is as follows:

```
<style type="text/css">
        body {
            padding: 20px 50px 150px;
```

```css
        text-align: center;
        background: white;
}

ul {
        text-align: left;
        display: inline;
        margin: 0;
        padding: 15px 4px 17px 0;
        list-style: none;
        box-shadow: 0 0 5px rgba(0, 0, 0, 0.15);
}

ul li {
        font: bold 12px/18px sans-serif;
        display: inline-block;
        margin-right: -4px;
        position: relative;
        padding: 15px 20px;
        background: mediumpurple;
        cursor: pointer;
        transition: all 0.3s;
}

ul li:hover {
        background: purple;
        color: white;
}

ul li ul {
        padding: 0;
        position: absolute;
        top: 48px;
        left: 0;
        width: 150px;
        box-shadow: none;
        display: none;
        opacity: 0;
        visibility: hidden;
        -transition: opacity 0.3s;
}

ul li ul li {
        background: #555;
        display: block;
        color: white;
        text-shadow: 0 -1px 0 black;
}
```

```
ul li ul li:hover {
    background: dimgrey;
}

ul li:hover ul {
    display: block;
    opacity: 1;
    visibility: visible;
}
</style>
```

If you load this up in a browser, you will see that when you hover your mouse over the **Services** option, another menu will appear and you will be given three new menu options. In this case, we want to try and click on the **Web Development** submenu option.

These sorts of menus can be horrible to automate. You can't trigger a CSS :hover event with JavaScript (no matter what some people on the internet would want you to believe). So, we need to find an alternative option. This is often where people get stuck and then get told on some forum somewhere to use Auto It...

We don't want to do this, because the Selenium developers have already come up with a solution! We are going to use the Actions class instead.

So, what actions do we need to perform? Well, we need to make Selenium act like a human would. We need to perform a series of steps that emulate the way a human would use this page:

1. First of all, we are going to move the mouse and make it hover over the **Services** menu option.
2. Once we hover over the **Services** menu option, we need to wait for the submenu to appear.
3. Now that the submenu has appeared, we are going to move the mouse down to the **Web Development** submenu option.
4. While hovering over the **Web Development** submenu option, we are going to click on it.

This may seem like a very verbose way of describing what we want to do, but it is important to be very clear about the actions taken because we need to code each of these steps into our Selenium test.

Let's go ahead and write some code that does this. First of all, we will need to get the page and set up an `Actions` object and a `WebDriverWait` object, as follows:

```
driver.get("http://web.masteringselenium.com/cssMenu.html");
Actions advancedActions = new Actions(driver);
WebDriverWait wait = new WebDriverWait(driver, 5, 100);
```

Then, we need to find the elements on the page that we want to interact with, as follows:

```
WebElement servicesMenuOption = driver.findElement(By.id("services"));
WebElement webDevelopmentSubMenuOption =
driver.findElement(By.cssSelector("#services > ul > li:nth-child(2)"));
```

Finally, we will use the `Actions` class to perform the four steps that were outlined in the preceding section, as follows:

```
advancedActions.moveToElement(servicesMenuOption)
        .perform();

wait.until(ExpectedConditions.visibilityOf(webDevelopmentSubMenuOption));

advancedActions.moveToElement(webDevelopmentSubMenuOption)
        .click()
        .perform();
```

As you can see, the `Actions` class allows you to chain actions. Unfortunately, it does not let you chain waits. Due to this, we need to break our `Actions` chain into two parts and put a wait in-between these two parts.

The reason behind using a wait is to make sure that the browser has had a chance to render the submenu before we move on and try to interact with it. If you don't do this, you will see intermittent errors occasionally. We don't want flakey tests. We want to be sure that the submenu has rendered before we try and interact with it. Hence, the wait is important.

> Remember to code your tests defensively. If you have a modern, powerful machine and you are only testing on a modern browser such as Chrome, things will generally work without adding waits to check whether things have happened. These same tests will probably not work so well on a VM that is running Internet Explorer 8 when you start doing some cross-browser compatibility checks.

Hopefully, this looks quite simple. So, are there any caveats? Unfortunately, yes. Browsers that do not have support for native events may not work.

As mentioned earlier, you cannot use JavaScript to trigger a CSS `:hover` event. This means that a driver that does not support native events cannot emulate the conditions required to trigger a CSS `:hover` event, and the test will not work. An example of a driver that does not support native events is Safari on macOS X. This code will not work in Safari.

To get it working in Safari, you will need to write some code to start moving the mouse cursor around the screen, and once you start doing this, things start getting quite complicated. We will have a look at things that you can't do, and possible workarounds, in `Chapter 8`, *Keeping It Real*.

Working with drag and drop

Another HTML construct that is hard to work with is a page that allows you to drag and drop elements. For this example, we will create a simple HTML page that uses jQuery to allow us to drag some elements around the screen. We are also going to add an element that will destroy any of the draggable elements that we drop onto it so that these draggable elements can be removed from the page. Let's start off with the basic HTML:

```html
<!DOCTYPE html>
<html lang="en">
<head>
    <meta charset=utf-8>
    <title>Drag and drop</title>
    <style type="text/css">${TBC}</style>
    <script src="https://ajax.googleapis.com/ajax/libs/jquery
    /2.1.3/jquery.min.js"></script>
    <script src="https://ajax.googleapis.com/ajax/libs/jqueryui
    /1.11.3/jquery-ui.min.js"></script>
</head>
<body>
<header>
    <h1>Drag and drop</h1>
</header>


<div>
    <p>Drop items onto the red square to remove them</p>

    <div id="obliterate"></div>
    <ul>
        <li>
            <div id="one" href="#" class="draggable">one</div>
        </li>
        <li>
```

```
            <div id="two" href="#" class="draggable">two</div>
        </li>
        <li>
            <div id="three" href="#" class="draggable">three</div>
        </li>
        <li>
            <div id="four" href="#" class="draggable">four</div>
        </li>
        <li>
            <div id="five" href="#" class="draggable">five</div>
        </li>
    </ul>
</div>
</body>
<script type="application/javascript">${TBC}</script>
</html>
```

This HTML code has some links to the jQuery libraries that we are going to use and a couple of ${TBC} tags, where we are going to add in some styling and JavaScript. Let's add the styling.

This will transform our elements into some nice boxes that will be easy to interact with. As we did before, we can put this styling inline or link into an external file. The choice is yours:

```
<style type="text/css">
    li {
        list-style: none;
    }

    li div {
        text-decoration: none;
        color: #000;
        margin: 10px;
        width: 150px;
        border: 2px groove black;
        background: #eee;
        padding: 10px;
        display: block;
        text-align: center;
    }

    ul {
        margin-left: 200px;
        min-height: 300px;
    }

    #obliterate {
```

```
            background-color: red;
            height: 250px;
            width: 166px;
            float: left;
            border: 5px solid #000;
            position: relative;
            margin-top: 0;
        }
    </style>
```

Finally, we need to add the jQuery code to make the drag-and-drop parts actually work. It's simple code and should be quite easy to follow:

```
<script type="application/javascript">
    $(function () {
        $(".draggable").draggable();

        $('#obliterate').droppable({
            drop: function (event, ui) {
                ui.draggable.remove();
            }
        });
    });
</script>
```

We now have a page that has a big red box and five smaller boxes. The smaller boxes can be dragged around the screen, and if we drop one of the smaller boxes on the big red box, it will be destroyed. Give it a go to make sure that it's all working correctly:

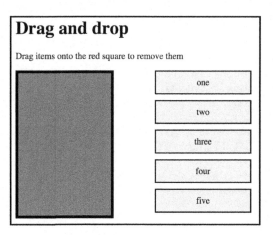

The drag-and-drop web page

Now, we need to write our Selenium test. We are going to write a simple test that checks how many smaller boxes exist. This test will then check whether they are destroyed when we drag them over the big red box.

We will start by getting the test page, setting up the objects that we are going to need to interact with, and checking whether we have five draggable boxes to start with, as follows:

```
@Test
public void automateJavaScriptDragAndDrop() {
    driver.get("http://web.masteringselenium.com/jsDragAndDrop.html");
    Actions advancedActions = new Actions(driver);
    final By destroyableBoxes = By.cssSelector("ul > li > div");
    WebElement obliterator =
    driver.findElement(By.id("obliterate"));
    WebElement firstBox = driver.findElement(By.id("one"));
    WebElement secondBox = driver.findElement(By.id("two"));

    assertThat(driver.findElements(destroyableBoxes).size()).isEqualTo(5);
}
```

We are now happy that everything is in place, and we are ready to start checking whether the drag-and-drop functionality that destroys the smaller boxes works. We have already set up the advancedActions object and found all of the elements that we are going to interact with. So, the rest of the code should be clean, simple, and clear:

```
@Test
public void automateJavaScriptDragAndDrop() {
    driver.get("http://web.masteringselenium.com
    /jsDragAndDrop.html");
    Actions advancedActions = new Actions(driver);
    final By destroyableBoxes = By.cssSelector("ul > li > div");
    WebElement obliterator =
    driver.findElement(By.id("obliterate"));
    WebElement firstBox = driver.findElement(By.id("one"));
    WebElement secondBox = driver.findElement(By.id("two"));

    assertThat(driver.findElements(destroyableBoxes).
    size()).isEqualTo(5);

    advancedActions.clickAndHold(firstBox)
            .moveToElement(obliterator)
            .release()
            .perform();

    assertThat(driver.findElements(destroyableBoxes).
    size()).isEqualTo(4);
}
```

The preceding code performs three steps to drag an element over the red box. First of all, we find the element that we want to drag, and click and hold our left mouse button on it. Then, we move (or drag) the element over to the red box. Finally, we let go of the mouse, which will cause the element to be dropped.

After we have dragged our box onto the red box and destroyed it, we count the number of boxes available on the screen again to check whether we now have four instead of five. We can also check whether the element that we were dragging has become stale (that is, it is not in the DOM anymore), but for the purposes of this example, the count is adequate.

It all works and it's quite clear what is going on, but we can make our code even simpler. Seeing that drag and drop is a reasonably common action, a shortcut was put in, which does all of the aforementioned commands for you.

Let's expand our test to destroy another box, but this time, we will use the `dragAndDrop()` method to add the following code to our test:

```
advancedActions.dragAndDrop(secondBox, obliterator).perform();

assertThat(driver.findElements(destroyableBoxes).size()).
isEqualTo(3);
```

The `dragAndDrop()` method takes two parameters—the element that we want to drag and the element we are going to drag it to.

We now have a nice, small piece of code that has given us the ability to do very powerful things.

Working with offsets

Let's make the drag-and-drop code a little bit more complicated. We are going to change the main page markup and the JavaScript slightly to make it more challenging to automate.

First of all, we are going to change the HTML code by adding a `<span>` element in each draggable element. We are going to move the text for the element into this `<span>`, as follows:

```
<ul>
    <li>
        <div id="one" href="#" class="draggable">
            <span>one</span>
        </div>
    </li>
```

```
    <li>
        <div id="two" href="#" class="draggable">
            <span>two</span>
        </div>
    </li>
    <li>
        <div id="three" href="#" class="draggable">
            <span>three</span>
        </div>
    </li>
    <li>
        <div id="four" href="#" class="draggable">
            <span>four</span>
        </div>
    </li>
    <li>
        <div id="five" href="#" class="draggable">
            <span>five</span>
        </div>
    </li>
</ul>
```

Next, we are going to tweak the JavaScript and change it so that you cannot drag the `<div>` element by using the `<span>` element. Instead, we are going to force the user to move their mouse cursor toward the left or the right so that it is not hovering over the text, as follows:

```
<script type="application/javascript">
    $(function () {
        $(".draggable").draggable({cancel: "span"});

        $('#obliterate').droppable({
            drop: function (event, ui) {
                ui.draggable.remove();
            }
        });
    });
</script>
```

Once you have updated the code, reload the page in your browser and give it a try. It should still work as before, as long as you try to drag the element from the side of the box and not from where the text is displayed.

Now, try and run the test script that you previously wrote to automate this page. You will see that it fails. The problem is that when you use the Advanced Interactions API to try and drag an element around the screen, the default point used to click and hold on the element is its center. We have now placed a <span> element over the center of the <div> element, and the <span> element is not draggable. To fix this, we need to find a way to click and hold our left mouse button down on the <div> element while avoiding the <span> element. Let's have a look at some code that can do this for us:

```
@Test
public void automateJavaScriptDragAndDropWithOffset() {
    driver.get("http://web.masteringselenium.com/
    jsDragAndDropWithHandle.html");
    Actions advancedActions = new Actions(driver);
    final By destroyableBoxes = By.cssSelector("ul > li > div");
    WebElement obliterator =
    driver.findElement(By.id("obliterate"));
    WebElement firstBox = driver.findElement(By.id("one"));

    assertThat(driver.findElements(destroyableBoxes).
    size()).isEqualTo(5);

    advancedActions.moveToElement(firstBox)
            .moveByOffset(-40, 0)
            .clickAndHold()
            .moveToElement(obliterator)
            .release()
            .perform();

    assertThat(driver.findElements(destroyableBoxes).
    size()).isEqualTo(4);
}
```

This time, instead of using the `clickAndHold(firstBox)` method to move the mouse cursor to the element and perform the left click, we are breaking it down a bit more. First, we move our mouse to the element. Then, we shift the mouse to the left by 40 pixels. Finally, we hold down our left mouse button.

Why 40 pixels? Well, I had a look at the markup, and after visually inspecting the <span> elements, I saw that none of them were larger than 32 pixels in width. This meant that moving 40 pixels to the left would always ensure that I'm not hovering over span, but I am still hovering over the button.

Try running the preceding updated test. This time, it will drag the boxes as expected and everything will pass. Now, there is a potential flaw in this test that you should be aware of. Let's modify the test code again and make it look like this:

```
advancedActions.moveToElement(firstBox)
            .moveByOffset(-40, 0)
            .clickAndHold(firstBox)
            .moveToElement(obliterator)
            .release()
            .perform();
```

If you now run the test again, it will fail. Why did it fail? If you pass an element to the clickAndHold() method, it will move the mouse to the center of that element. So, what we did in the preceding code is as follows:

1. Moved the mouse to the center of our <div> element
2. Moved it 40 pixels to the left
3. Moved it back to the center of the <div> element
4. Clicked and held down the left mouse button

It's a common mistake. The code looks correct, and you can spend hours trying to debug something that should work, but it just doesn't.

Remember that if you are using offsets, don't pass elements into the clickAndHold() method.

So, can we simplify the preceding code? Let's change our code to set the offset in the moveToElement() command instead of breaking it into two pieces, as follows:

```
advancedActions.moveToElement(firstBox, -40, 0)
            .clickAndHold()
            .moveToElement(obliterator)
            .release()
            .perform();
```

If we run the test again, everything should continue to work as expected.

I mentioned earlier that I had set arbitrary offset values to make the tests pass. However, this is something that I should not have done. This is the offset equivalent of using Thread.sleep(), and this is something that you shouldn't ever do. Instead, you should write a function that can figure out where you can safely place the mouse cursor before performing a click action.

If you are going to put a hardcoded value into one of your tests, stop and think first. You are probably creating a future failure for no good reason.

Now, we also know that this function should take into account two different starting positions for our mouse cursor: the center of the element and the top-left corner of the element. Unfortunately, there is no real, generic function for this. It will all depend on how the elements are rendered.

Let's put together an example class to work out the cursor location with the current markup. Hopefully, this will give you something that you can build upon if you ever come across this problem in the real world. First of all, we need to make some assumptions. Here are our assumptions for this class:

- The <div> element is a quadrilateral
- The <span> element is a quadrilateral
- The <span> element is always centered within <div>

Now that we have our assumptions let's write some code and work through it, as follows:

```
package com.masteringselenium.tests;

import org.openqa.selenium.ElementNotVisibleException;
import org.openqa.selenium.WebElement;

import static com.masteringselenium.tests.CalculateOffsetPosition.
CursorPosition.CENTER;
import static com.masteringselenium.tests.CalculateOffsetPosition.
CursorPosition.TOP_LEFT;

public class CalculateOffsetPosition {

    public enum CursorPosition {
        TOP_LEFT,
        CENTER
    }

    final WebElement parentElement;
    final WebElement childElement;
    final CursorPosition cursorPosition;
    private int xOffset = 0;
    private int yOffset = 0;

    public CalculateOffsetPosition(WebElement parentElement,
```

```java
        WebElement childElement, CursorPosition cursorPosition) {
            this.parentElement = parentElement;
            this.childElement = childElement;
            this.cursorPosition = cursorPosition;
            calculateOffset();
        }

    public int getXOffset() {
        return xOffset;
    }

    public int getYOffset() {
        return yOffset;
    }

    private void calculateOffset() throws ElementNotVisibleException {
        int parentHeight = parentElement.getSize().getHeight();
        int parentWidth = parentElement.getSize().getWidth();
        int childHeight = childElement.getSize().getHeight();
        int childWidth = childElement.getSize().getWidth();

        if (childHeight >= parentHeight && childWidth >=
        parentWidth) {
            throw new ElementNotVisibleException("The
            child element is totally covering
            the parent element");
        }

        if (cursorPosition.equals(TOP_LEFT)) {
            xOffset = 1;
            yOffset = 1;
        }
        if (cursorPosition.equals(CENTER)) {
            if (childWidth < parentWidth) {
                xOffset = (childWidth / 2) + 1;
            }
            if (childHeight < parentHeight) {
                yOffset = (childHeight / 2) + 1;
            }
        }
    }
}
```

When working with offsets, we need to be able to return an *X* and a *Y* offset. So, rather than writing a method, we have a class. The class constructor reads in the parent element and the child element and an enum value, telling us whether the current mouse position is at the top left or the center.

The first thing that we do is throw an `ElementNotVisibleException` if the child element is bigger than the parent element. In this situation, we are not going to be able to drag an element around. So, we may as well fail fast.

Figuring out `TOP_LEFT` is simple. If the child element is not the same size as that of the parent element, an offset of 1, 1 should always work, as this will put us in the top-left corner of the parent element.

Working our `CENTER` is a little more complicated. We need to take the existing height and width of the child element and then work out how far up, or towards the right, we need to go to move the mouse cursor off the child element. If one of the dimensions of the child element is the same as that of the parent element, we don't bother changing the offset for the dimension as there is no point.

We now have a couple of getters so that we can pull out the X and the Y offsets and use them in our test. Let's plug this class into our test using a center offset and see it in action:

```
@Test
public void automateJavaScriptDragAndDropWithOffsets() {
    driver.get("http://web.masteringselenium.com/
    jsDragAndDropWithHandle.html");
    Actions advancedActions = new Actions(driver);
    final By destroyableBoxes = By.cssSelector("ul > li > div");
    WebElement obliterator =
    driver.findElement(By.id("obliterate"));
    WebElement firstBox = driver.findElement(By.id("one"));
    WebElement firstBoxText =
    driver.findElement(By.cssSelector("#one > span"));

    assertThat(driver.findElements(destroyableBoxes).
    size()).isEqualTo(5);

    CalculateOffsetPosition op =
            new CalculateOffsetPosition(firstBox,
            firstBoxText, CursorPosition.CENTER);

    advancedActions.moveToElement(firstBox)
            .moveByOffset(op.getXOffset(), op.getYOffset())
            .clickAndHold()
            .moveToElement(obliterator)
            .release()
            .perform();

    assertThat(driver.findElements(destroyableBoxes).
    size()).isEqualTo(4);
}
```

As you can see, we have made a couple of small changes. We need to find the text element so that we can correctly calculate the offset. Then, we just calculate the offset and plug it in. It all works, and it makes sure that when the text of the span element expands in the future or the <div> container shrinks, our test won't start failing for no obvious reason.

 You could try modifying the HTML at this point to make the center element different sizes. Once you have done this, run this test again to make sure it still works as expected.

Working with access keys

We are going to focus on access keys for this section. You could use the Advanced User Interactions API to fill in fields, but .sendKeys() generally works without any problems, so it's really not worth the effort. Something that we do have problems interacting with is access keys because they don't rely on a specific element in the DOM.

Access keys can be controversial. Some people see them as a requirement for an accessible website, while others see them as well-intentioned, but badly implemented and unusable. Regardless of your views on them, it is quite possible that you will come across access keys at some point in your career and it's always useful to know how to deal with them.

Access keys can be tricky to work with; when you use an access key, you aren't really interacting with an element, you are just firing a key event into the web page and hoping that the browser picks up on it. This is an unusual way to implement automation using Selenium; we usually split the page up into components by building page objects that represent visual elements that we want to interact with. Since an access key is not a visual piece of the page, and we don't need to interact with a specific part of the page to trigger it, we need to come up with a slightly different way of dealing with it.

What we are going to do is write an access key handler that we can bind to our base page object, which all other page objects can inherit. First of all, we need a website to automate that has some access keys. Here are a couple of simple HTML pages that have access keys set up to navigate to each other. By hitting the access key combination and the number *1*, you will be taken to the home page; if you hit the access key modifier and the number *9*, you will be taken to the **About** page.

First of all, we have the code for our `accessKeysHome.html`:

```
<!DOCTYPE html>
<html lang="en">
<head>
    <meta charset="UTF-8">
    <title>Title</title>
</head>
<body>
<nav>
    <a href="accessKeysHome.html" accesskey="1">Home</a>
    <a href="accessKeysAbout.html" accesskey="9">About</a>
</nav>
<h1>Home page</h1>
<div id="home">This is the home page</div>
</body>
</html>
```

Then, we have the code for our `accessKeysAbout.html`:

```
<!DOCTYPE html>
<html lang="en">
<head>
    <meta charset="UTF-8">
    <title>Title</title>
</head>
<body>
<nav>
    <a href="accessKeysHome.html" accesskey="1">Home</a>
    <a href="accessKeysAbout.html" accesskey="9">About</a>
</nav>
<h1>About page</h1>
<div id="about">This is the home page</div>
</body>
</html>
```

The pages are very similar; they just have slight text variations. Next, we need to write some code to trigger the access keys and make sure that we can navigate between these two pages. I'm a Mac user and my browser of choice for automation work is Google Chrome, so let's get started with an initial implementation that works with this operating system or browser combination:

```
private void triggerAccessKey(String accessKey) {
    Actions advancedActions = new Actions(driver);
    advancedActions.keyDown(Keys.CONTROL)
```

```
        .keyDown(Keys.ALT)
        .sendKeys(accessKey)
        .perform();
}
```

We have a very simple piece of code that holds down *Ctrl* and *Alt* (the access key activation code for Chrome on macOS X) and then types the single key passed into the function. As before, we are just using `.perform()` because the `.build()` part is implicit. We can now plug this function into a test:

```
@Test
public void testThatUsingAccessKeysWorks() {
    driver.get("http://web.masteringselenium.com/accessKeysHome.html");
    WebDriverWait wait = new WebDriverWait(driver, 5, 100);
    List<WebElement> home = driver.findElements(By.id("home"));

    assertThat(home.size()).isEqualTo(1);

    triggerAccessKey("9");
    WebElement access =
    wait.until(ExpectedConditions.visibilityOfElementLocated
    (By.id("about")));

    home = driver.findElements(By.id("home"));
    assertThat(home.size()).isEqualTo(0);
    assertThat(access.isDisplayed()).isTrue();
}
```

Once more, we have a very simple test. It loads up our home page and checks that it has successfully rendered. Next, we trigger the access key that will navigate us to the about page. Finally, we check that the access page is now displayed, and that the home page is not. It all looks very simple, but we have some problems!

Let's start with our first problem. If you look back at our `.triggerAccessKey()` function, you will note that we are holding down the *Ctrl* and *Alt* keys, but what we didn't do was release them. What if our about page had something like a feedback form that we wanted to fill in? The second we try to type the number 1 into it, it will invoke the access key to navigate us back to the home page. Now, this is really simple to fix, but it's a good reminder to always check that you are cleaning up after yourself when you start using the Advanced Interactions API to trigger various keystrokes. Here is the updated `.triggerAccessKey()` method:

```
private void triggerAccessKey(String accessKey) {
    Actions advancedActions = new Actions(driver);
    advancedActions.keyDown(Keys.CONTROL)
```

```
.keyDown(Keys.ALT)
.sendKeys(accessKey)
.keyUp(Keys.CONTROL)
.keyUp(Keys.ALT)
.perform();
}
```

Our second problem is a little bit harder to fix. If you tried to execute the preceding example, but you aren't using Google Chrome and OS X, you may have found that it just doesn't work. With access keys, there is no W3C recommendation to tell browser manufacturers which key combination they should use to activate access keys. This means that each browser manufacturer picked one and went with it. To make matters even more complicated, different operating systems use the keys on your keyboard in different ways. This means that the access key activation combination may differ as you switch operating systems, even if you continue to use the same browser.

It looks like we have some work ahead of us to make this code work reliably in a cross-platform way.

 The **Mozilla Developer Network (MDN)** has a useful page about access keys that provides up-to-date information on the available access keys (`https://developer.mozilla.org/en-US/docs/Web/HTML/Global_attributes/accesskey`). It's worth having a look at this page when trying to implement the following example yourself, just in case things have changed.

Let's start off with a matrix of key combinations that are used to invoke access keys:

Browser	Windows	Linux	macOS X
Firefox	*Alt + Shift + <Key>*	*Alt + Shift + <Key>*	*Ctrl + Alt + <Key>*
Internet Explorer	*Alt + <Key>*	N/A	N/A
Edge	*Alt + <Key>*	N/A	N/A
Google Chrome	*Alt + <Key>*	*Alt + <Key>*	*Ctrl + Alt + <Key>*
Safari	N/A	N/A	*Ctrl + Alt + <Key>*
Opera	*Alt + <Key>*	*Alt + <Key>*	*Ctrl + Alt + <Key>*

Now, looking at the preceding table, it would appear that the browser manufacturers, with the exception of Firefox, seem to be pretty much in alignment across operating systems. Just by working out if the tests are running on OS X or not, we have pretty much got all we need; we will obviously need some exceptions for Firefox, though. Let's write some code.

First of all, we are going to create an OperatingSystem enum that will allow us to work out which OS we are running our tests on:

```
package com.masteringselenium.accessKeys;

public enum OperatingSystem {

    WINDOWS("windows"),
    OSX("mac"),
    LINUX("linux");

    private String operatingSystemName;

    OperatingSystem(String operatingSystemName) {
        this.operatingSystemName = operatingSystemName;
    }

    String getOperatingSystemType() {
        return operatingSystemName;
    }

    public static OperatingSystem getCurrentOperatingSystem() {
        String currentOperatingSystemName =
        System.getProperties().getProperty("os.name");
        for (OperatingSystem operatingSystemName : values()) {
            if (currentOperatingSystemName.toLowerCase()
            .contains(operatingSystemName.getOperatingSystemType()))
            {
                return operatingSystemName;
            }
        }

        throw new IllegalArgumentException("Unrecognised operating
        system name '" + currentOperatingSystemName + "'");
    }
}
```

Then, we will need a Browser enum that we can use to calculate the type of browser the tests are running in:

```
package com.masteringselenium.accessKeys;

import org.openqa.selenium.remote.BrowserType;

public enum Browser {
    FIREFOX(BrowserType.FIREFOX),
    GOOGLECHROME(BrowserType.CHROME),
```

```
SAFARI(BrowserType.SAFARI),
OPERA(BrowserType.OPERA_BLINK),
IE(BrowserType.IEXPLORE),
EDGE(BrowserType.EDGE);

private String type;

Browser(String type) {
    this.type = type;
}

public static Browser getBrowserType(String browserName) {
    for (Browser browser : values()) {
        if (browserName.toLowerCase().contains(browser.type)) {
            return browser;
        }
    }

    throw new IllegalArgumentException("Unrecognised
    browser name
    '" + browserName + "'");
    }
}
```

Note that we are pulling in the `BrowserType` definitions from Selenium; this is because we are going to use the capabilities of the driver object to work out what sort of browser is currently running the tests. This means that if the names used inside the capabilities ever change, we will get the updates for free. Now, we need to update our `.triggerAccessKey()` function and bring this all together:

```
import com.masteringselenium.accessKeys.Browser;
import com.masteringselenium.accessKeys.OperatingSystem;
private void triggerAccessKeyLocal(String accessKey) {
    Actions advancedActions = new Actions(driver);
    OperatingSystem currentOS =
    OperatingSystem.getCurrentOperatingSystem();
    String currentBrowserName =
    driver.getCapabilities().getBrowserName();
    Browser currentBrowser =
    Browser.getBrowserType(currentBrowserName);

    switch (currentOS) {
        case OSX:
            advancedActions.keyDown(Keys.CONTROL)
                    .keyDown(Keys.ALT)
                    .sendKeys(accessKey)
                    .keyUp(Keys.ALT)
```

```
                    .keyUp(Keys.CONTROL)
                    .perform();
            break;
        case LINUX:
        case WINDOWS:
            if (currentBrowser.equals(FIREFOX)) {
                advancedActions.keyDown(Keys.ALT)
                        .keyDown(Keys.SHIFT)
                        .sendKeys(accessKey)
                        .keyUp(Keys.SHIFT)
                        .keyUp(Keys.ALT)
                        .perform();
            } else {
                advancedActions.keyDown(Keys.ALT)
                        .sendKeys(accessKey)
                        .keyUp(Keys.ALT)
                        .perform();
            }
            break;
        default:
            throw new IllegalArgumentException("Unrecognised
            operating
            system name '" + currentOS + "'");
    }
}
```

We have made some assumptions in this code to keep it simple. First of all, we are assuming that you will never come across a Linux or macOS X system running Internet Explorer or Edge, so we have just ignored those scenarios. Secondly, we have assumed you aren't going to come across Safari in Windows or Linux and also ignored those scenarios. This means that really the only browser we care about is Firefox. In the future, if this changes, we could start nesting switch statements inside each case block of our current switch statement, but we really don't need to do that right now.

If you run the test again, everything should now work, no matter which browser or operating system combination you are running to write your tests. Excellent!

However, we have one more problem; what about using this code on a Selenium-Grid? The grid machine that you are connecting to may not be running the same operating system as you! Don't worry, we can fix that as well. The RemoteWebDriver instances should have a desired capability called Platform.

The reason that we didn't use it at first is because it's not always set (however in the future it should be, so this should stop being a problem). We need to make a couple of modifications to use it; let's start by looking at our OperatingSystem enum. Selenium supplies an enum, Platform, which provides a series of possible platforms and maps them to platform families (Windows, Unix, Mac, and so on). We can actually use this to replace our OperatingSystem enum since a RemoteWebDriver object has a method called driver.getCapabilities().getPlatform().

So, let's delete that already useless OperatingSystem enum straight away! Next, we will need to tweak our triggerAccessKey() function to use this Platform enum provided by Selenium:

```
private void triggerAccessKey(String accessKey) {
    Actions advancedActions = new Actions(driver);
    Platform currentOS = driver.getCapabilities().getPlatform();
    Platform currentOSFamily = (null == currentOS.family() ?
    currentOS : currentOS.family());
    String currentBrowserName =
    driver.getCapabilities().getBrowserName();
    Browser currentBrowser =
    Browser.getBrowserType(currentBrowserName);

    switch (currentOSFamily) {
        case MAC:
            advancedActions.keyDown(Keys.CONTROL)
                    .keyDown(Keys.ALT)
                    .sendKeys(accessKey)
                    .keyUp(Keys.ALT)
                    ..keyUp(Keys.CONTROL)
                    .perform();
            break;
        case UNIX:
        case WINDOWS:
            if (currentBrowser.equals(FIREFOX)) {
                advancedActions.keyDown(Keys.ALT)
                        .keyDown(Keys.SHIFT)
                        .sendKeys(accessKey)
                        .keyUp(Keys.SHIFT)
                        .keyUp(Keys.ALT)
                        .perform();
            } else {
                advancedActions.keyDown(Keys.ALT)
                        .sendKeys(accessKey)
                        .keyUp(Keys.ALT)
                        .perform();
            }
```

```
                        break;
            default:
                throw new IllegalArgumentException("Unrecognised
                operating system name '" + currentOS + "'");
        }
    }
```

You can see that we needed to do a bit of work to make sure we were returning a valid family. If you have a base family type returned (such as Windows) from your capabilities, you will get a `null` returned if you invoke `.family()`. We have dealt with this by inserting a ternary statement that will ensure the base family object is returned if calling `.family()` returns a `null`.

 Not sure what a ternary statement is? It's a conditional operator that's really just a shorthand way of writing an `if-then-else` statement. You can read more about it at `https://docs.oracle.com/javase/tutorial/java/nutsandbolts/op2.html`.

Now, if we run the same test again and connect it to a remote grid, everything should start working again. We probably have some edge cases here; it is possible to instantiate a driver object without setting a platform capability. We could probably extend it further so that if we cannot get a `Platform` name from the driver object capabilities, we can then fall back to getting the local operating system name and try that instead.

 Have a go at extending the `.triggerAccessKey()` function so that it can fall back and use the local operating system if the capabilities of the current `driver` object don't have a `Platform` type specified.

One of the main lessons to take away from this exercise is that it's hard work covering all the angles!

 Interacting with the keyboard sounds like a simple thing to do; however, in practice it's actually much harder than you would initially think, due to cross-platform compatibility issues. We usually don't have to worry about this sort of thing because the methods already supplied to you by the Selenium API have been written to work across various browsers and various platform combinations. A lot of people are quick to reach for their own solution rather than using one that has already been provided to them. The next time you think about doing this, it's worth remembering how much of a pain it can be to get a cross-platform solution working properly. Ask yourself, "Do I really need to do this?"

The Advanced Interactions API doesn't always work for me

The Advanced Interactions API is powerful, but it's not perfect. Sometimes, things just won't work.

Let's take our last example (the drag-and-drop page). The code works because we are using JavaScript to create the drag-and-drop functionality.

You can rewrite that example page by using the HTML5 `draggable` attribute and adding some event listeners. However, if you did this, the Advanced Interactions API would not be able to drag and drop the boxes anymore, because it doesn't yet (as of Selenium Version 3.12.0) support this.

As new technologies come out, it takes time for the core Selenium bindings to support them. So, what do you do when something doesn't work for you and you need to write a script? Well, you have a couple of options, which are as follows:

- Write a patch for Selenium and submit it
- Work around the issue

One of the most common ways to work around limitations in Selenium is to start using a JavaScript executor. In the next chapter, we will have a look at how JavaScript executors work and what you can do with them to get around problems.

Summary

In this chapter, we worked through a series of scenarios that are awkward to perform in Selenium without using a physical mouse or keyboard. A lot of people reach for third-party tools, or hacks that interact with the physical mouse or keyboard, in these situations.

After reading this chapter, you will no longer need to do that; instead, you will be able to use the Advanced Interactions API to its full potential to interact with both the mouse and the keyboard. There will be cases where things don't work due to limitations in the API, but you will be able to identify these scenarios.

In the next chapter, we will see how we can work around some of the limitations that we have come across so far. To do this we will examine how we can utilize the `JavascriptExecutor` class to its full potential. In doing so we will examine what it is capable of doing, and ask ourselves whether we should be doing these things.

7
JavaScript Execution with Selenium

In this chapter, we will look at how we can directly execute JavaScript snippets in Selenium. We will explore what you can do and how they can help you work around some of the limitations that you will come across while writing your scripts. We will also have a look at some examples of things that you should avoid doing.

The topics we will cover in this chapter will be:

- Using JavaScript to interact with the website loaded in your browser
- Injecting JavaScript libraries into the currently loaded website
- Performing complex actions using JavaScript
- Providing a way to allow user interaction with your tests by using JavaScript

To start off with, we are first going to have a look at how the `JavascriptExecutor` has been implemented in Selenium.

Introducing the JavaScript executor

Selenium has a mature API that handles the majority of automation tasks that you may want to throw at it. That being said, you will occasionally come across problems that the API doesn't really seem to support. This was very much on the development team's mind when Selenium was written. So, they provided a way for you to easily inject and execute arbitrary blocks of JavaScript. Let's have a look at a basic example of using a JavaScript executor in Selenium:

```
driver.executeScript("console.log('I logged something to the Javascript
console');");
```

Now it's possible that this didn't work for you; it depends on what sort of object you are passing around. If you are passing around an instance of `RemoteWebDriver` (that includes `FirefoxDriver` and `ChromeDriver`) it will have worked fine. However, if you are passing around a `WebDriver` instance it will have failed to compile. If you are passing around a `WebDriver` object, you will need to do the following:

```
JavascriptExecutor js = (JavascriptExecutor) driver;
js.executeScript("console.log('I logged something to the Javascript
console');");
```

The `WebDriver` object does not implement the `JavascriptExectutor` interface, so the execute script functions will not be available unless we perform this cast. If you are directly using an instance of `RemoteWebDriver` or something that extends it, you will have direct access to the `.executeScript()` function. The main driver implementations all extend `RemoteWebDriver` now so you probably won't need to cast your object into one of the `JavascriptExecutor` type. For the rest of the examples in this chapter, we are going to assume you are passing around a `RemoteWebDriver` object (if you are using the base framework we created in Chapter 1, *Creating a Fast Feedback Loop,* and Chapter 2, *Producing the Right Feedback When Failing,* you will already be doing this). Here's an example using `FirefoxDriver` directly, just to prove that it works:

```
FirefoxDriver driver = new FirefoxDriver(new FirefoxProfile());
driver.executeScript("console.log('I logged something to the Javascript
console');");
```

The second line (in both the preceding examples) is just telling Selenium to execute an arbitrary piece of JavaScript. In this case, we are just going to print something to the JavaScript console in the browser.

We can also get the `.executeScript()` function to return things to us. For example, if we tweak the JavaScript script in the first example, we can get Selenium to tell us whether it managed to write to the JavaScript console or not, as follows:

```
driver.executeScript("return console.log('I logged something to the
Javascript console');");
```

In the preceding example, we will get a `true` result coming back from the JavaScript executor.

Why does our JavaScript start with a `return` statement? Well, the JavaScript executed by Selenium is executed as a body of an anonymous function. This means that, if we did not add a `return` statement to the start of our JavaScript snippet, we would actually be running this JavaScript function using Selenium:

```
var anonymous = function () {
    console.log('I logged something to the Javascript console');
};
```

This function does log to the console, but it does not return anything. So, we can't access the result of the JavaScript snippet. If we prefix it with a `return` statement, it will execute the `anonymous` function:

```
var anonymous = function () {
    return console.log('I logged something to the Javascript
    console');
};
```

This does return something for us to work with. In this case, it will be the result of our attempt to write some text to the console. If we succeed in writing some text to the console, we will get back a `true` value. If we fail, we will get back a `false` value.

Note that in our example, we saved the response as an object, not a string or a Boolean. This is because the JavaScript executor can return lots of different types of objects. What we get as a response can be one of the following:

- If the result is `null` or there is no return value, a `null` will be returned
- If the result is an HTML element, a `WebElement` will be returned
- If the result is a decimal, a `double` will be returned
- If the result is a non-decimal number, a `long` will be returned
- If the result is a Boolean, a `Boolean` value will be returned
- If the result is an array, a `List` object with each object that it contains, along with all of these rules, will be returned (nested lists are supported)
- In all other cases, a `string` type will be returned

It is an impressive list, and it makes you realize just how powerful this method is. There is more as well. You can also pass arguments into the `.executeScript()` function. The arguments that you pass in can be any one of the following:

- `Number`
- `Boolean`

- `String`
- `WebElement`
- `List`

They are then put into a magic variable called `arguments`, which can be accessed by JavaScript. Let's extend our example a little bit to pass in some arguments, as follows:

```
String animal = "Lion";
int seen = 5;
driver.executeScript("console.log('I have seen a ' +
arguments[0] + ' ' + arguments[1] + ' times(s)');", animal, seen);
```

This time, you will see that we managed to print the following text into the console:

I have seen a Lion 5 times(s)

As you can see, there is a huge amount of flexibility with the JavaScript executor. You can write some complex bits of JavaScript code and pass in lots of different types of arguments from your Java code.

Think of all the things that you can do!

Let's not get carried away

We now know the basics of how one can execute JavaScript snippets in Selenium. This is where some people can start to get a bit carried away.

If you go through the mailing list of Selenium users, you will see many instances of people asking why they can't click on an element. Most of the time, this is due to the element that they are trying to interact with not being visible, which is blocking a click action. The real solution to this problem is to perform an action (the same one that they would perform if they were manually using the website) to make the element visible so that they can interact with it.

However, there is a shortcut offered by many, which is very bad practice. You can use a JavaScript executor to trigger a click event on this element. Doing this will probably make your test pass. So why is it a bad solution?

The Selenium development team has spent quite a lot of time writing code that works out if a user can interact with an element. It's pretty reliable. So, if Selenium says that you cannot currently interact with an element, it's highly unlikely that it's wrong. When figuring out whether you can interact with an element, lots of things are taken into account, including the z-index of an element. For example, you may have a transparent element that is covering the element that you want to click on and blocking the click action so that you can't reach it. Visually, it will be visible to you, but Selenium will correctly see it as not visible.

If you now invoke a JavaScript executor to trigger a click event on this element, your test will pass, but users will not be able to interact with it when they try to manually use your website.

However, what if Selenium got it wrong and you can interact with the element that you want to click manually? Well, that's great, but there are two things that you need to think about.

First of all, does it work in all browsers? If Selenium thinks that it is something that you cannot interact with, it's probably for a good reason. Is the markup, or the CSS, overly complicated? Can it be simplified?

Secondly, if you invoke a JavaScript executor, you will never know whether the element that you want to interact with really will get blocked at some point in the future. Your test may well keep passing when your application is broken. Tests that can't fail when something goes wrong are worse than no test at all!

If you think of Selenium as a toolbox, JavaScript executor is a very powerful tool that is present in it. However, it really should be seen as a last resort when all other avenues have failed you. Too many people use it as a solution to any slightly tricky problem that they come across.

If you are rewriting the code supplied by Selenium to use with a JavaScript executor, you are doing it wrong! Your code is unlikely to be better. The Selenium development team has been doing this for a long time with a lot of input from a lot of people, many of them being experts in their fields. If you are writing methods to find elements on a page, there is a good chance that you are doing it wrong. Use the .findElement() method provided by Selenium.

Occasionally, you may find a bug in Selenium that prevents you from interacting with an element in the way you would expect to. Many people first respond by reaching for a JavascriptExecutor to code around the problem in Selenium.

Hang on for just one moment, though. Have you upgraded to the latest version of Selenium? Did you just upgrade to the latest version of Selenium when you didn't need to? Using a slightly older version of Selenium that works correctly is perfectly acceptable. Don't feel forced to upgrade for no reason, especially if it means that you have to write your own hacks around problems that didn't exist before.

The correct thing to do is to use a stable version of Selenium that works for you. You can always raise bugs about functionalities that don't work, or even code a fix and submit a **pull request**. Don't give yourself the additional work of writing a workaround, which is probably not the ideal solution, unless you really need to.

So, what should we do with it?

Let's have a look at some examples of the things that we can do with the JavaScript executor that aren't really possible using the base Selenium API.

First of all, we will start off by getting the element text.

Wait a minute, element text? That's easy. You can use the existing Selenium API with the following code:

```
WebElement myElement = driver.findElement(By.id("foo"));
String elementText = myElement.getText();
```

So, why would we want to use a JavaScript executor to find the text of an element?

Getting text is easy using the Selenium API, but only under certain conditions. The element that you are collecting the text from needs to be displayed. If Selenium thinks that the element from which you are collecting the text is not displayed, it will return an empty string. If you want to collect some text from a hidden element, you are out of luck. You will need to implement a way to do it with a JavaScript executor.

Why would you want to do this? Well, maybe you have a responsive website that shows different elements based on different resolutions. You may well want to check whether these two different elements are displaying the same text to the user. To do this, you will need to get the text of the visible and invisible elements so that you can compare them. Let's create a method to collect some hidden text for us:

```
private String getHiddenText(WebElement element) {
    JavascriptExecutor js = (JavascriptExecutor)
    ((RemoteWebElement) element).getWrappedDriver();
    return (String) js.executeScript("return arguments[0].text",
    element);}
```

We have a bit of cleverness in this method. First of all, we took the element that we wanted to interact with and then extracted the `driver` object associated with it. We did this by casting the `WebElement` into a `RemoteWebElement`, which allowed us to use the `getWrappedDriver()` method. This removed the need to pass a `driver` object around the place all the time (this is something that happens a lot in some code bases).

Unfortunately, we get a base `WebDriver` object, not a `RemoteWebDriver` object, so we have to take this `WebDriver` object and cast it into a `JavascriptExecutor` object to gain the ability to invoke the `.executeScript()` method. Next, we execute the JavaScript snippet and pass in the original element as an argument. Finally, we take the response of the `executeScript()` call and cast it into a string that we can return as a result of the method.

> Generally, getting text is a **code smell**. Your tests should not rely on specific text to be displayed on a website, because content always changes. Maintaining tests that check the content of a site is a lot of work, and it makes your functional tests brittle. The best thing to do is test the mechanism that injects the content into the website. If you use a CMS that injects text into a specific template key, you can test whether each element has the correct template key associated with it.

A more complex example

So you want to see something more complicated. Well, you may remember that we had a look at how we could use the Advanced User Interactions API to interact with a page, allowing you to drag and drop elements, in Chapter 6, *Utilizing the Advanced User Interactions API*. The implementation that we used in that chapter was based on jQuery rather than the native HTML5 code. The Advanced User Interactions API cannot deal with HTML5 drag and drop. So, what happens if we come across an HTML5 drag-and-drop implementation that we want to automate? Well, we can use the `JavascriptExecutor`. Let's have a look at the markup for the HTML5 drag-and-drop page:

```
<!DOCTYPE html>
<html lang="en">
<head>
    <meta charset=utf-8>
    <title>Drag and drop</title>
    <style type="text/css">
        li {
            list-style: none;
        }
```

```
        li a {
            text-decoration: none;
            color: #000;
            margin: 10px;
            width: 150px;
            border-width: 2px;
            border-color: black;
            border-style: groove;
            background: #eee;
            padding: 10px;
            display: block;
        }

        *[draggable=true] {
            cursor: move;
        }

        ul {
            margin-left: 200px;
            min-height: 300px;
        }

        #obliterate {
            background-color: green;
            height: 250px;
            width: 166px;
            float: left;
            border: 5px solid #000;
            position: relative;
            margin-top: 0;
        }

        #obliterate.over {
            background-color: red;
        }
    </style>
</head>
<body>
<header>
    <h1>Drag and drop</h1>
</header>


<article>
    <p>Drag items over to the green square to remove them</p>

    <div id="obliterate"></div>
    <ul>
```

```
            <li><a id="one" href="#" draggable="true">one</a></li>
            <li><a id="two" href="#" draggable="true">two</a></li>
            <li><a id="three" href="#" draggable="true">three</a></li>
            <li><a id="four" href="#" draggable="true">four</a></li>
            <li><a id="five" href="#" draggable="true">five</a></li>
        </ul>
    </article>
    </body>
    <script>
        var draggableElements = document.querySelectorAll('li > a'),
                obliterator = document.getElementById('obliterate');

        for (var i = 0; i < draggableElements.length; i++) {
            element = draggableElements[i];
            element.addEventListener('dragstart', function (event) {
                event.dataTransfer.effectAllowed = 'copy';
                event.dataTransfer.setData('being-dragged', this.id);
            });
        }

        obliterator.addEventListener('dragover', function (event) {
            if (event.preventDefault) event.preventDefault();
            obliterator.className = 'over';
            event.dataTransfer.dropEffect = 'copy';
            return false;
        });

        obliterator.addEventListener('dragleave', function () {
            obliterator.className = '';
            return false;
        });

        obliterator.addEventListener('drop', function (event) {
            var elementToDelete = document.getElementById(
              event.dataTransfer.getData('being-dragged'));
            elementToDelete.parentNode.removeChild(elementToDelete);
            obliterator.className = '';
            return false;
        });
    </script>
    </html>
```

Note that the page looks pretty much identical to the one that we used in `Chapter` 6, *Utilizing the Advanced User Interactions API*. However, the implementation is different.

Note that you need a browser that supports HTML5/CSS3 for this page to work. The latest versions of Google Chrome, Opera Blink, Safari, and Firefox will work. You may have issues with Internet Explorer (depending on the version that you are using). For an updated list of HTML5/CSS3 support, have a look at `http://caniuse.com`.

If you try to use the Advanced User Interactions API to automate this page, you will find that it just doesn't work because the Advanced User Interactions API doesn't fire all the required triggers. It looks like it's time to reach for the power and flexibility of the `JavascriptExecutor`.

Executing complex blocks of JavaScript with the JavascriptExecutor

First of all, we need to write some JavaScript code that can simulate the events that we need to trigger to perform the drag-and-drop action. To do this, we are going to create three JavaScript functions (note that these three functions are not Java code). The first function is going to create a JavaScript `event`:

```
function createEvent(typeOfEvent) {
    var event = document.createEvent("CustomEvent");
    event.initCustomEvent(typeOfEvent, true, true, null);
    event.dataTransfer = {
        data: {},
         setData: function (key, value) {
            this.data[key] = value;
        },
         getData: function (key) {
            return this.data[key];
        }
    };
    return event;
}
```

We then need to write a function that will fire `event` instances that we have created. This also allows you to pass in the `dataTransfer` value set on an element. We need this to keep track of the element that we are dragging:

```
function dispatchEvent(element, event, transferData) {
    if (transferData !== undefined) {
        event.dataTransfer = transferData;
    }
    if (element.dispatchEvent) {
```

```
        element.dispatchEvent(event);
    } else if (element.fireEvent) {
        element.fireEvent("on" + event.type, event);
    }
}
```

Finally, we need something that will use these two functions to simulate the drag-and-drop action:

```
function simulateHTML5DragAndDrop(element, target) {
    var dragStartEvent = createEvent('dragstart');
    dispatchEvent(element, dragStartEvent);
    var dropEvent = createEvent('drop');
    dispatchEvent(target, dropEvent, dragStartEvent.dataTransfer);
    var dragEndEvent = createEvent('dragend');
    dispatchEvent(element, dragEndEvent, dropEvent.dataTransfer);
}
```

Note that the simulateHTML5DragAndDrop function needs us to pass in two elements—the element that we want to drag, and the element that we want to drag it to.

It's always a good idea to try out your JavaScript in a browser first. You can copy the preceding functions into the JavaScript console in a modern browser and then try using them to make sure that they work as expected. If things go wrong in your Selenium test, you then know that it is most likely an error invoked via the JavascriptExecutor rather than a bad piece of JavaScript.

We now need to take these scripts and put them into a JavascriptExecutor along with something that will call the simulateHTML5DragAndDrop function (this is now Java code):

```
private void simulateDragAndDrop(WebElement elementToDrag, WebElement
target) {
    driver.executeScript("function createEvent(typeOfEvent)
    {\n" + "    var event = document.createEvent(\"CustomEvent\");
    \n" + "    event.initCustomEvent(typeOfEvent, true, true, null);
    \n" +
                "    event.dataTransfer = {\n" +
                "        data: {},\n" +
                "        setData: function (key, value) {\n" +
                "            this.data[key] = value;\n" +
                "        },\n" +
                "        getData: function (key) {\n" +
                "            return this.data[key];\n" +
                "        }\n" +
                "    };\n" +
```

```
"      return event;\n" +
"}\n" +
"\n" +
"function dispatchEvent(element, event,
transferData) {\n" +
"      if (transferData !== undefined) {\n" +
"          event.dataTransfer = transferData;\n"
+   "      }\n" +
"      if (element.dispatchEvent) {\n" +
"          element.dispatchEvent(event);\n" +
"      } else if (element.fireEvent) {\n" +
"          element.fireEvent(\"on\" + event.type,
event);\n" +
"      }\n" +
"}\n" +
"\n" +
"function simulateHTML5DragAndDrop(element,
target) {\n" +
"      var dragStartEvent =
createEvent('dragstart');\n" +
"      dispatchEvent(element, dragStartEvent);
\n" +
"      var dropEvent = createEvent('drop');\n" +
"      dispatchEvent(target, dropEvent,
       dragStartEvent.dataTransfer);\n" +
"      var dragEndEvent =
createEvent('dragend');\n" +
"      dispatchEvent(element, dragEndEvent,
       dropEvent.dataTransfer);\n" +
"}\n" +
"\n" +
"var elementToDrag = arguments[0];\n" +
"var target = arguments[1];\n" +
"simulateHTML5DragAndDrop(elementToDrag,
target);",
elementToDrag, target);
  }
```

This method is really just a wrapper around the JavaScript code. We take a `driver` object and cast it into a `JavascriptExecutor`. We then pass the JavaScript code into the executor as a string. We have made a couple of additions to the JavaScript functions that we previously wrote. Firstly, we set a couple of variables (mainly for code clarity; they can quite easily be inlined) that take the `WebElements` that we have passed in as arguments. Finally, we invoke the `simulateHTML5DragAndDrop` function using these elements.

The final piece of the puzzle is to write a test that utilizes the `simulateDragAndDrop` method, as follows:

```
@Test
public void dragAndDropHTML5() {
    driver.get("http://web.masteringselenium.com/dragAndDrop.html");

    By destroyableBoxes = By.cssSelector("ul > li > a");
    WebElement obliterator =
    driver.findElement(By.id("obliterate"));
    WebElement firstBox = driver.findElement(By.id("one"));
    WebElement secondBox = driver.findElement(By.id("two"));

    assertThat(driver.findElements(destroyableBoxes).size()).isEqualTo(5);

    simulateDragAndDrop(firstBox, obliterator);

    assertThat(driver.findElements(destroyableBoxes).size()).isEqualTo(4);

    simulateDragAndDrop(secondBox, obliterator);

    assertThat(driver.findElements(destroyableBoxes).size()).isEqualTo(3);
}
```

This test is very similar to the one that we wrote in Chapter 6, *Utilizing the Advanced User Interactions API*. It finds a couple of boxes and destroys them one by one using the simulated drag and drop. As you can see, the `JavascriptExcutor` is extremely powerful.

Can I use JavaScript libraries?

The logical progression is of course to write your own JavaScript libraries that you can import instead of sending everything over as a string. Alternatively, maybe you would just like to import an existing library.

Let's write some code that allows you to import a JavaScript library of your choice. It's not particularly complex JavaScript. All that we are going to do is create a new `<script>` element in a page and then load our library into it. First of all, let's make sure we have access to a `driver` object in this class:

```
private RemoteWebDriver driver;
@BeforeMethod
public void setup() {
    driver = getDriver();
}
```

Then we will need to add some code that will let us inject a `<script>` element:

```
private void injectScript(String scriptURL) {
    driver.executeScript("function injectScript(url) {\n" +
            "    var script =
            document.createElement('script');\n" +
            "    script.src = url;\n" +
            "    var head =
            document.getElementsByTagName('head')[0];
            \n" +
            "    head.appendChild(script);\n" +
            "}\n" +
            "\n" +
            "var scriptURL = arguments[0];\n" +
            "injectScript(scriptURL);"
            , scriptURL);
}
```

We have again set `arguments[0]` to a variable before injecting it for clarity, but you can inline this part if you want to. All that remains now is to inject this into a page and check whether it works. Let's write a test!

We are going to use this function to inject jQuery into the Google website. The first thing that we need to do is write a method that can tell us whether jQuery has been loaded or not, as follows:

```
private Boolean isjQueryLoaded() {
    return (Boolean) driver.executeScript("return typeof jQuery
    != 'undefined';");
}
```

We are also going to write an `ExpectedCondition` to help us work out when the script has been successfully injected (you will notice that the JavaScript we use is identical to the preceding one):

```
private static ExpectedCondition<Boolean> jQueryHasLoaded() {
    return webDriver -> {
        JavascriptExecutor js = (JavascriptExecutor) webDriver;
        return Boolean.valueOf(js.executeScript("return typeof
        jQuery !=
        'undefined';").toString());
    };
}
```

Now you will see that the expected condition is a little bit more complex than you may have expected. This is because this expected condition is going to be plugged into the `.until()` method of a `WebDriverWait` object. Unfortunately, `WebDriverWait` objects are instantiated with a `WebDriver` object, not a `RemoteWebDriver` object. If you remember, we talked about this at the start of the chapter. We need to cast the `WebDriver` object into something that has the `.executeScript()` method. Next we need to put all of this together in a test, as follows:

```
@Test
public void injectjQueryIntoGoogle() {
    WebDriverWait wait = new WebDriverWait(driver, 15, 100);

    driver.get("http://www.google.com");

    assertThat(isjQueryLoaded()).isEqualTo(false);

    injectScript("https://code.jquery.com/jquery-latest.min.js");
    wait.until(jQueryHasLoaded());

    assertThat(isjQueryLoaded()).isEqualTo(true);
}
```

It's a very simple test. We loaded the Google website. Then, we checked whether jQuery existed. Once we were sure that it didn't exist, we injected jQuery into the page. Finally, we waited for jQuery to load, and then for completeness we have an assertion to be absolutely positive that jQuery now exists.

We have used jQuery in our example, but you don't have to use jQuery. You can inject any script that you desire.

Should I inject JavaScript libraries?

It's very easy to inject JavaScript into a page, but stop and think before you do it. Adding lots of different JavaScript libraries may affect the existing functionality of the site. You may overwrite the existing functions with the same name and break the core functionality.

If you are testing a site, it may make all of your tests invalid. Failures may arise because there is a clash between the scripts that you inject and the existing scripts used on the site. The flip side is also true—injecting a script may make the functionality that is broken, work.

If you are going to inject scripts into an existing site, be sure that you know what the consequences are.

If you are going to regularly inject a script, it may be a good idea to add some assertions to ensure that the functions that you are injecting do not already exist before you inject the script. This way, your tests will fail if the developers add a JavaScript function with the same name at some point in the future without your knowledge.

What about asynchronous scripts?

Everything that we have looked at so far has been a synchronous piece of JavaScript. However, what if we wanted to perform some asynchronous JavaScript calls as a part of our test? Well, we can do this. The `JavascriptExecutor` also has a method called `executeAsyncScript()`. This will allow you to run some JavaScript that does not respond instantly. Let's have a look at some examples.

First of all, we are going to write a very simple bit of JavaScript that will wait for 25 seconds before triggering a callback, as follows:

```
@Test
private void javascriptExample() {
    driver.manage().timeouts().setScriptTimeout(60,
    TimeUnit.SECONDS);
    driver.executeAsyncScript("var callback =
    arguments[arguments.length - 1];
    window.setTimeout(callback, 25000);");
    driver.get("http://www.google.com");
}
```

Note that we defined a JavaScript variable named `callback`, which uses a script argument that we have not set. For asynchronous scripts, Selenium needs to have a callback defined, which is used to detect when the JavaScript that you are executing has finished. This `callback` object is automatically added to the end of your arguments array. This is what we have defined as the `callback` variable.

If we now run the script, it will load our browser and then sit there for 25 seconds as it waits for the JavaScript snippet to complete and call the callback. It will then load the Google website and finish.

We have also set a script timeout on the `driver` object that will wait for up to 60 seconds for our piece of JavaScript to execute.

Let's see what happens if our script takes longer to execute than the script timeout:

```
@Test
private void javascriptExample() {
    driver.manage().timeouts().setScriptTimeout(5,
    TimeUnit.SECONDS);
    driver.executeAsyncScript("var callback =
    arguments[arguments.length - 1];
    window.setTimeout(callback, 25000);");
    driver.get("http://www.google.com");
}
```

This time, when we run our test, it waits for 5 seconds and then throws a `ScriptTimoutException`. This highlights how important it is to set a script timeout on the `driver` object when running asynchronous scripts to give them enough time to execute.

What do you think will happen if we execute this as a normal script? Let's look:

```
@Test
private void javascriptExample() {
    driver.manage().timeouts().setScriptTimeout(5,
    TimeUnit.SECONDS);
    driver.executeScript("var callback = arguments
    [arguments.length - 1];
    window.setTimeout(callback, 25000);");
    driver.get("http://www.google.com");
}
```

You may have been expecting an error, but that's not what you got. The script got executed as normal because Selenium was not waiting for a callback; as a result it did not wait for it to complete. Since Selenium did not wait for the script to complete, it didn't hit the script timeout. Hence, no error was thrown.

Wait a minute. What about the callback definition? No argument was used to set the `callback` variable. Why didn't it blow up?

Well, JavaScript isn't as strict as Java. What it does do is try and work out what `arguments[arguments.length - 1]` will resolve and realizes that it is not defined. Since it is not defined, it sets the `callback` variable to null. Our test then completed before `setTimeout()` had a chance to complete its call. So, you won't see any console errors.

As you can see, it's very easy to make a small error that stops things from working when working with asynchronous JavaScript. It's also very hard to find these errors because there can be very little user feedback. Always take extra care when using the `JavascriptExecutor` to execute asynchronous bits of JavaScript. Now we know the basics of using asynchronous scripts, let's put that knowledge to use to do something a bit more interesting.

Building user interaction into your automation

We don't always use automation for writing tests. Sometimes we also want to automate repetitive tasks. A lot of these repetitive tasks can be easily automated, whereas others are not completely repetitive and require some form of user input that regularly changes. How useful would it be to be able to write a Selenium script that can take some user input so that you don't need to keep rewriting the script for that regular task you have to perform?

Well, we can do that; let's put together an example. First of all, we are going to write a snippet of JavaScript that will allow us to insert an input field into a page:

```
var dataInput = document.createElement('div');
dataInput.id = "se_temp_markup";
dataInput.setAttribute("style","width: 200px; height: 100px; background-
color: yellow; z-index: 99999999; position: fixed; padding: 1rem;");
dataInput.innerHTML = "<p>Enter some text to use in the Selenium
test:</p>\n" +
    "<input type=\"text\" id=\"setest_collect_data\">\n" +
    "<button onclick=\"returnDataToSelenium()\">submit</button>";
```

There are a couple of important parts in this script. First of all, we are using the CSS styling `position: fixed;` and `z-index: 99999999`. This makes sure that the piece of HTML that we are injecting into the page is layered on the top of everything else. Next, we have specified an ID in our input element so that we can identify it later on when we want to pull data out of it. Finally, notice that we have added an `onclick` event to the button that calls another function. This is the function that is going to trigger the return of data to Selenium so that we can use it in our test. Let's take a look at it:

```
var script = document.createElement('script');
script.innerHTML = "function returnDataToSelenium() {\n" +
    "    var userInput =
    document.getElementById('setest_collect_data').value;
        \n" +
```

```
"        document.getElementById(\"se_temp_markup\").remove();\n" +
"        window.callback(userInput);\n" +
"}";
```

You will notice that this snippet of JavaScript is being written to the page HTML instead of just being injected into memory. This is so that it's in the right context for the previous bit of HTML that we injected to be able to call it. What it does is pretty simple—it collects the data that the user has input, deletes all of the injected HTML, and then calls the callback that Selenium is going to inject. Finally, we need to write all of this into the DOM:

```
var body = document.getElementsByTagName('body')[0];
body.appendChild(script);
body.appendChild(dataInput);
```

This finds the <body> tag of the current page and then injects our preceding custom pieces. The only outstanding part is to bind the Selenium callback to the window object so that the function we previously wrote can interact with it:

```
window.callback = arguments[arguments.length - 1];
```

We now need to do something useful with all of this, so let's create an example of how it can be used using the Google search page:

```
@Test
public void interactiveCallback() {
    driver.manage().timeouts().setScriptTimeout(45,
    TimeUnit.SECONDS);
    driver.get("http://www.google.com");

    String searchTerms = (String)
    driver.executeAsyncScript("window.callback =
    arguments[arguments.length - 1];\n" +
            "var dataInput = document.createElement('div');\n" +
            "dataInput.id = \"se_temp_markup\";\n" +
            "dataInput.setAttribute(\"style\", \"width: 200px;
            height: 100px;
            background-color: yellow; z-index: 99999999;
            position: fixed; padding: 1rem;\");\n" +
            "dataInput.innerHTML = \"<p>Enter some text to
            use in the
            Selenium test:</p>\\n\" +\n" +
    "        \"<input type=\\\"text\\\"
    id=\\\"setest_collect_data\\\">
            \\n\" +\n" +
    "        \"<button
            onclick=\\\"returnDataToSelenium()\\\">
            submit</button>\";\n" +
```

```
        "\n" +
        "\n" +
        "var script = document.createElement('script');\n" +
        "script.innerHTML = \"function returnDataToSelenium()
        {\\n\" +\n" +    "    \"    var userInput =
        document.getElementById('setest_collect_data').value;
        \\n\" +\n" +    "    \"
document.getElementById(\\\"se_temp_markup\\\")
.remove();\\n\" +\n" +
        "    \"    window.callback(userInput);\\n\" +\n" +
        "    \"}\"}\\";\n" + "\n" +
        "var body = document.getElementsByTagName('body')[0];
        \n" + "body.appendChild(script);\n" +
        "body.appendChild(dataInput);");

    WebElement googleSearchBox = driver.findElement(By.name("q"));
    googleSearchBox.sendKeys(searchTerms);
    googleSearchBox.submit();
}
```

This should all look very familiar. We have created a `JavascriptExecutor` object and set our script timeout to 45 seconds. This should give us long enough to enter some text before the script times out. We are casting the result of the script into a string and then we are using that string to enter some data into the Google Search box, and then submitting it. When you run this test, you should see a small yellow box in the top left of your screen asking for input. Once you have submitted some text, the box will disappear again and then that text will be used in the Google search. It does run quickly, so if you have a fast machine you may want to add an explicit wait that checks for the search results page to load.

Now, displaying a textbox so that we can type in some text and inject it into the textbox is not the most useful of scripts, but it does highlight the possibilities available to us. You don't have to supply a textbox for the user; you could pop up a radio button and let the user choose from a selection of existing flows or predefined datasets. You could put the script in a loop that asks if you want to run it again at the end of each run. The possibilities are only limited by your imagination and your ability to write JavaScript.

Summary

In this chapter, we explored some of the many possibilities that are opened up to you when using `JavascriptExecutor`. We have really just scratched the surface of what is possible, but this chapter should have given you a good solid platform to expand upon.

After reading through this chapter you should be confident in executing JavaScript snippets through the browser and know how to pass in arguments. As well as using synchronous pieces of JavaScript, you will also be able to enhance your tests with asynchronous pieces of JavaScript that will allow you to build user interaction into your automated scripts. Finally you should be aware of when we should and when we shouldn't use a JavaScript executor.

In the next chapter, we are going to have a look at some of the limitations of Selenium. We will also have a look at the ways in which we can work around these limitations and enhance Selenium by using additional tools.

8
Keeping It Real

In this chapter, we will have a look at some of the things that you cannot do with Selenium, and some of the things that you should not do with Selenium. We will have a look at some solutions that will work around its limitations. The topics we will cover in this chapter are:

- File downloads
- Checking network traffic
- Load testing

The first topic we are going to look at is something that I regularly end up talking about—downloading files with Selenium.

File downloads with Selenium

At some point in your career, you are probably going to work with a website that allows the user to download something. There are many different types of things that may be downloadable. The most common things are probably:

- PDF files
- Pictures (PNG, JPG, and GIF)
- Archives
- Installers

When you are working on a site that allows you to download files of some type, you will be expected to test that this functionality works and, at some point, the idea of writing some automated checks for this functionality will probably come up.

The scenario

You are working in a small, agile team and are in a pre-planning session with your tech lead, business analyst, and product owner. The product owner would like to give your users some new functionality that enables them to download PDFs from the website that you are working on. These PDFs are going to have legal terms and conditions in them to satisfy statutory requirements, so it is important that they are available. If they are not downloadable, your company may be liable for some fairly significant fines. During planning, your team agrees that this is a relatively trivial bit of functionality for the developers to implement. You also agree that it will be easy for you to run a quick manual test to check that the functionality works by clicking on the download link in your browser. You don't know what the content of these documents is going to be yet because the legal department hasn't got back to you.

The functionality is written, and the PDF download works fine; it's tested manually and looks good for sign off. The next day, you grab the product owner so that you can test the new piece of functionality with her, but something has gone wrong. A new build was pushed to your test environment this morning and it seems that the PDFs are no longer there. A quick investigation shows that the files were accidentally removed and the changes reverted; however, it still doesn't work when it hits your test environment! Further investigation shows that the links to the PDFs have also been changed in error; they are now linking to files that don't exist. That issue is fixed and eventually the new functionality is successfully shown to your product owner. Overall, this has been a messy day that nobody is very proud of, and it has highlighted the fact that this could very easily go wrong in the future.

The problem

Your product owner knows that the functionality works, but her faith has been shaken somewhat and she wants you to find a way to ensure that this will not happen again in the future. As a team, you all agree that the build should become red on the Linux CI server if changes the developers make break the new PDF download functionality.

So, what's next?

Writing the automated checks falls to you. You open up your development IDE and start writing Selenium code. Your plan is to replicate the actions that you would perform manually in an automated script:

1. You load the page with the download link
2. You find the <a> element on the page
3. You click on it

Wait! It's a trap. As soon as you click on the download link, your test stops because Selenium cannot interact with an OS-level dialog box.

You go and have a look at the Selenium mailing lists and see lots of posts talking about your problem. Most of them seem to be advocating the use of another tool called AutoIT and there is some talk about using a Java Robot class. Almost everything you read talks about finding a way to interact with your OS-level dialog box.

Stop right there!

Now is the time to take a step backward and work out exactly what you want to test.

Do you really need to download that file?

When I ask people if they really need to download the file, they normally say, "Yes, I do! I need to make sure that the download functionality works, and continues to work after a code change."

That sounds pretty reasonable so far. I then pose the following questions:

- How many files are you planning to download?
- How big are these files?
- Do you have enough disk space to hold all of these files?
- Do you have network capacity to continually download these files?
- What are you planning to do with the file(s) once you have downloaded them?

The answer to the last question is the most interesting one. People I talk to usually say something along the lines of this: "Well, I don't know. Delete it? I just need to know that it downloads; I'm not actually planning to do anything with it."

So the real question is: Do you really need to download a file to perform this test? What you are really saying is that, when you click on the PDF download link, you want to be sure that you are getting a valid response from the server.

You are not really checking that you can download the file, you are checking for broken links.

This is a worthwhile test, but it doesn't actually require you to download anything. So let's forget about trying to interact with that OS-level dialog box for now and see how we can check to see if the link is valid.

Checking that links are valid

It's actually pretty simple to check links. All you need to do is find the link on the page, extract a URL from its `href` attribute, and then check to see if sending an HTTP `GET` request to that URL results in a valid response.

Let's create some code to do this for us.

First of all, we are going to need to add some dependencies to our POM:

```
<properties>
    <commons-io.version>2.6</commons-io.version>
    <httpclient.version>4.5.5</httpclient.version>
</properties>

<dependency>
    <groupId>org.apache.httpcomponents</groupId>
    <artifactId>httpclient</artifactId>
    <version>${httpclient.version}</version>
    <scope>test</scope>
</dependency>
<dependency>
    <groupId>commons-io</groupId>
    <artifactId>commons-io</artifactId>
    <version>${commons-io.version}</version>
    <scope>test</scope>
</dependency>
```

Now that we have the libraries that are required, it's time to look at some code:

```
package com.masteringselenium.downloader;

import org.apache.http.client.methods.*;

public enum RequestType {
```

```
    OPTIONS(new HttpOptions()),
    GET(new HttpGet()),
    HEAD(new HttpHead()),
    PATCH(new HttpPatch()),
    POST(new HttpPost()),
    PUT(new HttpPut()),
    DELETE(new HttpDelete()),
    TRACE(new HttpTrace());

    private final HttpRequestBase requestMethod;

    RequestType(HttpRequestBase requestMethod) {
        this.requestMethod = requestMethod;
    }

    public HttpRequestBase getRequestMethod() {
        return this.requestMethod;
    }
}
```

First of all, we have an enum that will define all of the various types of HTTP requests that we could use to get the content from our website. We are probably going to use GET most of the time, but you will come across other requests at some point, so we may as well add them now. Let's now move on to the part that does the actual work; firstly, we have our basic class:

```
package com.masteringselenium.downloader;

import org.apache.http.HttpResponse;
import org.apache.http.NameValuePair;
import org.apache.http.client.HttpClient;
import org.apache.http.client.entity.UrlEncodedFormEntity;
import org.apache.http.client.methods.HttpEntityEnclosingRequestBase;
import org.apache.http.client.methods.HttpRequestBase;
import org.apache.http.impl.client.HttpClientBuilder;
import org.apache.http.protocol.BasicHttpContext;

import java.io.IOException;
import java.net.MalformedURLException;
import java.net.URI;
import java.util.List;

public class FileDownloader {

    private RequestType httpRequestMethod = RequestType.GET;
    private URI fileURI;
    private List<NameValuePair> urlParameters;
```

```
public void setHTTPRequestMethod(RequestType requestType) {
    httpRequestMethod = requestType;
}

public void setURLParameters(List<NameValuePair> urlParameters)
{
    this.urlParameters = urlParameters;
}

public void setURI(URI linkToFile) throws MalformedURLException
{
    fileURI = linkToFile;
}

}
```

We have created an object that we can instantiate once and then use multiple times to download different files. We have created some setters to allow you to set the URI you want to query, the type of request that you want to send, and some URL parameters if required for POST/PATCH/PUT requests. We have set our default request method to GET as it is probably the one you will use the most. The only thing you need to supply is the URI. The next step is to create the code that will negotiate with the remote server:

```
private HttpResponse makeHTTPConnection() throws IOException,
NullPointerException {
    if (fileURI == null) throw new NullPointerException("No file
    URI specified");

    HttpClient client = HttpClientBuilder.create().build();

    HttpRequestBase requestMethod =
    httpRequestMethod.getRequestMethod();
    requestMethod.setURI(fileURI);

    BasicHttpContext localContext = new BasicHttpContext();

    if (null != urlParameters && (
            httpRequestMethod.equals(RequestType.PATCH) ||
                httpRequestMethod.equals(RequestType.POST) ||
                httpRequestMethod.equals(RequestType.PUT)
    )) {
        ((HttpEntityEnclosingRequestBase) requestMethod)
                .setEntity(new UrlEncodedFormEntity(urlParameters));
    }

    return client.execute(requestMethod, localContext);
}
```

If you forget to specify a URI, this code will quickly fail and throw `NullPointerException`. The only complexity in there at the moment is adding some `urlParameters` if you are using a request type that would normally expect them.

Now that we can make a connection, we need to do something with it:

```
public int getLinkHTTPStatus() throws Exception {
    HttpResponse downloadableFile = makeHTTPConnection();
    int httpStatusCode;
    try {
        httpStatusCode =
        downloadableFile.getStatusLine().getStatusCode();
    } finally {
        if (null != downloadableFile.getEntity()) {
            downloadableFile.getEntity().getContent().close();
        }
    }

    return httpStatusCode;
}
```

This code uses the previous method to negotiate a connection with a remote server, and then gets the HTTP status code for the file that we are interested in. We can then use this HTTP status code to work out whether the file is there or if there is a problem. If the file is there, I would expect a 200 (OK) or maybe even a 302 (Redirect). If it's not there, I would expect a 404 (Not found) or maybe, if things really went badly, a 500 (Internal Server Error).

It's up to you to define which HTTP status code is a pass or a fail; the preceding code will simply tell you what the HTTP status code is.

While this code is useful, it's not yet perfect. Lots of websites do not allow you to just download files; they have protected content that can only be downloaded by somebody who has a valid account on the website.

Now, you should already have a Selenium script that is logging you into the website you are trying to test and allowing you to get the URI that you want to download. Let's use the information that Selenium has to trick the website into thinking that your Selenium session is actually performing the download. We are going to add a constructor to our `FileDownloader` class and make it require a `WebDriver` object:

```
private RemoteWebDriver driver;

public FileDownloader(RemoteWebDriver driverObject) {
    this.driver = driverObject;
}
```

Then, we need to use this driver object to get some information so that we can pretend our request is coming from the browser. We will copy the user agent:

```
private String getWebDriverUserAgent() {
    return driver.executeScript("return
    navigator.userAgent").toString();
}
```

Then, we need to copy the cookies:

```
private BasicCookieStore getWebDriverCookies(Set<Cookie> seleniumCookieSet)
{
    BasicCookieStore copyOfWebDriverCookieStore = new
    BasicCookieStore();
    for (Cookie seleniumCookie : seleniumCookieSet) {
        BasicClientCookie duplicateCookie = new
        BasicClientCookie(seleniumCookie.getName(),
        seleniumCookie.getValue());
        duplicateCookie.setDomain(seleniumCookie.getDomain());
        duplicateCookie.setSecure(seleniumCookie.isSecure());
        duplicateCookie.setExpiryDate(seleniumCookie.getExpiry());
        duplicateCookie.setPath(seleniumCookie.getPath());
        copyOfWebDriverCookieStore.addCookie(duplicateCookie);
    }

    return copyOfWebDriverCookieStore;
}
```

We now have all the bits that we need to pretend to be the browser that Selenium is driving, so let's tweak our `makeHTTPConnection()` method to use this information:

```
private HttpResponse makeHTTPConnection() throws IOException,
NullPointerException {
    if (fileURI == null) throw new NullPointerException("No file
    URI specified");

    HttpClient client = HttpClientBuilder.create().build();

    HttpRequestBase requestMethod =
    httpRequestMethod.getRequestMethod();
    requestMethod.setURI(fileURI);

    BasicHttpContext localContext = new BasicHttpContext();

    localContext.setAttribute(HttpClientContext.COOKIE_STORE,
    getWebDriverCookies(driver.manage().getCookies()));
    requestMethod.setHeader("User-Agent", getWebDriverUserAgent());
```

```
if (null != urlParameters && (
        httpRequestMethod.equals(RequestType.PATCH) ||
            httpRequestMethod.equals(RequestType.POST) ||
            httpRequestMethod.equals(RequestType.PUT))
        ) {
    ((HttpEntityEnclosingRequestBase) requestMethod)
    .setEntity(new UrlEncodedFormEntity(urlParameters));
}

return client.execute(requestMethod, localContext);
}
```

We are now duplicating the information set in the browser being driven by Selenium, so that our HTTP status checker code can use it when making our request. Now, if we use this code on a site that has protected content, the website will think that the Selenium session is making the call and present the file correctly.

This will work for most, but not all, sites. Some sites use HttpOnly cookies, which you should not be able to set locally and are not visible through JavaScript. If you are working with this type of cookie, you shouldn't be able to set it, but your mileage may vary. Some driver implementations make them visible, but others don't. You cannot set HttpOnly cookies locally, but some driver implementations let you set a normal cookie locally that has overridden the server-side one in the past. Generally, the best you can do is set a normal cookie and hope. If you type `document.cookies` in your JavaScript console, you will see a list of cookies that Selenium can reliably collect. You should be able to modify all of these cookies locally if you so desire.

Let's take all the code that we have written so far and put it into an example test to show how it would be used. We will need a very simple page for Selenium to read. Making a site that requires a login and uses cookies is not particularly simple, so we will create an example site that allows anybody to download the file. This HTML will need to be uploaded to a web server in order for Selenium to access it:

```
<!DOCTYPE HTML PUBLIC "-//W3C//DTD HTML 4.01 Transitional//EN"
"http://www.w3.org/TR/html4/loose.dtd">
<html>
<head>
    <title>Download Test</title>
</head>
<body>
    <h1>Download a Test PDF File!</h1>
    <p>To download it click <a id="fileToDownload"
    href="pdf/TestFile.pdf">Here</a>!</p>
```

```
            <img id="anImage" src="images/smyImage.png" alt="anImage">
        </body>
    </html>
```

Notice that the `href` attribute in the example HTML isn't a fully qualified URI, but actually a relative path. This is fine, Selenium will convert relative paths into a fully-qualified URI, so we don't need to add any additional code to do this for us. You can see that we have added a link to a PDF document. You can take any PDF document you like and save it in the relevant location to make sure that the link works (you can also try not saving anything there to test out some error scenarios as well).

Now we will need to write a Selenium test that uses our `FileDownloader` class to parse the page, get a link, and check whether it exists (note that you will need to modify the URL in the `driver.get()` statement to point to the location where you have uploaded the preceding HTML):

```java
    private RemoteWebDriver driver;
    @BeforeSuite
    public void setup() throws MalformedURLException {
        driver = getDriver();
    }

    @Test
    public void statusCodeFromEmbeddedFile() throws Exception {
        FileDownloader downloadHandler = new FileDownloader(driver);
        driver.get("http://web.masteringselenium.com/downloadTest.html");
        WebElement fileThatShouldExist =
        driver.findElement(By.id("fileToDownload"));
        URI fileAsURI = new
        URI(fileThatShouldExist.getAttribute("href"));

        downloadHandler.setURI(fileAsURI);
        downloadHandler.setHTTPRequestMethod(RequestType.GET);

        assertThat(downloadHandler.getLinkHTTPStatus()).isEqualTo(200);
    }
```

We now have a working test that will tell us whether our PDF exists on the server.

 You may have noticed that the example HTML also had an `<img>` tag in the markup. Try to modify the preceding example so that it checks to see if the image on the page exists instead of the PDF. Think about what sort of attribute an image has that holds the URI. Note that if an `<img>` tag does not have an `href` attribute, you will have to use something else instead.

If you managed to successfully modify the test script to check for the existence of an image, you will find that the test initially failed with output that looked like this:

```
org.junit.ComparisonFailure:
Expected :[200]
Actual :[404]
```

This tells us that the image that we were expecting to find does not exist (a 404 is an HTTP status code for *Not found*).

Obviously (as with the PDF example), you will need to save a PNG image of your choice to the correct location if you want to be able to actually find/download it. You should now have a good example of a test failing to find something, as well as one that managed to find something. I hope that gives you confidence that we can accurately check to see if the image exists or not, even though we aren't using any clever image comparison code.

 Now that you have got this working using a basic scenario, let's make things a little bit more complicated. You will need to find a website that allows you to only download a file/view an image when you are logged in and uses client-side cookies. Modify the previous test to log in to this site and try and check to see if a file/image is accessible when logged in. Try the same test without logging in and see what the difference is. You may find it useful to have lots of HTTP status codes to hand: `https://en.wikipedia.org/wiki/List_of_HTTP_status_codes`.

Let's go back to our original scenario. We now have a test that is capable of checking that the PDF files that we added to our website are available with every new build. To do this, we are checking that the `href` attribute of our anchor links does indeed refer to the correct URI. We are then taking this URI and checking that, when we request the file that it refers to, we get a valid HTTP status code.

We now have a happy product owner and a team that has much more confidence that they will not break something when they work with the code around the download functionality.

What if I do need to download the file?

In our previous scenario, we didn't actually need to download the file because we didn't know what the content was supposed to be. Let's extend that scenario. Our product owner has now been provided with the PDFs that need to be downloaded from our website. The legal department has made it very clear to her that, if we serve up the wrong file, there will be legal implications, and that we need to be sure that the correct file is there for every release.

We now have a new requirement: we really do need to download the file and check that the content is correct. So what do we do now? Well, we have a few options; let's take a look at them:

- Use AutoIt to click on the download dialog
- Write a Java Robot class to click on the download dialog
- Get our browser to automatically download files when we click on a link
- Extend our existing code

Well, we can extend our existing code, but are we going to be writing code for the sake of it? Let's have a look at the alternatives.

AutoIt

When we first did some investigation around the file download problem, everybody was raving about AutoIt on the Selenium users list, so that has got to be a good solution, right?

AutoIt is a scripting language that is only designed to automate a Windows GUI. This is great when you are working with Windows, but our CI server is running on Linux.

We could work around this problem by adding a build agent that runs Windows for our Selenium tests, but we would then have lost cross-browser compatibility. Dealing with downloads in Safari is going to be especially tricky since the only version worth supporting runs on OS X.

We also have to think about our developers. They are running a mixture of machines: Windows, Linux, and OS X. If we implement an AutoIt solution, we are stopping a large percentage of our developers from running the build locally unless we start supplying them with VMs. Creating VMs so that we can run a single-file download sounds a bit like overkill.

It looks like AutoIt is not for us.

Java Robot class

How about a Java Robot class, then?

From a compatibility point of view, this is much better; we can write cross-platform code that will work. However, we do still have some issues. The first problem that we will come across is that dialog boxes across operating systems differ, so we will probably have to write code branches for each operating system.

Let's assume that we decide to do that; does everything work for us now? Initially yes, but when we run our test twice we find out that we have some new problems. When a file already exists, we will be asked if we want to overwrite it or save it using a new filename. This means we have to start adding more logic into our Java Robot implementation. What if we specify an alternative filename that already exists? Do we want to clobber that file?

We are coming across more and more problems that we need to code solutions for; this is not going to be a simple, or quick, bit of code.

Browser auto download

What about configuring the browser to automatically download the file, then?

This will get rid of the dialog box completely so we no longer have to write any complicated code to interact with a dialog, or to deal with existing files that have the same name. If the file already exists, it will just append a number to the end of it.

This sounds great. We have removed all of the issues around dialog interaction and file naming; it sounds like we could have a winner.

Unfortunately, we still have some problems. If you download a file that already exists, how do you know what the name of the file you just downloaded is? Do we need to start checking file timestamps to see when it was downloaded?

Selenium is unaware of the download process because the browser controls it all. This injects some new problems into the mix. How do we know when the download has completed? Is our test going to finish and close the browser before the file download has completed?

It sounds like, if we are going to implement a browser auto download, we are going to have to implement some reasonably advanced logic to work out what the filename is and whether we managed to download it.

Extending our existing code

Our existing code already does a lot of the work we want a file download solution to do. We are already mimicking the browser state and negotiating a connection to the content we want to download. It shouldn't be too hard to extend this slightly further, should it?

We have already negotiated a connection with the server to get the file that we want; it's just a case of using that connection to download the file instead of just checking the HTTP status code. We can then call our file anything we want and we will know when the download has completed because our code is controlling it.

Is this the perfect solution? Not necessarily; as noted before, we may have some potential problems with HttpOnly cookies. However, it does seem to be the least complex solution so far.

Downloading a file with the help of Selenium

After looking at our available options, we are going to go with the least complex solution and extend our existing code. In our scenario, HttpOnly cookies are not a problem because we don't use them, so we don't have to worry about any potential issues relating to them.

 If you are planning on using this solution, you should first spike it out and check that you can mimic HttpOnly cookies successfully if you are using them. You don't want to write code that is not fit for purpose.

We don't need to change any of our existing code; instead we are going to write a new method that will take the connection we have already negotiated with the server and use it to complete the file download:

```
public File downloadFile() throws Exception {
    File downloadedFile = File.createTempFile("download", ".pdf");
    HttpResponse fileToDownload = makeHTTPConnection();
    try {
        FileUtils.copyInputStreamToFile(fileToDownload.getEntity()
        .getContent(), downloadedFile);
    } finally {
        fileToDownload.getEntity().getContent().close();
    }

    return downloadedFile;
}
```

This method will create a file in our temporary directory and then, using the connection we have already negotiated with the remote server, stream all the data from the remote file into it. We then close the connection to the remote server and return the file.

We are using a standard Java library to create a temporary file because this will guarantee that our file is unique. The other benefit is that, since we are putting this file in the `temp` directory, it will automatically get cleaned up by the operating system when required; we don't have to do the cleanup ourselves.

Let's plug this new code into a test to see how it works:

```
@Test
public void downloadAFile() throws Exception {
    FileDownloader downloadHandler = new FileDownloader(driver);
    driver.get("http://web.masteringselenium.com/
    downloadTest.html");
    WebElement fileThatShouldExist =
    driver.findElement(By.id("fileToDownload"));
    URI fileAsURI = new
    URI(fileThatShouldExist.getAttribute("href"));

    downloadHandler.setURI(fileAsURI);
    downloadHandler.setHTTPRequestMethod(RequestType.GET);

    File downloadedFile = downloadHandler.downloadFile();

    assertThat(downloadedFile.exists()).isEqualTo(true);
    assertThat(downloadHandler.getLinkHTTPStatus()).isEqualTo(200);
}
```

But that's not the same as clicking on a link and downloading the file

Well, actually it is. When you click on the link, your browser sends a HTTP GET request over to the web server and negotiates a connection. When it has negotiated a connection, it starts to download the file to a temporary location. It then tells your operating system that it's downloading a file and asks what to do with it. This is the point where you will see an OS-level dialog box as the operating system defers that request and asks you what to do.

Once you have told the operating system which filename and which download location to use, and decided if you want to overwrite any existing files, the operating system will pass this information back to the browser. The browser then copies the file it has downloaded to a temporary location, the location specified by the operating system.

What you are actually doing by implementing this solution is taking the browser and the operating system out of the equation. A lot of people don't feel comfortable with this solution when they first see it. If you are one of those people, have another read of the last two paragraphs.

Notice that the only interaction with the website is the action of clicking on the download link (usually an anchor element with an `href` attribute, or maybe a form post if it's a little bit more complex). The code that your developers have written does not have any download functionality; they are just providing a link that the browser recognizes and processes accordingly.

By bypassing the browser and the operating system code, you are only bypassing code that your development team has no control over. Let's face it, if you click on a valid anchor to download a file and the browser has a bug that prevents it from working, there is not much you can do about it anyway. You could raise a bug with the browser vendor, but you can't force them to fix it. Even if you could force them to fix it, it's unlikely you will be able to force all of your users to download this updated version of the browser.

Secondly, what are the chances of a browser vendor releasing a browser version that cannot download a file when you click on a link? I would suspect they are pretty slim; browser manufacturers have a pretty good idea of what they are doing and I would be shocked if they didn't have at least one test that checked that file download functionality worked correctly.

So we have successfully downloaded the file, and our test has passed. Are we done? Not quite—we still haven't checked to see if the file that we downloaded is the correct one.

Checking that the file we have downloaded is the correct one

This is actually the most important part of our test. Being able to download a file, or even actually downloading one, does not prove that you have the correct file.

So how do we prove that we have the correct one? Well, the file that we have downloaded is a PDF file, so maybe we need to write some code that can read in a PDF file. We could then scan all of the text in the file and see if it is correct.

How do we know that the text is correct? Well we could put all of the text of a PDF file into our test, but that's a lot of text. It's going to be horrible to update this test every time the PDF file changes, and we don't know how often the legal department is going to ask us to make updates. This is starting to sound like a bad idea.

Always avoid hardcoding content into your tests wherever possible. This will make your tests high-maintenance, high-cost, and brittle by design. People often want to tweak the text displayed to a user. If this minor tweak causes all of your tests to fail, you are doing it wrong. Focus on testing functionality and only check content where absolutely necessary!

The most simple and obvious way to check that the file is correct is to compare it to a known good copy of the file. This way, we don't need to store any of the text from the file in our tests. If the file we have downloaded matches the original file, it must be the correct file.

So now we have two PDF files: a known good file and the file that we have downloaded. The next step is to compare them. This is where, as mentioned earlier, people usually look for libraries that read in PDF files. They then scan both files and try and compare the text in them to highlight errors.

What would we need in order to do this?

Well, we would need some PDF libraries because we don't want to write our own. Apache has a library called PDFBox that allows you to extract text. This could work, but once we have extracted the text from the PDF files we will need to compare it to see if it is correct.

In our case, we want to check a PDF file. What if the file we want to compare isn't a PDF? What if it's a PNG, a JPG, or a Word document? We don't need to support any other files at the moment, but it's always worth keeping your code open-ended. A simple solution that can support multiple file types will always be good. So, when we look for our solution it's worth bearing in mind that we may need to start pulling in all sorts of different libraries to deal with all of these file formats.

The next question to answer is: Do we want to try and show the differences between these two files? That's even more code and libraries since we need a way to calculate and display the difference between our downloaded file and the known good file.

We also have another problem. That known good file could be quite large; where do we keep it? Source control? My personal view is that storing large files in source control is not ideal. I don't want to spend hours cloning a repository, and large files in source control have been known to cause problems if the server isn't configured correctly. You may not have to worry about this; whoever is administering your source control platform may have already thought about these problems, but it's something to keep in the back of your mind.

We are really just scratching the tip of the iceberg here. I'm sure you can think of many more questions and come up with many more problems that this generic solution needs to solve. It's starting to sound like we could have quite a lot of work here.

Let's stop right there and remember the KISS principle! We don't actually need to read in the file and compare the text line by line. We don't need to show diffs if our test fails. We just need to know if the file is correct or not. We can always save a copy of the file that we downloaded so that somebody can manually investigate any problems if the test fails.

 You don't have to *automate* everything. Some things are much easier for humans to check. There is nothing wrong with using an automated solution to get some information that can be easily checked by a person. Don't spend hours trying to get a computer to do a job that a human brain can do in seconds. If your tests fail, a human with a brain is going to look at them anyway.

So, how do you remove the complexity from this scenario and make the code simple? It's actually pretty easy because this problem has already been solved for us.

If you have downloaded files from the internet before, you may have seen lots of sites publishing an MD5, or SHA1, hash of the file they are hosting. You can take an MD5, or SHA1, hash of the file you have downloaded and compare it to the one they have published. If the hashes match, you know that you have the correct file and it has downloaded correctly. This works because taking an unsalted MD5 or SHA1 hash of a file will always produce the same hash for the same file. So, if we take a hash of the file you have downloaded, and compare it to a known good hash of the file, we can instantly tell if it is correct or not. If the hash doesn't match, you can fail the test and save the file for manual examination later on.

By doing this, we are massively simplifying our code. There are also hundreds of utilities available that will perform file comparisons for you and that can be used to manually inspect bad files that have caused your test to fail. If things go wrong, you can just pick up one of these utilities, which will quickly show you any differences.

This doesn't mean that you cannot write your own code to diff two files; this is not, however, something you need to write for the initial test. We generally wouldn't expect the wrong file to be downloaded so we don't want to spend lots of time writing code that will not be used. If the file regularly changes, that's not a problem. We can just get a copy of the updated file and get the MD5/SHA1 hash of the new file, and make some quick changes to our test. If this test fails regularly for unexpected reasons, that is when you may want to consider writing more complex code to help you diagnose the issue more easily.

So, let's write a small bit of code that can check the file hash of a file, and give you a quick answer as to whether the file is the one you are expecting or not:

```
package com.masteringselenium.hash;

public enum HashType {
    MD5,
    SHA1
}
```

We have started off with an enum that we will use in our hash checking class to determine the type of hash that we are using. If you are only going to perform one type of hash check, you probably won't need this extra bit of complexity, but for our example we are going to cater for both MD5 and SHA1. Next, we have the code that takes the file you have downloaded and generates a hash:

```
package com.masteringselenium.downloader;

import org.apache.commons.codec.digest.DigestUtils;

import java.io.File;
import java.io.FileInputStream;
import java.io.FileNotFoundException;

public class CheckFileHash {

    public static String generateHashForFileOfType(File
    fileToCheck, HashType hashType) throws Exception {
        if (!fileToCheck.exists()) throw new
        FileNotFoundException(fileToCheck + " does not exist!");

        switch (hashType) {
            case MD5:
                return DigestUtils.md5Hex(new
                FileInputStream(fileToCheck));
            case SHA1:
```

```
                return DigestUtils.sha1Hex(new
                FileInputStream(fileToCheck));
            default:
                throw new
                UnsupportedOperationException(hashType.toString()
                + " hash type is not supported!");
        }
    }
}
```

This is again a very simple snippet of code; you just pass in a file and a hash type and it returns you the hash. You can then use it in your test like so:

```
@Test
public void
downloadAFileWhilstMimickingSeleniumCookiesAndCheckTheSHA1Hash() throws
Exception {
    FileDownloader downloadHandler = new FileDownloader(driver);
    driver.get("http://web.masteringselenium.com/downloadTest.html");
    WebElement fileThatShouldExist =
driver.findElement(By.id("fileToDownload"));
    URI fileAsURI = new URI(fileThatShouldExist.getAttribute("href"));

    downloadHandler.setURI(fileAsURI);
    downloadHandler.setHTTPRequestMethod(RequestType.GET);
    File downloadedFile = downloadHandler.downloadFile();

    assertThat(downloadedFile.exists()).isEqualTo(true);
    assertThat(downloadHandler.getLinkHTTPStatus()).isEqualTo(200);
    assertThat(generateHashForFileOfType(downloadedFile, SHA1))
            .isEqualTo("8882e3d972be82e14a98c522745746a03b97997a");
}
```

You will notice that the preceding test is checking for a specific SHA1 hash. The hash displayed here will not match the PDF file you have uploaded, so you will need to generate the expected hash yourself. On OS X/Linux, it should be quite simple because you should have `openssl` installed. Just run `openssl sha1 <path/to/file>` or `openssl md5 <path/to/file>`. On Windows, you will need to download the **File Checksum Integrity Verifier (FCIV)** from Microsoft. Once you have done that, it's again very easy: run either `FCIV sha1 <path/to/file>` or `FCIV md5 <path/to/file>`.

Using a different type of hash is as simple as changing the hash type and your expectations:

```
@Test
public void downloadAFileWhilstMimickingSeleniumCookiesAndCheckTheMD5Hash()
throws Exception {
    FileDownloader downloadHandler = new FileDownloader(driver);
    driver.get("http://web.masteringselenium.com/downloadTest.html");
    WebElement fileThatShouldExist =
driver.findElement(By.id("fileToDownload"));
    URI fileAsURI = new URI(fileThatShouldExist.getAttribute("href"));

    downloadHandler.setURI(fileAsURI);
    downloadHandler.setHTTPRequestMethod(RequestType.GET);
    File downloadedFile = downloadHandler.downloadFile();

    assertThat(downloadedFile.exists()).isEqualTo(true);
    assertThat(downloadHandler.getLinkHTTPStatus()).isEqualTo(200);
    assertThat(generateHashForFileOfType(downloadedFile, MD5))
            .isEqualTo("d1f296f523b74462b31b912a5675a814");
}
```

You now have some clean and simple code that will help you check that the file you have downloaded is correct.

You cannot track network traffic with Selenium

A feature that Selenium does not support, and one that is requested time and again, is monitoring the browser network traffic. The Selenium development team has categorically stated that this will not be added to the WebDriver API, despite many cries of outrage. Their reasons for not adding it are actually quite sensible.

Selenium drives the browser; it does not interact with the underlying mechanisms that the browser uses. As such, when Selenium loads a page, it is actually asking the browser to load a page. It does not interact with the remote server that is hosting the page—the browser does that—and as a result it doesn't know how the browser is interacting with the remote server. This interaction is not within scope for WebDriver, and it never has been.

The issue is not completely straightforward, however. The old Selenium 1 API did have some functionality that allowed it to get network traffic, but only if you used Firefox. All involved agreed that this was probably a bad idea because it relied on a vendor-specific implementation and it was never cross-browser compliant. The fact that this kludge used to exist in the old Selenium 1 API is normally held up as proof that Selenium 2 (and moving forward, Selenium 3) should provide some support for tracking network traffic.

This does not, however, make sense. You have to remember that Selenium 2 was the merging of Selenium with `WebDriver`. The Selenium 1 API was officially deprecated when this happened (although, due to communication problems, it was decided to change the official position on that; it's now going to be officially deprecated with Selenium 3) and `WebDriver` was the new solution that everybody was supposed to use moving forward. One of the reasons that the Selenium 1 API was deprecated was because it was trying to be too many things to too many people and it was getting bloated and unwieldy.

Holding up something that was deprecated because it had become bloated and unwieldy, and using it as a reason to make something bloated and unwieldy, really makes no sense.

But I really want to track my network traffic!

Well, it's not all bad news. Selenium doesn't explicitly provide support for network traffic; however, it does provide support for proxies. If you want to track your network traffic, what's the best way to do it? Why, a proxy, of course!

There are many proxies available, but we will focus on one in particular: the `BrowserMob` proxy. The `BrowserMob` proxy has been written with test automation in mind and integrates very easily with Selenium. Let's look at a basic implementation:

```
package com.masteringselenium.tests;

import net.lightbody.bmp.BrowserMobProxy;
import net.lightbody.bmp.BrowserMobProxyServer;
import net.lightbody.bmp.client.ClientUtil;
import net.lightbody.bmp.core.har.Har;
import net.lightbody.bmp.core.har.HarEntry;
import org.openqa.selenium.Proxy;
import org.openqa.selenium.WebDriver;
import org.openqa.selenium.firefox.FirefoxDriver;
import org.openqa.selenium.firefox.FirefoxOptions;
import org.openqa.selenium.remote.CapabilityType;
import org.testng.annotations.AfterSuite;
import org.testng.annotations.Test;
```

```
import static org.assertj.core.api.Assertions.assertThat;

public class ProxyBasedIT {

    private static WebDriver driver;

    @AfterSuite
    public static void cleanUpDriver() {
        driver.quit();
    }

    @Test
    public void usingAProxyToTrackNetworkTraffic() {
        BrowserMobProxy browserMobProxy = new
        BrowserMobProxyServer();
        browserMobProxy.start();
        Proxy seleniumProxyConfiguration =
        ClientUtil.createSeleniumProxy(browserMobProxy);

        FirefoxOptions firefoxOptions = new FirefoxOptions();
        firefoxOptions.setCapability(CapabilityType.PROXY,
        seleniumProxyConfiguration);
        driver = new FirefoxDriver(firefoxOptions);
        browserMobProxy.newHar();
        driver.get("https://www.google.co.uk");
    }
}
```

Our basic implementation is really quite simple. We are creating an instance of
BrowserMobProxy, starting it up and then creating a Selenium proxy configuration using
the handy ClientUtil class provided by the BrowserMobProxy team. We then take this
proxy configuration and use the FirefoxOptions object to tell Selenium that we want to
use it. When Selenium starts up, all network traffic will now be routed through
BrowserMobProxy.

If we want to record the traffic, the first thing we need to do is to tell BrowserMobProxy to
create a **HTTP archive** (or **HAR**) of the network traffic. We then use Selenium to navigate
to a website and perform some actions. When we are done, we retrieve the HTTP archive
that has been created by BrowserMobProxy.

Earlier in the chapter, we wrote some code to check the HTTP status code for specific resources; we could use a proxy to do the same thing. Let's extend our test to do that and see how usable a solution it is.

First of all, we need to write some code to find a specific HTTP request and return the status code:

```
private int getHTTPStatusCode(String expectedURL, Har httpArchive)
{
    for (HarEntry entry : httpArchive.getLog().getEntries()) {
        if (entry.getRequest().getUrl().equals(expectedURL)) {
            return entry.getResponse().getStatus();
        }
    }
    return 0;
}
```

As you can see, parsing the HTTP archive is quite simple; we get a list of entries and then just iterate through them until we find the entry that we want.

However, this does expose a potential flaw. What if the archive is really big? With our example test here, it's not really a problem because we are only making a single request, so it won't take long to parse the archive. It's worth noting that (at the time of writing) this single request generated 17 entries; obviously this will vary depending on what Google has put on their home page when you try out this code. Imagine how big the archive could get with just one standard user journey, or even a couple.

Now that we have our function to find a status code for a URL, we need to extend our test to use this additional code:

```
@Test
public void usingAProxyToTrackNetworkTrafficStep2() {
    BrowserMobProxy browserMobProxy = new BrowserMobProxyServer();
    browserMobProxy.start();
    Proxy seleniumProxyConfiguration =
    ClientUtil.createSeleniumProxy(browserMobProxy);

    FirefoxOptions firefoxOptions = new FirefoxOptions();
    firefoxOptions.setCapability(CapabilityType.PROXY,
    seleniumProxyConfiguration);
    driver = new FirefoxDriver(firefoxOptions);
    browserMobProxy.newHar();
    driver.get("https://www.google.co.uk");

    Har httpArchive = browserMobProxy.getHar();
```

```
assertThat(getHTTPStatusCode("https://www.google.co.uk/",
httpArchive))
        .isEqualTo(200);
}
```

This is where we see another potential flaw. If you look closely at the test, the URL that we are getting is not the same as the URL that we are asserting on. The one that we are asserting on has an extra slash. The simple solution is to make sure that you specify all base URLs with a trailing slash, but it can easily catch you out.

In the preceding test, we are using BrowserMobProxy to collect HTTP status codes for specific calls. Try comparing this implementation with the original one we wrote at the start of this chapter. See how long it takes you to implement each one. When you have completed both of them, set up the same test, then time how long it takes for each one to complete. Which solution is faster? When you have done that, extend your tests so that they work through a longer user journey that will create more HTTP traffic and then time your tests again. How has this affected your test time? Which one would you prefer to have in your test code base?

It must be pointed out that collecting HTTP status codes is not the only thing you can do with network traffic. The fact that it's not a perfect solution for this use case does not mean that it isn't good for other things. There are things that you can only do by tracking network traffic.

For example, if you were writing a checkout application and you wanted to be sure that any transactions in flight were explicitly cancelled when you navigated to a different URL, tracking the network traffic would be ideal. Similarly, if you wanted to check that a specific network request was formatted in a specific way, you would need to scan the network traffic.

There are also other avenues that open up to you if you are using a proxy.

Maybe you would like to simulate a bad network connection. Well, you can do this by configuring your proxy to limit upload and download speeds. How about blocking some content and then taking screenshots of every step in your user journey? You can then quickly and easily view what a flow would look like if the images were not available.

There are many interesting and unusual things you can do if you have access to, and can manipulate, the network traffic.

We have a very basic proxy implementation, but in its current form it doesn't really work well with the test framework that we created earlier in this book. Let's have a look at how we can extend that framework to support proxies.

First of all, we are going to need to tweak our POM a little bit to allow us to set proxy details on the command line. To do this, we first need to add in some additional properties:

```
<properties>
    <project.build.sourceEncoding>UTF-
    8</project.build.sourceEncoding>
    <project.reporting.outputEncoding>UTF-
    8</project.reporting.outputEncoding>
    <java.version>1.8</java.version>
    <!-- Dependency versions -->
    <selenium.version>3.12.0</selenium.version>
    <testng.version>6.14.3</testng.version>
    <assertj-core.version>3.10.0</assertj-core.version>
    <query.version>1.2.0</query.version>
    <commons-io.version>2.6</commons-io.version>
    <httpclient.version>4.5.5</httpclient.version>
    <!-- Plugin versions -->
    <driver-binary-downloader-maven-plugin.version>1.0.17
    </driver-binary-downloader-maven-plugin.version>
    <maven-compiler-plugin.version>3.7.0
    </maven-compiler-plugin.version>
    <maven-failsafe-plugin.version>2.21.0
    </maven-failsafe-plugin.version>
    <!-- Configurable variables -->
    <threads>1</threads>
    <browser>firefox</browser>
    <overwrite.binaries>false</overwrite.binaries>
    <headless>true</headless>
    <remote>false</remote>
    <seleniumGridURL/>
    <platform/>
    <browserVersion/>
    <screenshotDirectory>${project.build.directory}
    /screenshots</screenshotDirectory>
    <proxyEnabled>false</proxyEnabled>
    <proxyHost/>
    <proxyPort/>
</properties>
```

As you can see, I have not set any default values, but if you have a good idea what the proxy details will be, feel free to add them. I have also set the `proxyEnabled` property to `false` by default; you can change this to true if you always want to use a proxy.

The next thing we need to do is to set these as system properties, so that our test can read them in:

```
<plugin>
    <groupId>org.apache.maven.plugins</groupId>
    <artifactId>maven-failsafe-plugin</artifactId>
    <version>${maven-failsafe-plugin.version}</version>
    <configuration>
        <parallel>methods</parallel>
        <threadCount>${threads}</threadCount>
        <systemPropertyVariables>
            <browser>${browser}</browser>
            <headless>${headless}</headless>
            <remoteDriver>${remote}</remoteDriver>
            <gridURL>${seleniumGridURL}</gridURL>
            <desiredPlatform>${platform}</desiredPlatform>
            <desiredBrowserVersion>${browserVersion}
            </desiredBrowserVersion>
            <screenshotDirectory>${screenshotDirectory}
            </screenshotDirectory>
            <proxyEnabled>${proxyEnabled}</proxyEnabled>
            <proxyHost>${proxyHost}</proxyHost>
            <proxyPort>${proxyPort}</proxyPort>
            <!--Set properties passed in by the driver binary
            downloader-->
            <webdriver.chrome.driver>${webdriver.chrome.driver}
            </webdriver.chrome.driver>
            <webdriver.ie.driver>${webdriver.ie.driver}
            </webdriver.ie.driver>
            <webdriver.opera.driver>${webdriver.opera.driver}
            </webdriver.opera.driver>
            <webdriver.gecko.driver>${webdriver.gecko.driver}
            </webdriver.gecko.driver>
            <webdriver.edge.driver>${webdriver.edge.driver}
            </webdriver.edge.driver>
        </systemPropertyVariables>
    </configuration>
    <executions>
        <execution>
            <goals>
                <goal>integration-test</goal>
                <goal>verify</goal>
            </goals>
        </execution>
    </executions>
</plugin>
```

We are now ready to start tweaking the rest of our code. First of all we need to update our `DriverFactory` class to read in our proxy settings. We do this by adding some additional class variables reading in the system properties we configured in our POM:

```
private final boolean proxyEnabled = Boolean.getBoolean("proxyEnabled");
private final String proxyHostname = System.getProperty("proxyHost");
private final Integer proxyPort = Integer.getInteger("proxyPort");
private final String proxyDetails = String.format("%s:%d", proxyHostname,
proxyPort);
```

Then we will need to modify our `instantiateWebDriver` method so that it configures our `DesiredCapabilities` to use a proxy if the `proxyEnabled` variable is true.

```
private void instantiateWebDriver(DriverType driverType) throws
MalformedURLException {
    System.out.println(" ");
    System.out.println("Local Operating System: " +
operatingSystem);
    System.out.println("Local Architecture: " + systemArchitecture);
    System.out.println("Selected Browser: " + selectedDriverType);
    System.out.println("Connecting to Selenium Grid: " +
useRemoteWebDriver);
    System.out.println(" ");

    DesiredCapabilities desiredCapabilities = new
    DesiredCapabilities();

    if (proxyEnabled) {
        Proxy proxy = new Proxy();
        proxy.setProxyType(MANUAL);
        proxy.setHttpProxy(proxyDetails);
        proxy.setSslProxy(proxyDetails);
        desiredCapabilities.setCapability(PROXY, proxy);
    }

    if (useRemoteWebDriver) {
        URL seleniumGridURL = new
        URL(System.getProperty("gridURL"));
        String desiredBrowserVersion =
        System.getProperty("desiredBrowserVersion");
        String desiredPlatform =
        System.getProperty("desiredPlatform");

        if (null != desiredPlatform && !desiredPlatform.isEmpty()) {
            desiredCapabilities.setPlatform
            (Platform.valueOf(desiredPlatform.toUpperCase()));
        }
```

```
        if (null != desiredBrowserVersion &&
        !desiredBrowserVersion.isEmpty()) {
            desiredCapabilities.setVersion(desiredBrowserVersion);
        }

        desiredCapabilities.setBrowserName(selectedDriverType.toString());
        webDriver = new RemoteWebDriver(seleniumGridURL,
        desiredCapabilities);
    } else {
        webDriver =
        driverType.getWebDriverObject(desiredCapabilities);
    }

}
```

That's it, the changes are actually very simple. We now have the ability to specify a proxy on the command line, and we can pre-configure one in our POM. This is great from the point of view of plugging corporate proxy details into your browser; however, it's not ideal if we want to use BrowserMobProxy. When we used BrowserMobProxy in our example test, you may have noticed that we were programmatically starting a BrowserMobProxy instance and interacting with it in our test. To do this, we really want to bake in support for BrowserMobProxy, and we also want to be able to forward on calls to our corporate proxy.

Let's extend our framework again to do exactly this. First of all, we will add a dependency to browsermob-core to our POM:

```
<dependency>
    <groupId>net.lightbody.bmp</groupId>
    <artifactId>browsermob-core</artifactId>
    <version>2.1.5</version>
    <scope>test</scope>
</dependency>
```

This will make all of the BrowserMobProxy libraries available for our implementation. Then we need to update DriverFactory so that it can support BrowserMobProxy. We will start off by adding a couple of class variables:

```
private BrowserMobProxy browserMobProxy;
private boolean useBrowserMobProxy = false;
```

We are going to use these later on to hold a reference to any `BrowserMobProxy` instance we start, and to track whether we are using it or not. The next step is to update our `instantiateWebDriver` method:

```
private void instantiateWebDriver(DriverType driverType, boolean
useBrowserMobProxy) throws MalformedURLException {
    System.out.println(" ");
    System.out.println("Local Operating System: " +
    operatingSystem);
    System.out.println("Local Architecture: " + systemArchitecture);
    System.out.println("Selected Browser: " + selectedDriverType);
    System.out.println("Connecting to Selenium Grid: " +
    useRemoteWebDriver);
    System.out.println(" ");

    DesiredCapabilities desiredCapabilities = new
    DesiredCapabilities();

    if (proxyEnabled || useBrowserMobProxy) {
        Proxy proxy;
        if (useBrowserMobProxy) {
            usingBrowserMobProxy = true;
            browserMobProxy = new BrowserMobProxyServer();
            browserMobProxy.start();
            if (proxyEnabled) {
                browserMobProxy.setChainedProxy(new
                InetSocketAddress(proxyHostname, proxyPort));
            }
            proxy = ClientUtil.createSeleniumProxy(browserMobProxy);
        } else {
            proxy = new Proxy();
            proxy.setProxyType(MANUAL);
            proxy.setHttpProxy(proxyDetails);
            proxy.setSslProxy(proxyDetails);
        }
        desiredCapabilities.setCapability(PROXY, proxy);
    }

    if (useRemoteWebDriver) {
        URL seleniumGridURL = new
        URL(System.getProperty("gridURL"));
        String desiredBrowserVersion =
        System.getProperty("desiredBrowserVersion");
        String desiredPlatform =
        System.getProperty("desiredPlatform");

        if (null != desiredPlatform && !desiredPlatform.isEmpty()) {
```

```
        desiredCapabilities.setPlatform(Platform.valueOf
        (desiredPlatform.toUpperCase())));
    }

    if (null != desiredBrowserVersion &&
    !desiredBrowserVersion.isEmpty()) {
        desiredCapabilities.setVersion(desiredBrowserVersion);
    }

    desiredCapabilities.setBrowserName(selectedDriverType.toString());
    webDriver = new RemoteWebDriver(seleniumGridURL,
    desiredCapabilities);
} else {
    webDriver =
    driverType.getWebDriverObject(desiredCapabilities);
    }
}
```

We are now also passing in a Boolean that tells us if we want to use BrowserMobProxy or not. This lets us configure our RemoteWebDriver object to use a proxy, or a BrowserMobProxy, or both. This ensures that if we need to use a corporate proxy server to get to the website we are testing we can still use our corporate proxy as well as our BrowserMobProxy. We have a bit more work to do though, we need to modify our getDriver() method to give us the ability to turn the BrowserMobProxy on or off.

```
public RemoteWebDriver getDriver(boolean useBrowserMobProxy)
throws MalformedURLException {
    if(useBrowserMobProxy != usingBrowserMobProxy){
        quitDriver();
    }
    if (null == webDriver) {
        instantiateWebDriver(selectedDriverType,
        useBrowserMobProxy);
    }

    return webDriver;
}

public RemoteWebDriver getDriver() throws MalformedURLException {
    return getDriver(usingBrowserMobProxy);
}

public void quitDriver() {
    if (null != webDriver) {
        webDriver.quit();
```

```
            webDriver = null;
            usingBrowserMobProxy = false;
        }
    }
```

We have a few changes here. To start off with we have created a new `getDriver(boolean useBrowserMobProxy)` method that takes in a boolean that allows you to specify if you want to use the `BrowserMobProxy` or not. We then compare this boolean to our `usingBrowserMobProxy` boolean stored in our `DriverFactory` to see if need to start up, or stop the `BrowserMobProxy`.

If we need to start up or stop the `BrowserMobProxy` we invoke `quitDriver()` to kill our current `WebDriver` instance and create a new one since proxy settings need to be specified when instantiating the `WebDriver` object.

Our old `getDriver()` method now calls the new one, but it always sets the `useBrowserMobProxy` value to the value stored internally in `DriverFactory` so that we continue to use what has already been set. This can be used by the `DriverFactory` method without any changes so that our existing code continues to work.

The final change we need to make in DriverFactory is to create a `getBrowserMobProxy()` method:

```
public BrowserMobProxy getBrowserMobProxy() {
    if (usingBrowserMobProxy) {
        return browserMobProxy;
    }
    return null;
}
```

This is used to return the `BrowserMobProxy` instance so that you can give it commands. This is so that you can start collecting traffic, or examine traffic it has already collected.

The final step is to expose this functionality by tweaking our `DriverBase` class. First of all we need a way to get hold of a `BrowserMobProxy` enabled driver instance:

```
public static RemoteWebDriver getBrowserMobProxyEnabledDriver() throws
MalformedURLException {
    return driverThread.get().getDriver(true);
}
```

Then we need a way to get hold of the `BrowserMobProxy` object:

```
public static BrowserMobProxy getBrowserMobProxy() {
    return driverThread.get().getBrowserMobProxy();
}
```

Now everything is ready for you to use in your tests. Why don't you try writing a test that will check the network traffic (like the one we wrote earlier in this chapter) to try it out?

Writing performance tests with Selenium

It is theoretically possible to run performance tests with Selenium. You could start up a great big Selenium grid and then point your grid at an application and run lots of tests against it.

So why don't people normally do this?

The sheer power that would be required to configure a grid that could actually hit your performance testing environment with enough traffic usually makes it a very expensive solution. You then also have the setup and maintenance costs of your grid. That being said, with the advent of cloud services and tools such as:

- Ansible (http://www.ansible.com)
- Chef (https://www.chef.io)
- Puppet (https://puppetlabs.com)

It is much cheaper than it used to be. Once you have done the groundwork, it's also pretty easy to spin up slaves that can attach themselves to the grid as and when required. So at the end of the day, it is now something you could do.

The question is: Should we do this?

Well, first of all, you have to stop and think about what you are actually testing. When the server that hosts your website is under load, what is it actually doing? Well, it is taking a request from a browser over the network, performing some calculations on the server, and then sending a response to your browser.

None of this actually requires any interaction with what you as a user see on your screen (what is generally called the presentation layer). Selenium is a tool that explicitly interacts with the presentation layer. Why would we want to use a tool that is designed to interact with the presentation layer to try and send lots of network traffic to a server?

If the only tool that you have in your toolbox is a hammer, everything starts to look like a nail. You see that screw, it's sort of nail shaped, and if you hit it hard enough with a hammer it will probably go into the wall. You will probably be able to successfully hang a picture from it as well.

This sort of scenario often happens with Selenium. You will find testers who have lots of Selenium experience but not much exposure to other tools. This is when Selenium starts to become their hammer. This is generally why people start to use a tool such as Selenium to do performance tests.

So, if it is a bad idea, why are we even talking about it? Well, we can still use Selenium to help us create our performance tests and, thanks to the proxy implementation that we wrote earlier in this chapter, it's really easy!

What we are going to do is start JMeter up as a proxy server that records network traffic. We will then get Selenium to run a test while connecting through this proxy. As the Selenium test drives the browser, network requests will be made to our server and the JMeter proxy will collect them and build a basic test plan.

Obviously, creating a performance test plan is not quite as simple as just recoding the requests that have been captured and then playing them back. It does, however, give us a solid base to build upon. This will be useful when we have a series of user journeys already written in Selenium and we would like to take these user journeys and use them as the basis for our performance testing.

The focus here is on how to use Selenium to create a solid base that can be either built upon, or passed over to the people who are going to build the performance test scripts to get them started.

So, first of all let's start up JMeter and set up the proxy that we are going to connect Selenium to. We need to add an HTTP(S) test script recorder to your test plan:

1. Add a test script recorder to your test plan:

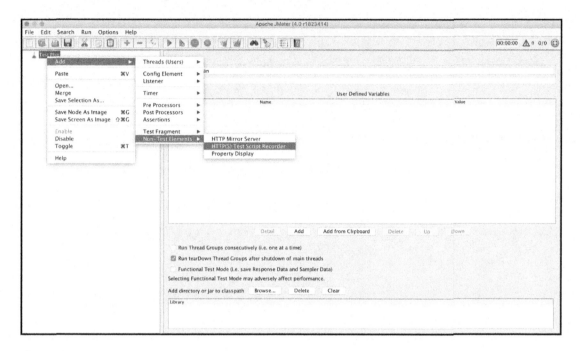

Then we need to set the port and the target controller so that JMeter can record network traffic:

2. Set the port and target controller:

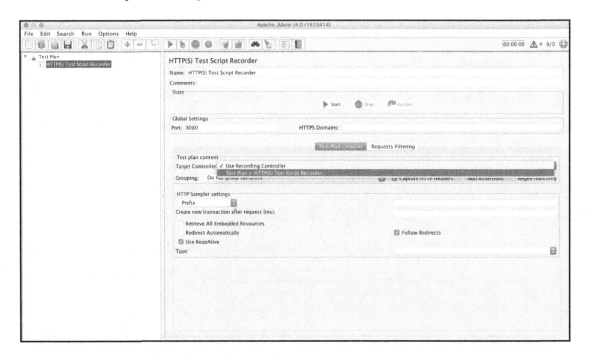

Finally, click on Start. You will then see a popup telling you where JMeter has saved a temporary root certificate (you may need to set this up as a trusted root certificate for some browsers); just click on **OK** to bypass it.

Now our JMeter proxy is up-and-running and ready to accept connections. We now need to run our Selenium tests and tell them to connect to the JMeter proxy. Since we have already extended our Selenium framework to support proxies, all we need to do is provide the proxy details on the command line:

```
mvn clean install -DproxyEnabled=true -DproxyHost=localhost -
DproxyPort=8080
```

Finally, wait for your tests to run and you're done. Stop the JMeter proxy, save the test plan, and you have the start of a performance test plan in JMeter that is all ready to be built upon. We can use Selenium in this way to record all sorts of user journeys in JMeter. It's a lot quicker than manually running through all the scenarios and saves loads of time when you are generating your initial set of data.

Don't use multiple threads when using a JMeter proxy to make things go faster. You want to capture user journeys that make sense and can be traced based upon the network requests. If you run more than one thread in parallel, you will mix up the network requests for all the tests running in parallel. It will be hard to read and not a very good base for a performance test suite in JMeter.

Penetration testing with Selenium

Penetration testing is one of those things that people don't often think about while they are building a product. It's usually seen as a phase of testing that is performed by a third party who has expertise in that area once a release has passed normal testing.

The problem with this view is that fixing security problems at this point may well be very expensive and requires large amounts of refactoring, or even rewrites. Wouldn't it be good if we could do as much penetration testing as possible in the early development phases? This would give us a fast feedback loop that would allow us to make changes earlier in the development life cycle at a greatly reduced cost.

Selenium does not have any penetration testing functionality built in, but we can use other tools to supplement it. One excellent tool that can work well with Selenium is the **Zed Attack Proxy (ZAP)**. For more information about ZAP, have a look at `https://www.owasp.org/index.php/OWASP_Zed_Attack_Proxy_Project`.

ZAP is a penetration testing tool that searches for vulnerabilities in web applications. It is a proxy that sits between your browser and the website you are testing. As you use the website you are testing, ZAP logs all of the network calls and uses them to build up a series of attack profiles. The more functionality on your website you use, the more information ZAP has to build these attack profiles.

Once you have walked through the functionality of your site, you can tell ZAP to build a series of attack profiles based on the information it has collected. ZAP then starts a series of attacks on your site and logs any potential vulnerability that it finds.

Obviously, the more functionality you use, the more information ZAP has and the better its attacks are. If you are testing your website with Selenium, it's probably a pretty safe bet that you cover a large percentage of functionality with your tests.

So what we are going to do is set ZAP up as a proxy and then use our proxy implementation to run our Selenium tests through ZAP so that it can generate an attack profile for our site.

Setting up ZAP is nice and simple:

1. First of all, open up ZAP:

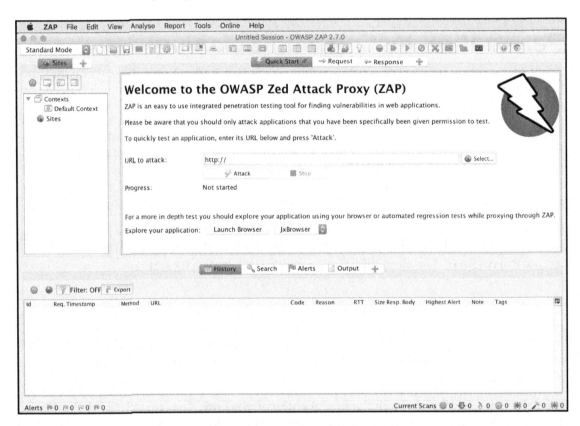

2. Then go to **Tools** | **Options**:

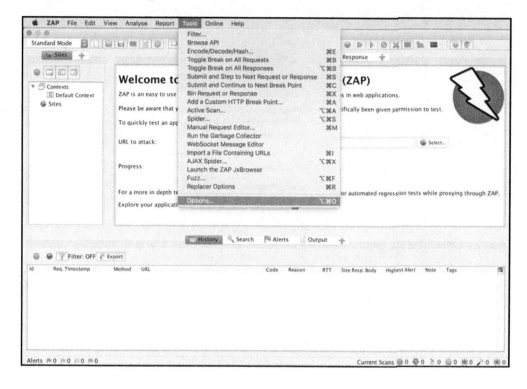

3. Next, select **Local proxy**:

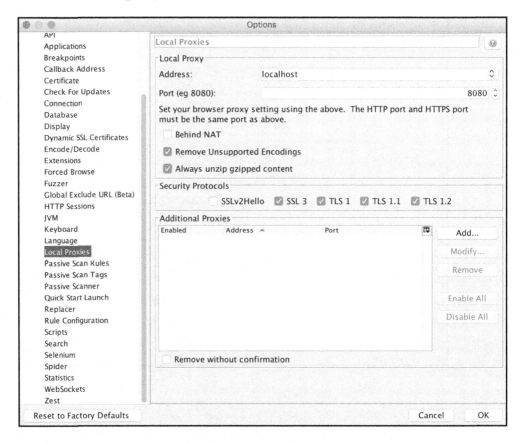

4. Finally, set the proxy address to **localhost**, and select a port; we will use **8080** for this example.

Now we need to run our Selenium tests using this proxy so that ZAP can monitor our network traffic and build attack profiles. Use the following command:

```
mvn clean install –DproxyEnabled=true –DproxyHost=localhost –
DproxyPort=8080
```

Now wait for your tests to complete and you're done. You can now tell ZAP to start attacking the site that you are testing. As it performs its attacks, it will highlight vulnerabilities and at the end will give you a list of things that need investigation.

ZAP can be very verbose and you should remember that it is reporting potential vulnerabilities. Not everything that it logs is a problem that needs a high-priority fix; some may be vulnerabilities in technologies that you aren't currently using. A lot of people get a nasty shock when they first run their website through ZAP.

Summary

In this chapter, we have had a look at the various things that Selenium cannot do. We have also explored the ways in which we can extend Selenium to work with other tools that can provide us with a more complete testing toolbox.

By the time you have reached the end of this chapter, you should have some good strategies to check for dead links on web pages you are testing. You should also have sensible solutions for downloading and validating files. We also learned how to integrate Selenium with various proxies. This then gave us the ability to use our Selenium tests as a base for performance tests in JMeter; as well as a way to build attack profiles for penetration tests using the OWASP Zed Attack Proxy.

In the next chapter, we are going to look at how we can use Docker with Selenium. We will see how easy it is to start spinning up your own grid in Docker. We will also look at how we can integrate Docker into our build process.

Hooking Docker into Selenium

9

This chapter will be a brief introduction to Docker and how it can be used with Selenium. It should give you an idea of the potential capabilities of Docker and get you thinking about ways in which you could integrate it into your current build process.

In this chapter, we will have a look at how we can get started with Docker and use it with Selenium. We will cover the following topics:

- Installing Docker on our machines
- Setting up Selenium-Grid using Docker
- Learning how to start Docker containers as a part of our build

Introducing Docker

So, what is Docker?

Well, Docker is like a **virtual machine** (**VM**), but it's not. In a traditional VM setup, you would take a machine, install an operating system on that machine, and then install a hypervisor, such as VirtualBox (for more information, visit `https://www.virtualbox.org`) or VMware (to know more about VMware, check out `http://www.vmware.com`). You could then create a VM image on the hypervisor, which pretends to be a computer. This image would have its own BIOS and emulated hardware. You would then install an OS on this image. This is generally referred to as the guest OS. Once this is done, you would boot up the guest OS and then treat it like any other computer.

If you want to isolate your applications, you can create multiple guest OSes, but this can be costly:

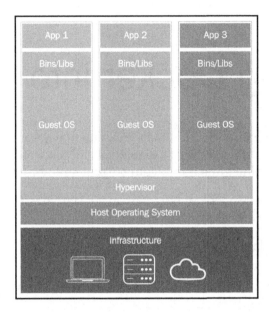

Docker is slightly different. It is a program that you install on the host machine instead of the hypervisor. Docker can then start up an application in what is known as a **container**. Containers are totally isolated, just like a virtual machine. However, Docker uses the host OS instead of a guest OS:

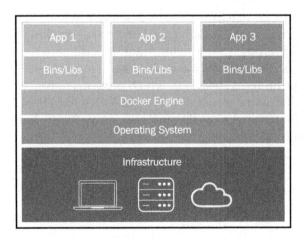

The Docker alternative

This gives you some advantages, which are as follows:

- Containers are not as resource-intensive as virtual machines
- Containers can start up much faster than virtual machines

So, how does Docker do this? Well, it uses a Linux technology called **namespaces**. The following are the Linux namespaces:

- `pid`: This is used for process isolation
- `net`: This is used to manage network interfaces
- `ipc`: This is used to manage interprocess communication
- `mnt`: This is used to manage mount points
- `uts`: This is used to isolate kernel and version identifiers

Docker uses these namespaces to isolate containers. This means that they are unaware of anything else that is running on the host OS. These containers have their own isolated process tree, their own isolated network stack, and so on.

The wonderful thing about Docker is that all of these containers can be made to interact with each other. This means that you can take lots of individual containers and stick them together to make something quite complex.

Let's use a basic **Linux, Nginx, MySQL, and PHP (LNMP**) setup as an example. Normally, you would create a Linux virtual machine and then install Nginx, PHP, and MySQL on it.

With Docker, you can split up this stack with multiple containers. The most common setup would be an Nginx container with added PHP support and a MySQL container. You can then link these two containers together to give you the LNMP stack.

For example, if you wanted to update MySQL, you would just delete the MySQL container and add a new one.

Wait a second! If I delete MySQL and start it up again, would I lose all my data?

Well, that's not a problem. Docker can also create data-only containers. So, you can create a data-only container that holds all the data that MySQL writes to the disk and is totally isolated from the MySQL install.

Docker can be extremely powerful. The hardest part is figuring out how to break your complex systems down into small containers that run a single process. People are so used to thinking along the lines of working systems with multiple components, it can be hard to break out of this mindset.

All of this sounds great, but how do we use it?

Well, first of all you will need to install Docker on your system. Docker is constantly evolving, so the best place to find out how to install it on your machine is to head on over to `http://www.docker.com/community-edition`. They have a good overview of all the options available for you and all the information you need to get you up and running with a basic install.

Once you have performed your basic install, you can check that everything is working by running `docker run hello-world` in your Terminal (or Command Prompt if you are on Windows).

Spinning up Selenium-Grid with Docker

At some point, most people who use Selenium have tried to get Selenium-Grid up and running. As with getting any service up and running, it's normally a real pain. Some pain points that you may have probably come across are as follows:

- What software do I need to install to get Selenium-Grid up and running?
- How do we keep Selenium up to date?
- How do we keep the browsers up to date?
- How do we deal with browsers becoming unresponsive on the nodes?
- How do we deal with unresponsive nodes in general?
- How do I ensure that the driver binaries (such as `ChromeDriver`) are kept up to date?

We can remove some of these pain points with Docker. Let's start off by spinning up Selenium-Grid with Docker.

The general philosophy behind Docker is to have small containers that do only one thing. Unfortunately, the Selenium Docker images are a bit bigger than most images, because they need to have access to some form of GUI as well as full-browser installs. The next step may take a while if you have a slow internet connection.

First of all, we will need to pull down some containers from the Docker registry (for more information, visit `https://registry.hub.docker.com`). There are three images that we will need to get, which are as follows:

- The Selenium-Grid hub
- The Firefox Selenium-Grid node
- The Chrome Selenium-Grid node

We can do this by using the `pull` command, as follows:

```
docker pull selenium/hub:3.11.0
docker pull selenium/node-firefox:3.11.0
docker pull selenium/node-chrome:3.11.0
```

This will download the three containers that we need to build up Selenium-Grid locally.

You don't need to specify a version; you could just use `docker pull selenium/hub`. This will pull down the latest version that is available. I've used specific versions in the examples in this chapter because it's not always a good idea to automatically pull down the latest and greatest version. There could be breaking changes in the implementation that require code changes.

Once we have downloaded these images, we can start them up. First of all, we will need to start up the Selenium-Grid hub, as follows:

```
docker run -d -p 4444:4444 --name selenium-hub selenium/hub:3.11.0
```

If you try to run a container before pulling an image, it will still work if you are connected to the internet. Docker is clever enough to realize that it does not have the image stored locally. When it realizes, it's in the state where it will automatically try to download it for you before trying to run it.

Let's work through this command. The `-d` parameter will ensure that the `selenium-hub` container runs as a daemon. Docker containers are designed to start up, perform their intended function, and then shut down again. If you don't use the `-d` parameter, switching containers will instantly shut it down. Next, we mapped a tunnel between the Docker container and the Docker host (the machine you are running Docker on) using port `4444` so that we can talk to the container using the host's IP address. Each Docker container has its own isolated network stack, and it will not be able to see anything that is not linked to it in some way.

There are multiple ways to link things to containers with Docker. You can open up a port to the host and communicate through that. You could use the `--link` switch to build explicit links between containers, or you could use a Docker compose file to build up a complete self-contained system.

We gave our container a name so that we can easily identify it. If you don't specify a name for your container, Docker will automatically assign one for you. While these random names can be fun, it's hard to remember what process each one is running. With this in mind, it's good practice to give your containers sensible descriptive names. In this case, we have called our container `selenium-hub`. Finally, we specified the name of the container image and the version that we then span up.

Once we have attempted to start a container, we can check to see whether it is there by using the following command:

```
docker ps
```

This will show us a list of all the containers that are currently running. Since we have opened up a tunnel between our machine and the container, we will also be able to open a web browser and browse to the Selenium-Grid console. It is as simple as navigating to the following URL in your browser:

```
http://127.0.0.1:4444/grid/console
```

If you navigate to this URL in your browser, it should look like this:

We now need to spin up some nodes to connect these to Selenium-Grid. Let's start with Firefox:

```
docker run -d --link selenium-hub:hub selenium/node-firefox:3.11.0
```

Like we did before, we are running the container as a daemon so that it does not shut down. However, we have not opened up a port between the container and the Docker host this time. Instead, we are linking this container to the container that we have already started, `selenium-hub`. We haven't specified a name for this node, but that's not a problem. If you don't specify a name, Docker will automatically allocate one for you. Finally, like the last command, we specify the container identifier and version.

If you refresh your browser, it should now look like this:

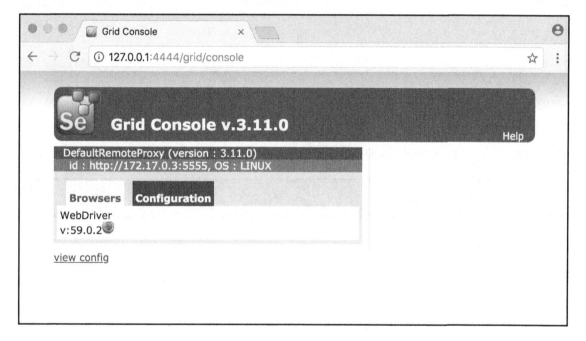

Next, we are going to add a Chrome node to give us an additional browser option, as follows:

```
docker run -d --link selenium-hub:hub selenium/node-chrome:3.11.0
```

The command is exactly the same as before. We just specified a different container ID this time. If you refresh your browser, it should now look like this:

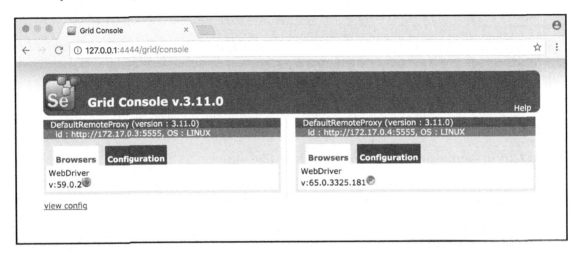

Now, in your Terminal, try typing the following:

```
docker ps
```

This will show you a list of containers that are currently active, as follows:

You will see that even though we didn't name the nodes that we started up, Docker has generated a unique name for them. Let's start up some more Chrome nodes, as follows:

```
docker run -d --link selenium-hub:hub selenium/node-chrome:3.11.0
docker run -d --link selenium-hub:hub selenium/node-chrome:3.11.0
docker run -d --link selenium-hub:hub selenium/node-chrome:3.11.0
docker run -d --link selenium-hub:hub selenium/node-chrome:3.11.0
```

Note that we used exactly the same command as before, but we didn't have any errors. If you refresh your browser, you will now see all the additional nodes that we started:

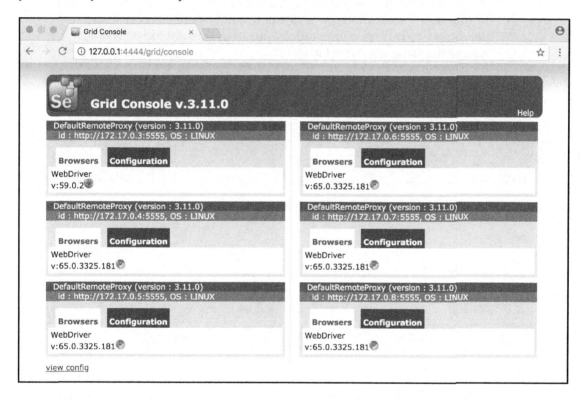

Now, if you rerun the `docker ps` command, you will see the following additional nodes in your Terminal:

You can spin up as many nodes as you like in this fashion. You are only limited by your computing power. If you decide that you don't need that many nodes, you can start shutting down some of them. Let's shut down one of the Chrome nodes because we have loads of them. The one that we are going to shut down has a container ID of `6f348932ef1d`:

```
docker stop 6f348932ef1d
```

 Different machines are capable of running a different number of containers. If your machine is struggling with five nodes, you may want to shut down some more. As a rule of thumb, figure out how many browsers you can open in parallel. Your machines should be able to handle the same number of nodes.

If you rerun the `docker ps` command, you will now see that we have only five nodes running:

```
Shar:~ fyres docker ps
CONTAINER ID   IMAGE                         COMMAND                CREATED         STATUS          PORTS                    NAMES
a1a5d2e70cd8   selenium/node-chrome:3.11.0   "/opt/bin/entry_poin…" 3 minutes ago   Up 3 minutes                             pensive_raman
9b7b5670698c   selenium/node-chrome:3.11.0   "/opt/bin/entry_poin…" 3 minutes ago   Up 3 minutes                             naughty_visvesvaraya
10105fbea83f   selenium/node-chrome:3.11.0   "/opt/bin/entry_poin…" 3 minutes ago   Up 3 minutes                             sad_shannon
c06c225f29fe   selenium/node-chrome:3.11.0   "/opt/bin/entry_poin…" 3 minutes ago   Up 3 minutes                             gracious_leakey
966b82c9c4d9   selenium/node-firefox:3.11.0  "/opt/bin/entry_poin…" 4 minutes ago   Up 4 minutes                             eager_pare
56add68c0f67   selenium/hub:3.11.0           "/opt/bin/entry_poin…" 5 minutes ago   Up 5 minutes    0.0.0.0:4444->4444/tcp   selenium-hub
```

However, try running the following command:

```
docker ps -a
```

In this case, we will see all six again, as follows:

```
Shar:~ fyres docker ps -a
CONTAINER ID   IMAGE                         COMMAND                CREATED         STATUS                      PORTS                    NAMES
a1a5d2e70cd8   selenium/node-chrome:3.11.0   "/opt/bin/entry_poin…" 3 minutes ago   Up 3 minutes                                         pensive_raman
9b7b5670698c   selenium/node-chrome:3.11.0   "/opt/bin/entry_poin…" 3 minutes ago   Up 3 minutes                                         naughty_visvesvaraya
10105fbea83f   selenium/node-chrome:3.11.0   "/opt/bin/entry_poin…" 3 minutes ago   Up 3 minutes                                         sad_shannon
c06c225f29fe   selenium/node-chrome:3.11.0   "/opt/bin/entry_poin…" 3 minutes ago   Up 3 minutes                                         gracious_leakey
6f348932ef1d   selenium/node-chrome:3.11.0   "/opt/bin/entry_poin…" 4 minutes ago   Exited (143) 59 seconds ago                          lucid_hopper
966b82c9c4d9   selenium/node-firefox:3.11.0  "/opt/bin/entry_poin…" 5 minutes ago   Up 5 minutes                                         eager_pare
56add68c0f67   selenium/hub:3.11.0           "/opt/bin/entry_poin…" 5 minutes ago   Up 5 minutes                0.0.0.0:4444->4444/tcp   selenium-hub
```

Docker doesn't remove your containers when you stop them, so that you can do things such as look at the logs or copy the contents of the container into a TAR file so that you can examine them. Once the container has stopped, it is dead; you cannot restart it. Once you have finished with your stopped container, you can remove it with the following command:

```
docker rm 6f348932ef1d
```

If you have stopped a container with a specific name (for example, the `selenium-hub` container), you will need to remove it before you can start another container with the same name.

If you have a lot of containers running, it can be very time-consuming to stop each one by container ID. However, there is a nice shortcut that we can use to stop all the containers:

```
docker stop $(docker ps -q)
```

 `$(docker ps -a)` is a bash trick called **command substitution**. It takes the output of any command and replaces itself with the output. See `http://www.tldp.org/LDP/abs/html/commandsub.html` for more information.

This also works if you want to remove images:

```
docker rm $(docker ps -qa)
```

So, we now have a quick and easy way to start up Selenium-Grid, and we can quickly tear it down again when we are finished with it.

Running tests against our new Selenium-Grid

We now know how to quickly spin up Selenium-Grid, but so far, we haven't seen it in action. Let's face it. It's not of much use if we can't use it to run some tests. If you have shut down Selenium-Grid, you will need to start it up again:

```
docker run -d -p 4444:4444 --name selenium-hub selenium/hub:3.11.0
docker run -d --link selenium-hub:hub selenium/node-firefox:3.11.0
docker run -d --link selenium-hub:hub selenium/node-chrome:3.11.0
```

Next, we are going to reuse the Selenium framework that we built in Chapter 1, *Creating a Fast Feedback Loop*, and Chapter 2, *Producing the Right Feedback When Failing*. It already supports connections to Selenium-Grid. So, we just need to specify the URL of the grid using the following command:

```
mvn verify -Dremote=true -Dbrowser=firefox -
DgridURL=http://127.0.0.1:4444/wd/hub
```

This will run our tests against Selenium-Grid, which has been set up in Docker. Refresh the grid console when you have started the tests and watch the status of the nodes change. You can try using multiple threads to use multiple nodes, as follows:

```
docker run -d -p 4444:4444 --name selenium-hub selenium/hub:3.11.0
docker run -d --link selenium-hub:hub selenium/node-chrome:3.11.0
docker run -d --link selenium-hub:hub selenium/node-chrome:3.11.0

mvn verify -Dremote=true -Dbrowser=chrome -DgridURL=http://127.0.0.1:4444/
wd/hub -Dthreads=2
```

Alternatively, you can even modify one of your tests to make it fail. If you do this, a screenshot will be taken to show you what was happening in the browser when the test failed.

This is a fully functional grid that can be used for real testing!

Starting up Docker containers as part of the build

As we have seen, it's really easy to spin up and shut down Docker containers. Wouldn't it be useful if we could do that as part of a build?

In a perfect world, our build process would build our application and then install it in a Docker container. We would then be able to run tests against this container, and if everything worked as expected, we could publish the container in a private Docker registry. We could then take this Docker container and pass it through our promotional model until it hits live. We then would have something in live that is identical to the container that we originally built and tested. Thus, we would know that it works. If we have any problems with it in live, we can easily spin up another instance of this container in a test environment to reproduce the problem. Rather than passing around application installers, we can instead pass around pre-installed and working applications.

Let's have a look at how we can spin up containers as a part of our build. For this example, we are going to spin up the same Selenium-Grid that we created earlier. Then, we are going to run a couple of tests against it to prove that it works. This process can of course be used to spin up any type of container for any purpose. This example is really just a quick exercise to get you up and running.

We are going to build a project structure that looks like this:

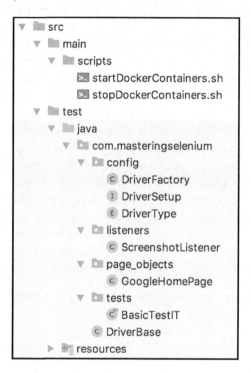

As you can see from the preceding screenshot, the first thing that we need to do is write a couple of shell scripts to control Docker. Our first script is going to start up our containers and will be called `startDockerContainers.sh`:

```
#!/usr/bin/env bash

set -euo pipefail

docker run -d -p 4444:4444 --name selenium-hub selenium/hub:3.11.0
docker run -d --link selenium-hub:hub selenium/node-firefox:3.11.0
docker run -d --link selenium-hub:hub selenium/node-chrome:3.11.0
```

Why have I used a shebang of `#!/usr/bin/env bash`? This tells your shell script to look for the bash binary in your current environment. If I had set a shebang of `#!/bin/bash/`, it would have set an explicit path for your bash binary. This path may not be correct on all systems. Using `#!/usr/bin/env bash` is more portable when passing a script around between multiple systems that may have slightly different bash installs. What does `set -euo pipefail` mean? The `-e` option causes the bash script to exit straight away when a command fails. This helps you identify failing commands and makes it easier to fix them. The `-o` `pipefail` option makes sure that your bash script exits with a sensible exit status when you are piping the result of one command into another. The `-u` makes bash treat unset variables as an error. If there are any unset variables, it will exit straight away. This is useful to help you keep track of assignment errors and will highlight unused variables that are just hanging around. There is also an `-x` version, which can be really useful for debugging. This will print every command to the console before executing it.

Our second script is going to shut down the containers and remove them. It will be called `stopDockerContainers.sh`:

```bash
#!/usr/bin/env bash

set -euo pipefail
docker stop $(docker ps -q)
docker rm $(docker ps -qa)
```

Since we are expanding upon the original Selenium implementation that we wrote in Chapter 1, *Creating a Fast Feedback Loop*, and Chapter 2, *Producing the Right Feedback When Failing*, we are using `maven-failsafe-plugin`. This means that all the tests are executed in the integration phase. Due to this, we are going to start up the Docker containers in the pre-integration phase and then shut them down again in the post-integration phase. It's a Maven project, so we are going to use a Maven plugin to execute these shell scripts in the relevant phases:

```xml
<plugin>
    <artifactId>exec-maven-plugin</artifactId>
    <groupId>org.codehaus.mojo</groupId>
    <version>1.6.0</version>
    <executions>
        <execution>
            <id>Start Docker</id>
            <phase>pre-integration-test</phase>
```

```
<goals>
    <goal>exec</goal>
</goals>
<configuration>
    <executable>
        ${project.build.scriptSourceDirectory}/
        startDockerContainers.sh
    </executable>
</configuration>
    </execution>
    <execution>
        <id>Stop Docker</id>
        <phase>post-integration-test</phase>
        <goals>
            <goal>exec</goal>
        </goals>
        <configuration>
            <executable>
                ${project.build.scriptSourceDirectory}/
                stopDockerContainers.sh
            </executable>
        </configuration>
    </execution>
</executions>
</plugin>
```

 Don't forget to make your shell scripts executable using `chmod +x`. If you don't, `exec-maven-plugin` will not be able to execute them!

We used a standard Maven project structure while creating our scripts. This means that we can use the `${project.build.scriptSourceDirectory}` Maven variable to locate our scripts easily in the POM.

We can now run our tests, and the containers will stop and start as part of the build. We haven't quite finished yet though. We need to know how to connect to Selenium-Grid, which will be spun up as part of the build. Don't worry; it's not hard. It is exactly the same command that you used when Selenium-Grid was not a part of the build:

```
mvn clean verify -Dremote=true -Dbrowser=firefox -
DgridURL=http://127.0.0.1:4444/wd/hub
```

Hopefully, everything worked correctly, but it's possible that you may have noticed some problems. Docker containers start up very quickly, but sometimes they aren't quite quick enough. Let's make sure that we won't see any problems by making sure that the container has started before moving on to the next step of actually using it. We can do this by modifying the startDockerContainers.sh file, as follows:

```bash
#!/usr/bin/env bash

set -euo pipefail

docker run -d -p 4444:4444 --name selenium-hub selenium/hub:3.11.0
docker run -d --link selenium-hub:hub selenium/node-chrome:3.11.0
docker run -d --link selenium-hub:hub selenium/node-firefox:3.11.0

echo -n "Waiting for grid to load."
while ! curl http://127.0.0.1:4444/grid/console > /dev/null 2>&1
do
  echo -n "."
  sleep 1
done
echo " "
echo "Connected to grid successfully"
```

This will add a curl command into the script that will attempt to query the Selenium-Grid hub. If it can't connect to it, it will sleep for one second and then try again. When it does manage to connect, it will drop out of the while loop and print a success message to the console. This is a very simple script; if the grid doesn't start up, it will sit there forever.

If you want to try your hand at some bash scripting, you can try to extend this script to give up after a set period of time. See if you can modify this script to time out after 45 seconds and print an appropriate message to the console. It's not that hard to do and you will probably find some bash scripting knowledge useful at some point in the future.

What we have looked at so far is very much script-based. Maybe we should explore options that are more Maven-centric, since our project is very heavily based upon Maven at the moment.

Using a Docker Maven plugin

There is `docker-maven` plugin available. In fact, there is more than one available. I found seven when I went looking, and there are probably more now. At the time of writing this book, all of the plugins suffered from one fatal flaw—they didn't support Linux sockets. This means that they are only really useful if you are running `boot2docker` at the moment. This really isn't ideal, but it's still worth investigating how we can use them. The first one that I tried that really met my needs was the one written by Wouter Danes, but unfortunately the project is no longer active. As a result, I've had to switch and the fabric8 one seems to meet my current needs (see `https://github.com/fabric8io/docker-maven-plugin`).

We are going to base this Maven implementation off the shell scripts that we wrote previously:

```
<plugin>
    <groupId>io.fabric8</groupId>
    <artifactId>docker-maven-plugin</artifactId>
    <configuration>
        <images>
            <image>
                <alias>hub</alias>
                <name>selenium/hub:3.11.0</name>
                <run>
                    <ports>
                        <port>4444:4444</port>
                    </ports>
                    <wait>
                        <log>Selenium Grid hub is up and
                        running</log>
                    </wait>
                </run>
            </image>
            <image>
                <alias>selenium-chrome</alias>
                <name>selenium/node-chrome:3.11.0</name>
                <run>
                    <links>
                        <link>hub</link>
                    </links>
                    <wait>
                        <log>The node is registered to the hub and
                            ready to use</log>
                    </wait>
                </run>
```

```
        </image>
        <image>
            <alias>selenium-firefox</alias>
            <name>selenium/node-firefox:3.11.0</name>
            <run>
                <links>
                    <link>hub</link>
                </links>
                <wait>
                    <log>The node is registered to the hub and
                          ready to use</log>
                </wait>
            </run>
        </image>
    </images>
</configuration>
<executions>
    <execution>
        <id>start</id>
        <phase>pre-integration-test</phase>
        <goals>
            <goal>start</goal>
        </goals>
    </execution>
    <execution>
        <id>stop</id>
        <phase>post-integration-test</phase>
        <goals>
            <goal>stop</goal>
        </goals>
    </execution>
</executions>
</plugin>
```

This can be broken down into two main parts. First of all, we have the `images` block where we can define our containers. In this case, we have the same three containers that we had with our shell script. The first one is hub (the plugin doesn't seem to like linking to aliases with hyphens in them, hence the minor name change). We have configured an external port mapping of `4444:4444` so that our tests can talk to the hub, and we have used the `wait` configuration element to specify an expected piece of log output from the container so that we can tell it has successfully started. We then have the two Selenium-Grid nodes, which are both linked to hub using the `links` configuration element.

We then have our two execution blocks. These are used to start the containers before the integration test phase, and then stop them again after the integration test phase has completed. This mirrors what our `exec-maven-plugin` was doing previously.

So far, the functionality looks identical to our previous implementation. We are going to make an extra little change this time though. We are going to tweak the `seleniumGridURL` property in the POM so that we don't have to set it on the command line:

```
<seleniumGridURL>http://127.0.0.1:4444/wd/hub</seleniumGridURL>
```

We are now going to cheat a little bit more. We know that we are going to run our tests by default against Selenium-Grid, which is spun up by Docker. So, we are going to change our remote property to default to true:

```
<remote>true</remote>
```

Now, we just need to run a test and see it in action:

```
mvn clean verify
```

We haven't specified a browser, because we don't really mind which one is picked up. So, it will probably pick up Firefox by default. You will see that our test ran as before, but the output looks a lot more like the standard Maven output this time.

Using Docker compose

So far, we have looked at writing scripts and using Maven plugins, but we haven't looked at the option that Docker currently suggests you to follow, Docker compose. **Docker compose** is a tool that lets you define a multiple container system using a YAML file. You can then use Docker compose to start and stop this system. Let's get this set up for our Selenium-Grid. First of all, we need to create a file called `docker-compose.yml`:

```yaml
version: '2.2'
services:
  selenium-hub:
    image: selenium/hub:3.11.0
    ports:
    - 4444:4444

  chrome:
    image: selenium/node-chrome:3.11.0
    links:
    - selenium-hub:hub

  firefox:
    image: selenium/node-firefox:3.11.0
    links:
    - selenium-hub:hub
```

Here, you can see that we have defined the same system again, only this time it's in YAML format. We can now use Docker compose to start up our Selenium-Grid:

```
docker-compose up -d
```

No surprises here; Docker compose ran, created our grid setup, and exited again. You can check that everything is working by navigating to `http://127.0.0.1:4444/grid/console` in your browser again, like you did before. You can also check that it's fully functional by running:

```
mvn clean verify -Dremote=true -Dbrowser=firefox -
DgridURL=http://127.0.0.1:4444/wd/hub
```

Once you are happy it's functionally equivalent to what we did before, you can tear it down again by running the following command:

```
docker-compose down
```

You will see that Docker compose will now shut down all of your containers; it will also remove them so that everything is ready for another run later on. Now the configuration for this is much easier than the previous two solutions, but how do we plug this into our Maven project? Luckily, the Maven plugin we are using has support for Docker compose. Let's modify the configuration in our POM file to take advantage of this. First of all, we need to create a `docker` directory under `src/test`, then we need to save our `docker-compose.yml` there. Then, we will modify the plugin configuration in our POM to point at our Docker compose file:

```xml
<plugin>
    <groupId>io.fabric8</groupId>
    <artifactId>docker-maven-plugin</artifactId>
    <configuration>
        <images>
            <image>
                <external>
                    <type>compose</type>
                    <basedir>src/test/docker</basedir>
                    <composeFile>docker-compose.yml</composeFile>
                </external>
            </image>
        </images>
    </configuration>
    <executions>
        <execution>
            <id>start</id>
            <phase>pre-integration-test</phase>
            <goals>
```

```
                <goal>start</goal>
            </goals>
        </execution>
        <execution>
            <id>stop</id>
            <phase>post-integration-test</phase>
            <goals>
                <goal>stop</goal>
            </goals>
        </execution>
    </executions>
</plugin>
```

As you can see, this is instantly much cleaner. We have changed our 40-line configuration block into an 11-line configuration block. Functionality, it is identical to our previous Maven plugin implementation, so the same command will still work to run tests against this Selenium-Grid:

```
mvn clean verify
```

I would suggest that Docker compose is the cleanest and easiest implementation of the lot.

What about the negatives?

Docker has lots of potential, but sadly it doesn't always live up to people's hopes and aspirations. Microsoft now has native support for Docker containers, but we never did see that much hope for an Internet Explorer container. If you still need to test in Internet Explorer, sadly it's still administering physical boxes or your own set of virtual machines. On the plus side of things, Internet Explorer is becoming less and less relevant, so hopefully we will never need them. What about Edge though? It would be nice to be able to spin up some Edge containers in Docker to get away from physical Windows machines, or virtual machines for Edge testing. Alas, that doesn't appear to be coming any time soon. Windows Docker containers don't support a Windows GUI at the moment and there probably aren't that many use cases where doing so is useful.

We can continue to keep our fingers crossed, but it does feel that from a browser automation point of view, Docker has failed to deliver all of its initial potential.

Summary

In this chapter, we spent some time installing docker and working out how to start up a Selenium-Grid. Although this chapter was very much focused on running a Selenium-Grid, you should be able to see many more potential applications of Docker.

By the end of this chapter, you should be able to use docker to start and stop containers as part of your build process. You will also have working implementations using bash scripts, docker compose, and a maven plugin.

In the next chapter, we are going to examine the constantly evolving fields of machine learning and artificial intelligence, and how they are going to affect the future of Selenium.

Selenium – the Future

10

Selenium 3 is finally out, so what does the future hold now? The next major release is going to be Selenium 4, which will align Selenium with the W3C WebDriver spec (`https://w3c.github.io/webdriver/`). After this has happened, currently there doesn't really seem to be much of a plan for future development. There will undoubtedly be enhancements to the W3C WebDriver in the future, which Selenium will need to align with, but W3C spec changes are not things that happen overnight. I think it's safe to say that the Selenium API will stabilize and the number of changes will reduce drastically.

So, if Selenium doesn't look like it's going to change all that much, what does the future hold? Well unless you have had your head buried in the sand, you will undoubtedly have heard lots of excitement around machine learning and artificial intelligence.

Machine learning — the new Holy Grail

Machine learning (eventually leading to artificial intelligence) is the current buzzword that's thrown around a lot in the automation sphere. It promises a lot, but what can it actually do for testing?

Well, theoretically, it can take over the job of a tester by learning how a system works and then using its knowledge to search through the system for known bugs. It sounds amazing (or scary depending upon your point of view), and it is also a bit of a nebulous statement; there are hundreds of different things that testers look at.

Now this all sounds like doom and gloom: the machine learning apocalypse is coming and all of us testers will soon be obsolete. Well, I don't think that is true. Machine learning systems need to be taught how to do things. If they are not properly trained, they will not work in the way they are expected to work. Also I've worked with lots of talented testers over the years with loads of experience and they have still missed problems in systems they have tested; I do it myself. I've never met a single person capable of finding every single bug in a system. What makes us think that machine learning will be any different? At the end of the day, we are a product of our experiences and the way we test is shaped partly by the way we were trained and partly by our experiences of things that have gone wrong in systems we have tested in the past.

Every single person will have slightly different training and experiences. This diversity is what allows us to find bugs that other people don't find. How would we provide artificial intelligence with all of this diversity and experience? Are we going to end up training multiple different artificial intelligences and then pointing a few of them at a system we want to test so that they can all find different things? If we have a couple of artificial intelligences looking at things, why not some humans as well to give us yet another point of view?

Then, we also have the task of validating that the machine learning algorithms used to create artificial intelligence work as expected. We will need to train these artificial intelligences and check that they have been trained correctly. How do you validate that you have trained somebody to find bugs when there are no concrete outcomes of the training?

Jobs in general always evolve as technology marches onward and I think that one of the ways that the job of a tester will change will be for us to spend more time teaching machines how to successfully test things. Some of this learning will be applicable across multiple different websites, some of it probably won't. I think the hardest thing for a machine to do is learn to check the look and feel of the system under test. At the end of the day look and feel are very emotive and what is right greatly depends upon a person's point of view. Secondly, depending upon your target audience, the look and feel of a website change greatly.

Let's explore this scenario a bit more. Imagine artificial intelligence that has been taught to look at sites that advertise soft drinks. Most of these sites are going to be colorful, cool, and aimed at the younger generation. They often also throw in eye-grabbing lifestyle statements that imply you will be the coolest extreme sports practitioner in the world if you drink that brand of soft drink.

Let's take this artificial intelligence and point it at a funeral site. The sort of site that has neutral colors and doesn't have statements littered around it that try to make it sound "cool" to use their services. It wouldn't know what to do, the entire style of the site would be completely alien to it. If you let this system loose to log all the look and feel errors it would have a field day, but most of what it found would be invalid. Imagine if it was sufficiently advanced to start changing the site to automatically fix all of these errors it had found. Can you imagine it? A funeral website with loud eye-grabbing colors and statements such as "Only the coolest people let us bury their loved ones!" It would be a complete disaster.

You could, of course, train your AI to work on funeral sites, but what if you then pointed it back at your soft drink site? As ever, context is key, and one of the skills we have as testers is being able to switch context for different sorts of sites. Now, I'm sure you could eventually get to the point where you could train an AI to work out what sort of site it is and then utilize algorithms specific to that types of site. But that's a lot of work to be able to identify and switch between the different types of sites. Also companies that sell soft drink aren't usually involved in the funeral business, or vice versa. Why would they want to spend lots of time training an AI to context-switch when there is little value in them having that ability? I think it's far more likely that companies will create their own artificial intelligences that are designed specifically for the sort of content that they create.

I think the key thing to take away here is that no matter what people say, machine learning (and by extension artificial intelligence) is not going to be a silver bullet that fixes everything. As I've said previously; when it comes to automation, there are no silver bullets!

Now this is a book about Selenium, so obviously we are going to be interested in how machine learning can help us with our Selenium tests. There are three main areas of help that I can think of:

- Machine learning that helps identify problems by examining the results of your tests
- Machine learning that tries to automatically fix errors with your tests
- Machine learning that tries to write your tests for you

You will notice that the three points I have listed kind of depend upon each other; if a machine learning system cannot identify problems by looking at results it will not be able to automatically fix errors with your tests. If it can't automatically fix errors with existing tests, how is it going to start writing its own tests?

So, let's have a look at these three areas of machine learning and see what they have actually delivered so far. Well you may already be using the first area of machine learning in your Selenium tests today; it's called visual validation.

Visual validation

I've never been a strong proponent of visual validation (the practice of using code to check if something that you are looking at on screen is what should be displayed on screen). It's something I have tried in the past and it never really seemed to live up to the hype. The idea of being able to take a screenshot of a site and then compare it to a known good copy sounds great, but the reality was always underwhelming.

In the past, I have diligently written code to take screenshots and then do a pixel-by-pixel comparison to see if they match. The problem was they very rarely did: variables such as different machines running at different resolutions came into play, slightly different rendering engines could result in color changes that were invisible to the human eye, but absolutely different to a computer. You then have to worry about brightness and contrast levels. The only way to make things work was by accepting that you had to allow a certain percentage of difference.

Using a percentage of difference to work out if the correct thing was displayed on screen turned out to be the Achilles heel of visual testing, a percentage difference on its own is just not meaningful. Imagine that you have three screenshots of a screen: your base image, image one, and image two. Both image one and image two are 75% similar to the base image; however, they are wildly different. One has an almost indistinguishable color change that you cannot see with the human eye, the other is showing a different header bar.

About four years ago, tools such as **Wraith** (`https://github.com/BBC-News/wraith`) started popping up, which only solidified my view that this was not a useful thing to add to my automation toolkit. The example that they show you on the `README.md` shows all the problems I'm used to seeing with visual validation:

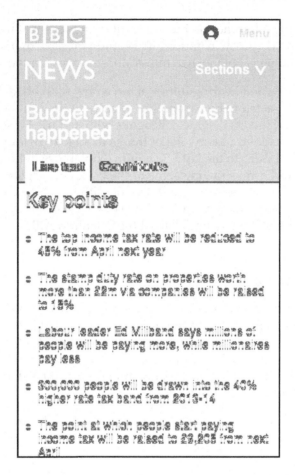

You can see that to the left of the menu text on the top-right of the screen we have a new visual artifact that has appeared that wasn't there before. That's a good reason to fail a test and investigate why that area of the screen has changed. However, as you continue down the screen you will see that all of the differences are due to minor rendering variations with pixels being pushed to the left or right slightly. You can actually read the text of the article just by looking at the difference. How can you base an automated pass or fail on that? In my opinion you can't.

It's still kind of useful to take these screenshots on every build and then store the images somewhere so that somebody can physically go and look at them to see if there are any worrying discrepancies. However, humans are not good at focusing on unexpected changes.

If I hadn't pointed out the difference on the top-right of the screen at the start of the previous paragraph would you have noticed it? Would you have marked this test as passed because the majority of blue is obviously a minor difference in rendering?

A couple of years ago, I started hearing things about a new tool called **Applitools Eyes**, which I initially expected to be yet another attempt to do visual validation that would probably disappoint me. However, some colleagues who had tried it seemed to be very enthusiastic about it, so I added it to my list of things to look at. Before I had really investigated it properly, I went to the 2016 Selenium Conference in London and there was a presentation from Adam Carmi showing some of the basics of Applitools Eyes. The presentation involved Adam live-coding and it went without a hitch. What impressed me most of all was that the code Adam had written was very clean and well formed. He clearly knew what he was doing and really understood the Selenium API.

Applitools Eyes

In this section, we will set up a basic Applitools Eyes implementation so that we can see what it can do for us. We will start with the code that we created in Chapter 1, *Creating a Fast Feedback Loop* and Chapter 2, *Producing the Right Feedback When Failing*, and add in our eyes code. You don't need to pay for a full Applitools Eyes subscription to try this out, they offer trial accounts with access to all the functionality (you will need to use either Chrome or Firefox to log into their website, however).

So first things first; let's add a dependency to the Applitools code into our POM:

```
<dependency>
    <groupId>com.applitools</groupId>
    <artifactId>eyes-selenium-java3</artifactId>
    <version>3.32.1</version>
</dependency>
```

Next, we will make some modifications to our `DriverFactory` class to allow us to have an `eyes` object as well as a driver object stored in it. We will need to add the following variables:

```
private String currentTestName;
private Eyes eyes;
private final String eyesAPIKey = System.getProperty("eyesAPIKey",
"<DEFAULT_KEY_HERE>");
private final Boolean disableEyes = Boolean.getBoolean("disableEyes");
```

The `currentTestName` is something that we will use to group the screenshots that `eyes` takes into screenshots for specific tests. The `eyes` object is the main control object that we will use to talk to the Applitools server and pass data across to them, as well as performing actions such as taking screenshots of the current screen.

We then have our `eyesAPIKey`, which we will need to authenticate with the Applitools server, and finally a Boolean called `disableEyes` that we can use to, yes you guessed it, disable eyes for the current test run. This gives us the ability to run our tests without taking screenshots and uploading them to the Applitools server every time. Since this is a paid service there are restrictions on how often you can use it depending on your subscription; as a result we want the ability to turn things off when we are debugging errors so that we don't rattle through our subscription minutes when we are not really interested in comparing screenshots.

Next, we have a few methods that we need to add:

```
public void setTestName(String testname) {
    currentTestName = testname;
}
```

We created a `currentTestName` variable to track the name of the current test; obviously we need a way to update it depending on the name of the current test and this small method will give us the ability to do that.

Finally, we have the code that does all the real work:

```
public Eyes openEyes() throws Exception {
    if (null == eyes) {
        eyes = new Eyes();
        eyes.setApiKey(eyesAPIKey);
        eyes.setIsDisabled(disableEyes);
        eyes.open(getDriver(), "Google Example", currentTestName);
    }

    return eyes;
}
```

This method is similar to our `getDriver()` method. When we invoke it we see if we already have a valid eyes object or not. If we do, we return it ready for use. If we don't we go about generating one. We instantiate the eyes object and add our API key. We then work out if we really want to start sending data over to the Applitools server or not using the `disableEyes` flag.

We still perform `eyes.open()` in every case because we want to send back a valid `eyes` object that will prevent us seeing null pointer errors if we have disabled eyes. You will notice that we pass our `getDriver()` method into `eyes.open()`, instead of just the `driver` variable we have stored in the class.

This is to ensure that we don't inadvertently send in a null driver object, which will prevent us from trying to take a screenshot before instantiating the driver (showing a blank driver screen demonstrating that we haven't loaded a web page is probably better than a slightly confusing null pointer exception). The next option is an app name that allows Applitools to filter tests into relevant buckets. If you are testing multiple apps using the same Applitools account, you can then have buckets of tests related to specific apps. Finally, we pass in the test name so that we know which tests screenshots are related to.

Finally, we need to add a clean up method:

```
public void closeEyes() {
    try {
        eyes.close();
    } finally {
        eyes.abortIfNotClosed();
    }
    eyes = null;
}
```

This just attempts to close our connection to the Applitools server. If we can't close it down cleanly we will perform a hard abort to make sure that we don't leave any connections open on our side. Finally, we set the `eyes` object to `null` again to guarantee that the next time we call `openEyes()` we go through the process of instantiating a new object again.

Now that we have made our modifications to our `DriverFactory`, we also need to tweak our `DriverBase`.

First of all we need to make sure that we successfully pass our test name into our `DriverFactory` at the start of each test as it's now going to be used to instantiate our `eyes` object:

```
@BeforeMethod(alwaysRun = true)
public static void setTestName(Method method) {
    driverThread.get().setTestName(method.getName());
}
```

TestNG makes this nice and easy for us. Since it has already scanned all the test methods so that it can throw them into one big bucket, it already has some basic information about them. It also provides the ability to pass this information into our own methods if we use the `@BeforeMethod` annotation. Here, we simply get `TestNG` to pass in the information it's storing about the method it is about to run, then we extract the name and set it as the current test name in our `DriverFactory`.

Next we need to provide a way for us to get the `eyes` object out of `DriverFactory` and into our test. This works in exactly the same way as our `getDriver()` method:

```
public static Eyes openEyes() throws Exception {
    return driverThread.get().openEyes();
}
```

Finally, we need to make sure that when we clean up at the end of our tests we also clean up the `eyes` object; this is a simple tweak to our `closeDriverObjects()` method to make sure that it also calls `closeEyes()`:

```
@AfterSuite(alwaysRun = true)
public static void closeDriverObjects() {
    for (DriverFactory webDriverThread : webDriverThreadPool) {
        webDriverThread.quitDriver();
        webDriverThread.closeEyes();
    }
}
```

We are now ready to add some screen comparison ability into our tests! We already have our basic Google example; let's add in a visual check:

```
private RemoteWebDriver driver;

@BeforeMethod
public void setup() throws MalformedURLException {
    driver = getDriver();
}

private void googleExampleThatSearchesFor(final String searchString) throws
Exception {
    driver.get("http://www.google.com");

    WebElement searchField = driver.findElement(By.name("q"));

    searchField.clear();
    searchField.sendKeys(searchString);

    System.out.println("Page title is: " + driver.getTitle());
```

```
        searchField.submit();

        WebDriverWait wait = new WebDriverWait(driver, 10);
        wait.until((ExpectedCondition<Boolean>) d ->
    d.getTitle().toLowerCase().startsWith(searchString.toLowerCase()));

        openEyes().setMatchLevel(MatchLevel.LAYOUT);
        openEyes().checkWindow("Search results for " + searchString);

        System.out.println("Page title is: " + driver.getTitle());
    }

@Test
public void googleCheeseExample() throws Exception {
    googleExampleThatSearchesFor("Cheese!");
}
```

We can now run this test to set up our baseline image.

 Every time you run a test and tell Applitools about it, some checks will be performed on the Applitools server. If it can't find any record of tests for the selected app and test name, it will assume that it is a new test and any screenshots that are taken will become the baseline for subsequent runs. As a result you need to be aware that if you change test names Applitools will think you want to create a new baseline. Be careful about changing test names; you may miss a visual change because a new baseline has been created instead of a comparison with your old screenshot.

You can log into the Applitools website and you will now see something like the following:

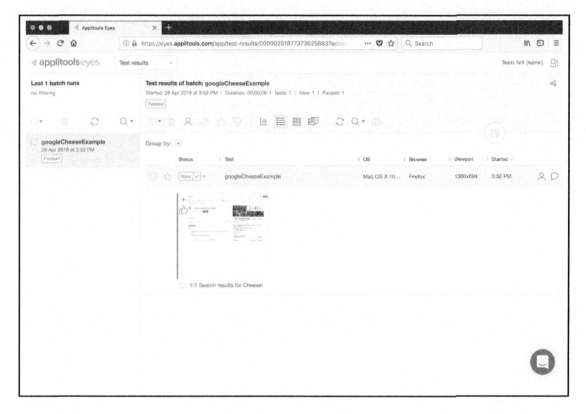

This is our initial baseline and all subsequent tests will be compared against this. Let's run the same test again.

This time, you will most likely see something like the following:

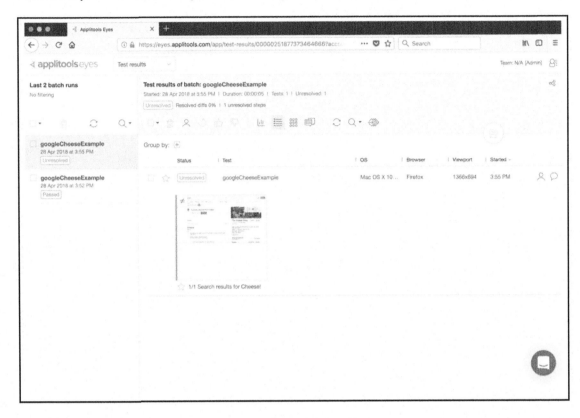

If you click on the thumbnail, you will be shown a bigger version of it so that you can work out exactly what went wrong:

As you can see, Google tells you how long it took to process the search. Since that number changes depending on a series of things (server load, network performance, if the search is cached, and so on) it's unlikely that you will always get the same number. So, we now need to mark this area as something that is known to change.

Select **X** and draw a box around this area so that Applitools knows it should ignore it, and then click on the thumbs-up icon and save it:

You will see that the test now goes green. Let's run it again to check that everything is working and that we aren't going to have any problems with subsequent runs of this test:

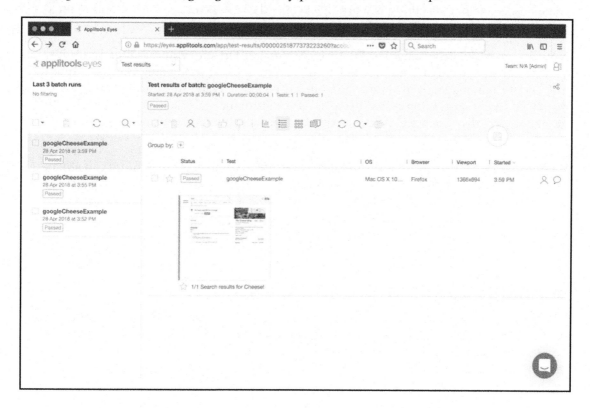

This time you will see that, as expected, the test has stayed green. If you look at the screenshot, you will see that the number showing how long it took to process the search has changed yet again. Everything is working excellently. We have a visual validation on a website and we have made sure that changes to page speed aren't classified as failures.

Now we are really just scratching the surface here, but I'm sure you can already see just how powerful this enhancement to Selenium is. When I first tried using this tool I found that I could remove loads of assertions from my code, checking that various things were displayed to the user. I don't need those assertions any more, I just need a screenshot that highlights any discrepancies. A tool like this can drastically cut down on the number of lines of code in your tests and that can only be a good thing.

Where Applitools Eyes really excels is mobile testing. Appium is great, but it can still be very slow depending upon the device you are running tests against. If you have 10 assertions on a page to check that various controls exist, things can really slow down. Replacing those 10 assertions with a single screenshot taken by Applitools Eyes that can check everything on the screen can really speed your tests up.

So what has this got to do with AI?

While what we have seen so far is useful, we haven't really seen anything that shows the usage of AI. Let's have a look at one of the more advanced bits of functionality that Applitools Eyes has. To show this off in all its glory we first of all need to modify our test to make it fail. Instead of looking for cheese, let's look for `Mango`:

```
@Test
public void googleCheeseExample() throws Exception {
    googleExampleThatSearchesFor("Mango!");
}
```

If we now run our test again, you will see that, as expected, it fails. Looking at the visual comparison, you will see that a lot has changed, as we would expect:

Let's tweak our test again and change the matching strategy that Applitools Eyes uses. By default, it uses the STRICT level, which will show you all visual changes. We are now going to switch this to the LAYOUT matching level:

```
private void googleExampleThatSearchesFor(final String searchString) throws
Exception {

    WebDriver driver = DriverBase.getDriver();

    driver.get("http://www.google.com");

    WebElement searchField = driver.findElement(By.name("q"));

    searchField.clear();
    searchField.sendKeys(searchString);

    System.out.println("Page title is: " + driver.getTitle());
```

```
searchField.submit();

(new WebDriverWait(driver, 10)).until(new
ExpectedCondition<Boolean>() {
    public Boolean apply(WebDriver driverObject) {
        return driverObject.getTitle().toLowerCase().
        startsWith(searchString.toLowerCase());
    }
});

openEyes().setMatchLevel(MatchLevel.LAYOUT);
openEyes().checkWindow("Search results for " + searchString);

System.out.println("Page title is: " + driver.getTitle());
}
```

If you now run your test again, you will see a big difference in the output:

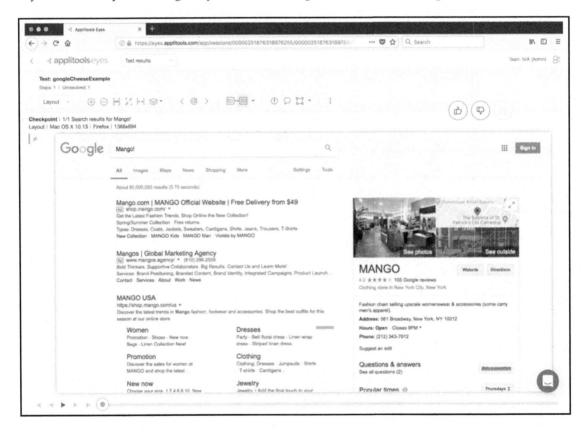

Applitools Eyes has still picked up some differences, but this time it has used its AI routines to try and work out if the physical layout of the page has changed or not. It is ignoring different text and different images and trying to just highlight structural changes in the visual layout. This is really not a very fair test either; I've used Google as an example and there are a lot of dynamic areas on a Google search result page that could change in slightly unexpected ways. Imagine using this on a generic shopping cart site that has a fairly fixed structure, or a generic blog site. In both of these cases Applitools Eyes would have passed the test.

I think this is a really exciting example that shows how the future of visual testing is effectively already here. When I first saw this it blew me away. There is still work to be done (after all, these tools are still at the early stages) but they are still extremely powerful right now and they will only get better. This functionality is almost bordering on the next area of machine learning, self-healing tests.

Self healing tests

One of the main areas of interest right now for artificial intelligence in the automation space seems to be the idea of self healing tests. This is where artificial intelligence can try and learn whether a change to the website you are testing that has caused your test to fail is something that is expected. If it is identified as an expected change, the artificial intelligence will then automatically modify your code to fix the problem.

There are a few tools offering this service at the moment; the three most popular seem to be:

- Mabl: `https://www.mabl.com`
- Testim: `https://www.testim.io/automate`
- Testcraft: `https://www.testcraft.io`

Out of the three, Testcraft is the only one that explicitly markets itself as using Selenium.

These tools generally work in two ways. On the one hand, they spider your website to try and work out what pages are available and build up an image of the website. On the other hand, they rely on record and play technology to train them. At the time of writing, there is no way to pass your own Selenium code over to these systems, which is kind of understandable. It's much easier to get you to record and play your scenarios and turn that into code that the AI understands. Attempting to parse custom code and work out the intent of it is actually quite hard.

The idea is that, once you have trained these tools, they will regularly check against your website and verify that everything still looks fine. If they detect changes they can then either flag the changes as errors that need to be fixed, or they can use their self-healing algorithms to modify the tests so that they don't fail. Examples of things that they provide for the self healing functionality are things such as minor locator changes, or element color changes.

This is where I start to get skeptical. In the past I've seen elements change color because it was a conscious design decision, I've also seen typos change the color of elements by mistake. How is an AI going to know which one of these your color change is? Well in my mind it can't unless it's aware of the stories in your backlog. If you have a backlog story to change the element color, the change is probably good. If you don't it's probably an error. How can artificial intelligence understand these different contexts without additional information?

At some point in the future, these systems may want to try and read in the story data in your backlog to work out what sort of changes are coming, but by the time we get to that point surely the artificial intelligence will just be able to write the actual code changes as well.

Now if you think back to the example with Applitools Eyes in the last section, you will remember that we finished off with an example that detected the screen layout. I think this is a good example of a self-healing test. We don't really care about the specific test or images shown on a certain page, but we do care that the layout is structured in a specific way. You can change the text and images as much as you like, but as soon as you break the layout the test fails. In a way you could say that self healing tests are already here.

I think the main point to remember here is that good testing involves many layers of tests and checks. Some of these advances in artificial intelligence will be able to give us useful self healing tests, but in other areas we are still going to need a human to make the final decision.

Having your tests written for you

This is what everybody is frantically working toward: creating artificial intelligence that you can point at a website and let it work out how to test it all by itself. I suspect this is something lots of hiring managers can't wait for because they think that they will be able to get rid of a bunch of staff who will no longer be required. I think that the reality is going to be very different!

Once we have created this amazing artificial intelligence that is capable of learning how a site works and creating test scripts automatically, it will still have to be trained. After it has been trained, it will also need to be checked to make sure that its training has worked. Our job will change from testing websites, to testing that artificial intelligence is testing websites properly.

I would encourage you to read this experience report from Angie Jones, one of the leading lights when it comes to machine learning in test automation. It does a great job of explaining the problems with machine learning and how it cannot be seen as infallible:

`http://angiejones.tech/test-automation-for-machine-learning/`

One day, we may be able to have our tests automatically written for us, but to get there we will still need to spend time training and validating artificial intelligences.

Summary

In this chapter, we have had a look at what the future may hold for Selenium and where we currently are in that journey. After reading this chapter, you will have a basic understanding of machine learning/artificial intelligence.

In this chapter we specifically focussed on visual testing and the various pros and cons. You will also have been introduced to Applitools, one of the more exciting implementations of visual testing backed by machine learning. Finally, we had a look at some of the self-healing testing systems that are available right now, which may have given you an idea of how the role of a tester may evolve in the future.

Appendix A: Contributing to Selenium

Selenium is amazing – how can I help make it better?

There are lots of ways in which you can help the Selenium project. Believe it or not, it's not just hardcore coding skills that are required.

The first and the most important thing that you can do is find problems with Selenium and report them. The Selenium developers do an awesome job, but they are not infallible. They need your help to find problems and raise defects so that they can fix them and make Selenium even better.

The problem with a lot of bugs that occur in Selenium is that they are unclear and range from hard to impossible to replicate. One of the best things that you can supply when you report a defect is a Selenium script that reproduces the problem. This gives the developers a way to see the issue first-hand, and it helps massively with regard to debugging. It can also form the basis of a test to ensure that once fixed, the problem doesn't raise its ugly head again in the future.

That being said, you don't need to have a prewritten script that shows your problem. However, you do need to be very clear about your problem. Bugs that sound kind of valid, but don't really have enough information so that they can be replicated, are the worst. If a developer takes a day trying to make sense of a badly written bug report and gets so frustrated that they don't want to look at the Selenium code base again for another week, we all lose out.

One of the biggest annoyances is people not providing the Selenium code. Your Selenium code is not special and secret. It's almost guaranteed that somebody else has done it before, and there is a good chance that they have made improvements in some areas. Share your code if you want to get it fixed.

When you report bugs on Selenium, make sure that you do the following:

- Investigate the issue before you raise it! Don't waste people's time with a one-line bug, saying that it doesn't work. Explain exactly what doesn't work and what you did to get to this non-working state.
- Write down the version of Selenium used, the language bindings, the browser, and the OS that you are using.
- Add as much information as possible. Stack traces, screenshots, and HTML code are great. They give people more information so that they are able to diagnose the issue.
- Try to create a Selenium script that reproduces the issue (the smaller the script, the better).

Great bugs mean issues that are easy to reproduce and which can be identified and fixed quickly. Everybody loves well-written bugs.

Getting set up to contribute to a Selenium repository

Selenium has quite a few repositories of code that you can check out, explore, and contribute to. The first thing that you will need to do to get a local copy is to install Git (for more information, visit `https://git-scm.com`). Git is available on all the major operating systems, so installing it should be a relatively pain-free process. If you don't just want to use the command line, you may want to have a look at the following additional clients. Some people like them, whereas others are fine with a Terminal:

- **TortoiseGit**: `https://code.google.com/p/tortoisegit/`
- **The GitHub Windows client**: `https://windows.github.com`
- **The GitHub Mac client**: `https://mac.github.com`

Once you have installed Git, you can check out any of the Selenium code bases. When you first start looking at them, don't worry about forking local copies. You'll only need to do this if you want to raise pull requests. All Selenium code repositories are now held on GitHub (for more information, visit `https://github.com/SeleniumHQ`). First of all, the best thing to do is just check out an individual code base and have a play. Let's do this right now. We will start with the Selenium website, `https://github.com/SeleniumHQ/www.seleniumhq.org`:

```
git clone https://github.com/SeleniumHQ/www.seleniumhq.org.git
```

To get everything up-and-running, we are going to need to install a couple of things:

- Maven
- Python (at least version 2.7.9 to ensure that `pip` is bundled with it)

Then, you will need to install Sphinx, as follows:

```
pip install -U Sphinx
```

Sphinx is a documentation generator that is used by the Selenium project to generate the Selenium website (visit `http://sphinx-doc.org` for more information). It will take `reStructuredText` files and convert them into other formats (in this case, HTML). Now you are ready to build the project:

```
mvn clean install
```

After this, you can start up the site in exploded mode:

```
mvn jetty:run-exploded
```

You can now navigate to the Selenium website in your local browser by visiting `http://localhost:8080/`. If you make changes, they should be automatically updated since you are running in the exploded mode. All that you will need to do is refresh the browser. Have a look around and see how easy it is to change things.

Aiding the documentation effort

Selenium is a very old project. The original work on it started in 2004. As a result, there have been many changes over the years and, as with all big and old projects, the documentation hasn't always stayed up to date or been as clear as it could be.

If you spend time going through the documentation, you will probably encounter the following:

- Minor errors (such as typos, grammar mistakes, and so on)
- Gaps where some available functionality has never been written about
- Documentation that is either no longer correct or no longer relevant

Documentation always needs to be updated, and there are never enough people to do it. This is the perfect place to start contributing to the Selenium project. The documentation is roughly split into two areas. There is the existing Selenium HQ site, which contains the current documentation (for more information, visit http://docs.seleniumhq.org/docs/). There is also the new documentation project, which was created in 2013. The idea was to start writing the documentation from scratch (visit http://seleniumhq.github.io/docs/ for additional information).

> The Selenium HQ site is more than just documentation. Don't think that you are limited to just enhancing the documentation. You are quite welcome to contribute a change to any aspect of the site.

Earlier in this chapter, we cloned a copy of the existing SeleniumHQ website. Hopefully, you have already examined and played around with it a bit. If we now want to take the next step and start contributing, we will need to turn our clone into a fork. The process is very simple.

First of all, go to the GitHub page for the documentation and then click on the **Fork** button:

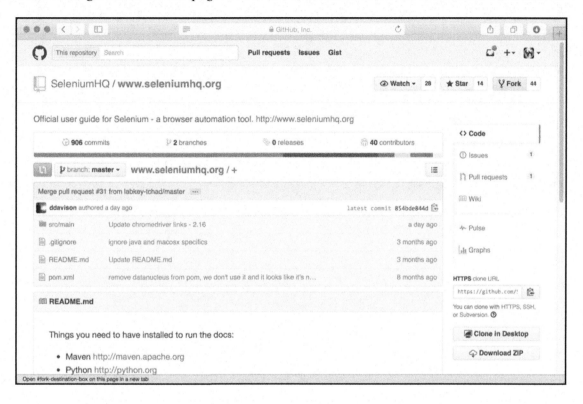

GitHub will then do all the work for you. When it has finished, it will load the forked version of the site:

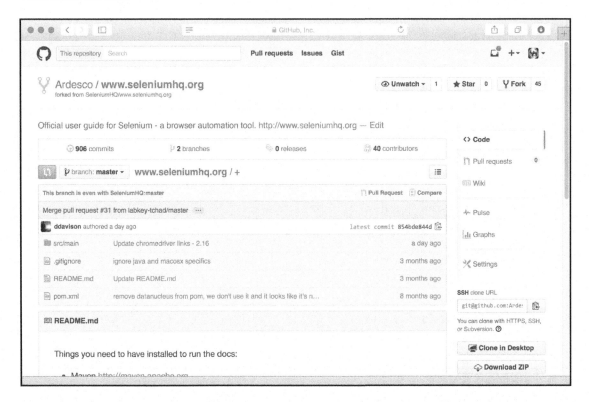

Note that on the right-hand side, you now have your own unique clone URL. There are two things that you can do at this point:

- Delete your existing local copy of the documentation and then clone your fork
- Change your `remote` to point at the new fork on GitHub

Deleting your local copy is easy. Just go to the parent directory that you originally ran your `clone` command in and use the following command:

```
rm -r www.seleniumhq.org
git clone <your personal clone url>
```

You will now have the forked version of the Selenium website cloned. You just need to set up an upstream remote, as shown in the following section.

Be very careful whenever you use an `rm -r` or `rm -rf` command. The `-r` stands for recursive (that is, it will delete the directory that you have told it to delete along with the files and directories in the original directory that you specified). The `-f` stands for force. It will do everything it can to delete the files. If you aren't paying attention and you run the command with elevated privileges, it's very easy to remove the wrong thing, or even everything on your hard drive by mistake!

Let's assume that you have some changes that you don't want to lose. The easiest thing to do in this situation is just change your `remote`.

We are going to do this in a couple of steps. First of all, we need to have a look at what we currently have set up in Git. We can do this by using the following command to list our remotes:

```
git remote -v
```

You will get something that looks like this:

```
Kezef:www.seleniumhq.org fyre$ git remote -v
origin  https://github.com/SeleniumHQ/www.seleniumhq.org.git (fetch)
origin  https://github.com/SeleniumHQ/www.seleniumhq.org.git (push)
```

We are going to change the existing `remote` to `upstream`. This will allow us to pull down any changes that are made in SeleniumHQ's copy of the code:

```
git remote add upstream
https://github.com/SeleniumHQ/www.seleniumhq.org.git
```

If you check your remotes again, you will now have an upstream and an origin both pointing at the same thing:

```
Kezef:www.seleniumhq.org fyre$ git remote -v
origin  https://github.com/SeleniumHQ/www.seleniumhq.org.git (fetch)
origin  https://github.com/SeleniumHQ/www.seleniumhq.org.git (push)
upstream        https://github.com/SeleniumHQ/www.seleniumhq.org.git (fetch)
upstream        https://github.com/SeleniumHQ/www.seleniumhq.org.git (push)
```

Now, if you want to get your fork up-to-date with SeleniumHQ's copy of the code, all you need to do is use the following command:

```
git fetch upstream
git rebase upstream/master
```

This will pull down the latest code from the origin and then rebase it onto your current branch (in this case, `origin/master`).

 We have used quite a few different Git commands so far; if you haven't used Git before you may be getting a bit lost. There is a good basic tutorial available at `https://git-scm.com/docs/gittutorial` which should give you most of the basics. Then you'll probably want to understand rebasing: `https://git-scm.com/book/en/v2/Git-Branching-Rebasing`. Git is a very powerful version control system, but it can be a little overwhelming at first if you don't know where to get more information.

The final step is to change our remote to point at the fork. First, copy the clone URL for your fork and then run the following command:

```
git remote set-url origin
git@github.com:Ardesco/www.seleniumhq.org.git
```

Your remotes should now look like this:

```
Kezef:www.seleniumhq.org fyre$ git remote -v
origin    git@github.com:Ardesco/www.seleniumhq.org.git (fetch)
origin    git@github.com:Ardesco/www.seleniumhq.org.git (push)
upstream         https://github.com/SeleniumHQ/www.seleniumhq.org.git (fetch)
upstream         https://github.com/SeleniumHQ/www.seleniumhq.org.git (push)
```

You are now ready to make changes to the documentation. When you are happy with a change, you can create a pull request to submit it back to the Selenium developers.

 It's always useful to create a new branch for the changes you make. When you perform a pull request, it is not for a static piece of code. You are requesting that the branch that you are currently working on should be pulled in. This means that if you make any changes to the branch after making your pull request, they will also be added to the list of things that are being offered. Having a separate branch for each pull request allows you to easily isolate changes.

So far, we have been looking at the old site. Also, we did briefly mention earlier that there is a new documentation project. If you want to add documentation, this is probably the best place to start. To do this, you will need to clone the new documentation project (for more information, visit `https://github.com/SeleniumHQ/docs.git`).

The process is basically identical to the one that we followed to clone the Selenium website. Once you are done, you are all ready to make changes to the document. Why not start updating the documentations and creating pull requests today?

Making changes to Selenium

We had a look at the various things that you can do to help the Selenium project. The big one is obviously adding code to Selenium itself. The first thing that you will need to do is fork the Selenium project and check it out locally. It's exactly the same process as before.

Once we have the code checked out, the first challenge is to build it. Selenium has lots of moving parts, and it's not always clear what you need to run. The two targets that will probably be useful for somebody working with Java are as follows:

```
./go test_java_webdriver -trace
./go test_firefox --trace
```

What you want to build will depend on which part of the code you are working on. There is a Rakefile in the root of the project, and if you look through this, you will see the various targets that are available to you.

One thing that I always try to do is run a `./go` command and then expect everything to work. If it won't, there is code in Selenium for multiple operating systems, and you will not be able to run everything on your machine. Focus on the bits that you are changing, and trust CI to catch anything else.

If you get stuck and have any questions, the best way to get them answered is to go to the #selenium IRC channel on `irc.freenode.net` and have a chat with various people from the Selenium community. They are all very helpful and will probably have seen your problem before.

Now that we have got Selenium building projects locally, let's do something useful. Let's add something that is missing and then submit a pull request. The Selenium team has created a document to aid people who want to contribute to the project. It's available at `https://github.com/SeleniumHQ/selenium/blob/master/CONTRIBUTING.md`. The most important thing to do is sign the **CLA (Contributor License Agreement)**. If you don't sign this, your code cannot be accepted in the project. Once this has been signed, we can get on with making a pull request.

Selenium has a support class to convert colors from one format to another. It also has a predefined list of colors, as specified at `http://www.w3.org/TR/css3-color/#html4`. Since this list was created, an additional color has been added to the W3C spec, rebeccapurple. So, we are going to add this color to the `Colors` enum inside the support package.

The first thing that we are going to do is create a new local branch. This means that when we make changes and raise a pull request, we can switch to another branch and make more changes without affecting the pull request. Creating a branch is simple. You just use the following command:

```
git checkout -b rebeccapurple
```

Normally, when adding a change to the Selenium code base, we would start off by writing a failing test that uses the functionality that we are about to implement. However, in this case, the change is just the addition of a constant to an enum. It's a simple code change. So, we don't expect it to have any side effects, and we don't really need to add any more tests. Let's start with the additional code that we are going to add:

```
POWDERBLUE(new Color(176, 224, 230, 1d)),
PURPLE(new Color(128, 0, 128, 1d)),
REBECCAPURPLE(new Color(102, 51, 153, 1d)),
RED(new Color(255, 0, 0, 1d)),
ROSYBROWN(new Color(188, 143, 143, 1d)),
```

Everything else is currently there. So, the only color that we are adding is rebeccapurple. Now that we have added our change, we need to run tests to make sure that we didn't break anything. It would be a big surprise if our change did break something, but always run the tests anyway:

```
./go test_java_webdriver -trace
```

Now, we need to commit the change, as follows:

```
git commit -m "Add rebeccapurple to the Colors enum"
```

We are now ready to raise our pull request, but we have a bit more work to do. We need to make sure that our fork is up to date with the main Selenium repository. To do this, we need to add a remote and then pull in all the changes that have happened since we pulled down our copy of the Selenium repository. Let's add the remote first:

```
git remote add upstream https://github.com/SeleniumHQ/selenium.git
```

Then, pull down the latest code from the main Selenium repository and add it to our branch, as follows:

```
git fetch upstream
git rebase upstream/master
```

We now have the latest code on our local branch as well as the change. We need to push all of this up to our fork on GitHub, as follows:

```
git push origin rebeccapurple
```

We are now ready to make the pull request. Load your fork in GitHub with a browser, and you should see a big green button called **Compare & pull request**:

It's as simple as clicking the button. You will then be asked to confirm the branch that you want to generate the pull request with and the fork that you want to send it to:

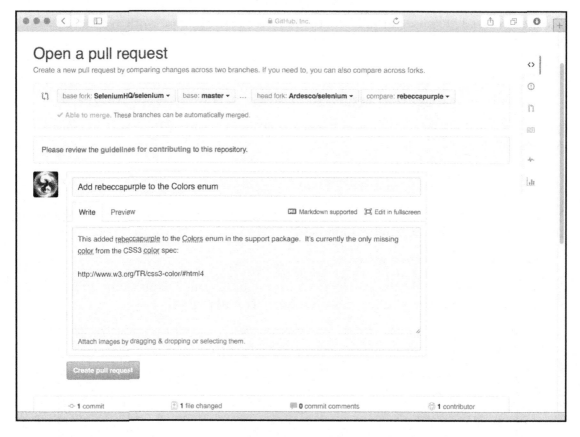

Creating a pull request

When you are happy, click on **Create pull request**, and your pull request will be generated for you. You will get a summary that tells you the state of your pull request, and a Travis CI build will be triggered:

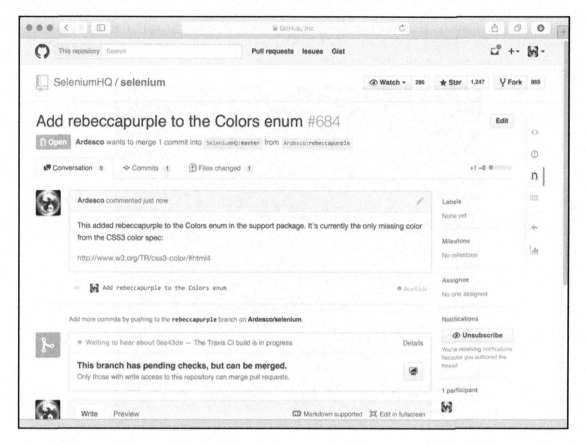

When this is complete, it's all ready to be merged. You can sit back and wait, or jump into the #selenium IRC channel and check whether you can find a core committer.

Keeping your history clean

Selenium is a large project with lots of contributors. Due to this, there are lots of commits happening all the time. To keep the commit history clean, the developers try to ensure that each pull request that they merge into the main branch is just a single commit. We didn't have a problem with our change, because it was very simple. However, if you have made some quite far-reaching changes and have many commits, you will probably find out that you have some tidying up to do.

First of all, don't worry. It's not a big problem. GIT has the ability to squash these multiple commits into one change. Let's have a look at how we can do this. We will start off with a project that has four commits that we want to squash into one:

```
commit 0eea1e81d8382d3add84e219b057c251b41d85fb
Author: Mark Collin <mark.collin@lazeryattack.com>
Date:   Thu Jun 18 20:45:51 2015 +0100

    Final bit of tidying, everything works and all the tests pass

commit dd3ccdf8cd9454dcee452ac0b27970fe290d7355
Author: Mark Collin <mark.collin@lazeryattack.com>
Date:   Thu Jun 18 20:45:17 2015 +0100

    Nearly done.

commit 498f31a372d1025e70da26556b4355fed0188fed
Author: Mark Collin <mark.collin@lazeryattack.com>
Date:   Thu Jun 18 20:45:01 2015 +0100

    It's all going well so far.

commit ad7ae7e6df169a323ad9995dc981e2db161afd1b
Author: Mark Collin <mark.collin@lazeryattack.com>
Date:   Thu Jun 18 20:44:16 2015 +0100

    Start of my great big change.

commit 0e67b7b688b505173264d4ba552b110a1985475b
Author: Daniel Davison <daniel.jj.davison@gmail.com>
Date:   Thu Jun 18 10:51:56 2015 -0400

    fix broken tests
```

Our four initial commits

We know that we have four commits. So, we are going to use the `rebase` command to interactively change these four commits and squash them into one, as follows:

```
git rebase -i HEAD~4
```

When you use the `rebase` command, Git will take the commits that you are interested in, show a screen that lists the commits, and ask what you want to do with them.

You may want to get hold of a VI cheat sheet from the internet at this point. If you are not used to VI, it can be quite frustrating. A reasonably good one is available at http://www.viemu.com/vi-vim-cheat-sheet.gif.

```
pick ad7ae7e Start of my great big change.
pick 498f31a It's all going well so far.
pick dd3ccdf Nearly done.
pick 0eea1e8 Final bit of tidying, everything works and all the tests pass

# Rebase 0e67b7b..0eea1e8 onto 0e67b7b (4 command(s))
#
# Commands:
# p, pick = use commit
# r, reword = use commit, but edit the commit message
# e, edit = use commit, but stop for amending
# s, squash = use commit, but meld into previous commit
# f, fixup = like "squash", but discard this commit's log message
# x, exec = run command (the rest of the line) using shell
#
# These lines can be re-ordered; they are executed from top to bottom.
#
# If you remove a line here THAT COMMIT WILL BE LOST.
#
# However, if you remove everything, the rebase will be aborted.
#
# Note that empty commits are commented out
```

We now need to tell Git to squash all the commits into just one commit. The commit at the top of the file was the original one. So, this is the one that we are going to leave as it is. The other commits will be squashed into this original commit:

```
pick ad7ae7e Start of my great big change.
squash 498f31a It's all going well so far.
squash dd3ccdf Nearly done.
squash 0eea1e8 Final bit of tidying, everything works and all the tests pass

# Rebase 0e67b7b..0eea1e8 onto 0e67b7b (4 command(s))
#
# Commands:
# p, pick = use commit
# r, reword = use commit, but edit the commit message
# e, edit = use commit, but stop for amending
# s, squash = use commit, but meld into previous commit
# f, fixup = like "squash", but discard this commit's log message
# x, exec = run command (the rest of the line) using shell
#
# These lines can be re-ordered; they are executed from top to bottom.
#
# If you remove a line here THAT COMMIT WILL BE LOST.
#
# However, if you remove everything, the rebase will be aborted.
#
# Note that empty commits are commented out
```

Now, we just need to save our changes. The easiest way to do this is by holding down *Shift* and pressing Z twice. You will then be presented with a screen asking you to specify a commit message for your newly squashed commit. You can either join together all the old commit messages, or you can use a completely new one:

```
# This is a combination of 4 commits.
My change squashed into one commit.

# Please enter the commit message for your changes. Lines starting
# with '#' will be ignored, and an empty message aborts the commit.
#
# Date:      Thu Jun 18 20:44:16 2015 +0100
#
# rebase in progress; onto 0e67b7b
# You are currently editing a commit while rebasing branch 'master' on '0e67b7b'.
#
# Changes to be committed:
#        modified:   .idea/compiler.xml
#        modified:   .idea/misc.xml
#
# Untracked files:
#        .idea/shelf/
#        android/
#        node_modules/
#
```

Again, we need to save our changes. Hold down *Shift* and press Z twice again. We have now squashed all the changes into one commit. We can check whether the whole process worked by checking out `git log` again:

```
commit e6a1b1fa4e3b5aff87088ce240a1576d0c3dd0ab
Author: Mark Collin <mark.collin@lazeryattack.com>
Date:    Thu Jun 18 20:44:16 2015 +0100

    My change squashed into one commit.

commit 0e67b7b688b505173264d4ba552b110a1985475b
Author: Daniel Davison <daniel.jj.davison@gmail.com>
Date:    Thu Jun 18 10:51:56 2015 -0400

    fix broken tests
```

Now that we have just the one change, let's push this to GitHub so that we can make our pull request, as follows:

```
git push
```

If you pushed the four commits to GitHub before you squashed your history, the push was probably rejected. It was rejected because rewriting the history for your code base can cause problems if somebody else is also using your repository and they have already pulled the latest revision of code.

In our case, we don't have to worry about this problem because nobody else is using our branch. To get the code pushed up to GitHub, we will force `push`, as follows:

```
git push -f
```

Now that our code has been pushed up to our fork on GitHub, we are ready to raise another pull request.

Now it's your turn

All in all, the commit process is quite simple. So, why don't you make some changes and submit a pull request right now? The Selenium developers have added a filter to the bug tracker on GitHub to identify the bugs that look like they may be quite simple.

These bugs are good candidates for people who want to work on the Selenium code base but aren't sure where to start. Have a look at `https://github.com/SeleniumHQ/selenium/issues?q=is%3Aopen+is%3Aissue+label%3AE-easy`.

Appendix B: Working with JUnit

In this appendix, we are going to have a look at the changes required to move away from TestNG and start using JUnit instead. These modifications are based on the code produced previously in the book. It assumes that you have all the modifications up to Chapter 8, *Keeping It Real*. However it should be easy to also just use the basic implementation you will have by the end of Chapter 2, *Producing the Right Feedback When Failing*, which gives you a basic test framework with a listener that will take screenshots if tests fail.

There are some caveats with the JUnit implementation; we will discuss these here as we modify the code.

Switching from TestNG to JUnit

First of all, we need to make some changes to our POM.xml to use JUnit instead of TestNG; we will start with the properties block:

```xml
<properties>
    <project.build.sourceEncoding>UTF-8</project.build.sourceEncoding>
    <project.reporting.outputEncoding>UTF-
8</project.reporting.outputEncoding>
    <java.version>1.8</java.version>
    <!-- Dependency versions -->
    <selenium.version>3.12.0</selenium.version>
    <junit.version>4.12</junit.version>
    <assertj-core.version>3.10.0</assertj-core.version>
    <query.version>1.2.0</query.version>
    <commons-io.version>2.6</commons-io.version>
    <httpclient.version>4.5.5</httpclient.version>
    <!-- Plugin versions -->
    <driver-binary-downloader-maven-plugin.version>1.0.17</driver-
binary-downloader-maven-plugin.version>
    <maven-compiler-plugin.version>3.7.0</maven-compiler-
plugin.version>
    <maven-failsafe-plugin.version>2.21.0</maven-failsafe-
plugin.version>
    <!-- Configurable variables -->
    <threads>1</threads>
    <browser>firefox</browser>
    <overwrite.binaries>false</overwrite.binaries>
    <headless>true</headless>
```

```
            <remote>false</remote>
            <seleniumGridURL/>
            <platform/>
            <browserVersion/>
            <screenshotDirectory>${project.build.directory}
            /screenshots</screenshotDirectory>
            <proxyEnabled>false</proxyEnabled>
            <proxyHost/>
            <proxyPort/>
        </properties>
```

Then we need to modify our dependencies. We are going to remove the testNG dependency and instead add in a Unit dependency:

```
<dependency>
        <groupId>junit</groupId>
        <artifactId>junit</artifactId>
        <version>${junit.version}</version>
        <scope>test</scope>
</dependency>
```

For the final changes to our POM.xml, we need to modify our plugin configuration:

```
<plugin>
        <groupId>org.apache.maven.plugins</groupId>
        <artifactId>maven-failsafe-plugin</artifactId>
        <version>${maven-failsafe-plugin.version}</version>
        <configuration>
            <parallel>methods</parallel>
            <threadCount>${threads}</threadCount>
            <perCoreThreadCount>false</perCoreThreadCount>
            <properties>
                <property>
                    <name>listener</name>
                    <value>com.masteringselenium.
                    listeners.ScreenshotListener</value>
                </property>
            </properties>
            <systemPropertyVariables>
                <browser>${browser}</browser>
                <headless>${headless}</headless>
                <remoteDriver>${remote}</remoteDriver>
                <gridURL>${seleniumGridURL}</gridURL>
                <desiredPlatform>${platform}</desiredPlatform>
                <desiredBrowserVersion>${browserVersion}
                </desiredBrowserVersion>
                <screenshotDirectory>${screenshotDirectory}
                </screenshotDirectory>
```

```
                <proxyEnabled>${proxyEnabled}</proxyEnabled>
                <proxyHost>${proxyHost}</proxyHost>
                <proxyPort>${proxyPort}</proxyPort>
                <!--Set properties passed in by the driver binary
                downloader-->
                <webdriver.chrome.driver>${webdriver.chrome.driver}
                </webdriver.chrome.driver>
                <webdriver.ie.driver>${webdriver.ie.driver}
                </webdriver.ie.driver>
                <webdriver.opera.driver>${webdriver.opera.driver}
                </webdriver.opera.driver>
                <webdriver.gecko.driver>${webdriver.gecko.driver}
                </webdriver.gecko.driver>
                <webdriver.edge.driver>${webdriver.edge.driver}
                </webdriver.edge.driver>
            </systemPropertyVariables>
        </configuration>
        <executions>
            <execution>
                <goals>
                    <goal>integration-test</goal>
                    <goal>verify</goal>
                </goals>
            </execution>
        </executions>
    </plugin>
```

The first change is to add the
`<perCoreThreadCount>false</perCoreThreadCount>` configuration setting. When
using the surefire plugin with JUnit, the plugin applies the thread count to each CPU core
you have in your machine. We want to make sure that we are supplying a total number of
browsers, not defaulting to eight browsers if you have an eight-core machine.

The second change is to specify the location of our `ScreenshotListener` class; we can't
apply it using an annotation in code, like we did with TestNG. As a result, we are using the
Maven Failsafe plugin configuration block to apply it instead.

Now we need to make some changes to our `DriverBase` class:

```
package com.masteringselenium;

import com.masteringselenium.config.DriverFactory;
import net.lightbody.bmp.BrowserMobProxy;
import org.junit.After;
import org.junit.AfterClass;
import org.junit.BeforeClass;
import org.openqa.selenium.remote.RemoteWebDriver;

import java.net.MalformedURLException;
import java.util.ArrayList;
import java.util.Collections;
import java.util.List;

public class DriverBase {

    private static List<DriverFactory> webDriverThreadPool =
    Collections.synchronizedList(new ArrayList<DriverFactory>());
    private static ThreadLocal<DriverFactory> driverThread;

    @BeforeClass
    public static void instantiateDriverObject() {
        driverThread = new ThreadLocal<DriverFactory>() {
            @Override
            protected DriverFactory initialValue() {
                DriverFactory webDriverThread = new DriverFactory();
                webDriverThreadPool.add(webDriverThread);
                return webDriverThread;
            }
        };
    }

    public static RemoteWebDriver getBrowserMobProxyEnabledDriver()
    throws MalformedURLException {
        return driverThread.get().getDriver(true);
    }

    public static RemoteWebDriver getDriver() throws
    MalformedURLException {
        return driverThread.get().getDriver();
    }

    public static BrowserMobProxy getBrowserMobProxy() {
        return driverThread.get().getBrowserMobProxy();
    }
```

```
    @After
    public void clearCookies() {
        try {
            getDriver().manage().deleteAllCookies();
        } catch (Exception ex) {
            System.err.println("Unable to delete cookies: " + ex);
        }
    }

    @AfterClass
    public static void closeDriverObjects() {
        for (DriverFactory webDriverThread : webDriverThreadPool) {
            webDriverThread.quitDriver();
        }
    }
}
```

There aren't many changes here. We have switched out the TestNG annotations for JUnit ones, and we have removed the @Listener annotation because JUnit doesn't have an equivalent. This does mean that whilst running our tests through an IDE, we will no longer get screenshots on failure. Don't worry though, it will still work when running the build on the command line using Maven. You will still be able to collect screenshots on your CI server if things go wrong.

Finally, we need to modify our ScreenshotListener class to work with JUnit instead of TestNG:

```
package com.masteringselenium.listeners;

import org.junit.runner.notification.Failure;
import org.junit.runner.notification.RunListener;
import org.openqa.selenium.OutputType;
import org.openqa.selenium.TakesScreenshot;
import org.openqa.selenium.WebDriver;
import org.openqa.selenium.remote.Augmenter;

import java.io.File;
import java.io.FileOutputStream;
import java.io.IOException;

import static com.masteringselenium.DriverBase.getDriver;


public class ScreenshotListener extends RunListener {

    private boolean createFile(File screenshot) {
        boolean fileCreated = false;
```

```java
            if (screenshot.exists()) {
                fileCreated = true;
            } else {
                File parentDirectory = new File(screenshot.getParent());
                if (parentDirectory.exists() || parentDirectory.mkdirs()) {
                    try {
                        fileCreated = screenshot.createNewFile();
                    } catch (IOException errorCreatingScreenshot) {
                        errorCreatingScreenshot.printStackTrace();
                    }
                }
            }

        return fileCreated;
    }

    private void writeScreenshotToFile(WebDriver driver, File
    screenshot) {
        try {
            FileOutputStream screenshotStream = new
            FileOutputStream(screenshot);
            screenshotStream.write(((TakesScreenshot)
            driver).getScreenshotAs(OutputType.BYTES));
            screenshotStream.close();
        } catch (IOException unableToWriteScreenshot) {
            System.err.println("Unable to write " +
            screenshot.getAbsolutePath());
            unableToWriteScreenshot.printStackTrace();
        }
    }

    @Override
    public void testFailure(Failure failure) {
        try {
            WebDriver driver = getDriver();
            String screenshotDirectory =
            System.getProperty("screenshotDirectory",
            "target/screenshots");
            String screenshotAbsolutePath = screenshotDirectory +
            File.separator + System.currentTimeMillis() + "_" +
            failure.getDescription().getMethodName() + ".png";
            File screenshot = new File(screenshotAbsolutePath);
            if (createFile(screenshot)) {
                try {
                    writeScreenshotToFile(driver, screenshot);
                } catch (ClassCastException
                weNeedToAugmentOurDriverObject) {
                    writeScreenshotToFile(new
```

```
                    Augmenter().augment(driver), screenshot);
            }
            System.out.println("Written screenshot to " +
            screenshotAbsolutePath);
        } else {
            System.err.println("Unable to create " +
            screenshotAbsolutePath);
        }
    } catch (Exception ex) {
        System.err.println("Unable to capture screenshot: " +
        ex.getCause());

    }
  }
}
```

Again, the changes are minimal. We now extend `RunListener`, which is part of JUnit, instead of `TestListenerAdaptor` provided by TestNG. The name of the class we need to override has changed and it passes in a different variable. This means that we need to slightly change the code that gets the name of the failing test.

The only thing that is left to do is to modify the imports on our tests; you use the JUnit `@Test` annotation instead of the TestNG `@Test` annotation. To do this, we need to find all instances of the following:

```
import org.testng.annotations.Test;
```

We replace them with the following:

```
import org.junit.Test;
```

You are now ready to try running your tests again; let's perform the following in the Terminal to check that everything still works:

`mvn clean verify`

Let's check that threading still works as well:

`mvn clean verify -Dthreads=2`

Excellent. Everything seems to be working correctly; we now have a working JUnit implementation.

I did, however, mention that there would be some caveats, and unfortunately they are not instantly obvious. JUnit does not have a concept of `@BeforeSuite` like TestNG, so we have used the `@BeforeClass` annotation instead. When you have a single test class, it would appear to work in the same way as `@BeforeSuite`, however, that's not true. When we were using before suite, we could configure our thread pool before any tests were run and then clean it up after all tests were run. With the JUnit implementation, we configure our thread pool before each class is run and then clean it up after each class is run. It's a small difference, but it does result in more browser startup/shutdown time.

The easiest way to show this is by adding another test class. Copy the existing one and give it a slightly different name. Once you have done that, tweak the tests to search with a slightly different criteria. Now try running the following code again:

```
mvn clean verify -Dthreads=2
```

You will notice that, this time, two browser windows opened, the tests in the first class were run, and then the browser windows shut again. They then opened up again and ran the tests for the second class. You can add more tests to each of your test classes to reassure yourself that the browsers are being reused inside the class.

Summary

In this chapter, we took our original TestNG Selenium implementation and looked at how it needed to be modified to support Unit. By the end of this chapter, you will have a working JUnit implementation with functionality that is very similar to the TestNG implementation.

Appendix C: Introduction to Appium

In this appendix, we are going to look at how we can build up a basic Appium implementation that will look very similar to the Selenium implementation, we have been creating throughout the rest of the book. This should provide you with a springboard to start expanding from Selenium automation to Appium automation.

Creating an Appium framework

We are going to structure our Appium framework in a very similar way to our Selenium framework. We will have a base method that our tests can inherit from, some familiar looking configuration classes and a very similar POM.xml to hold our dependencies. Let's start off with our POM file:

```xml
<?xml version="1.0" encoding="UTF-8"?>
<project xmlns="http://maven.apache.org/POM/4.0.0"
         xmlns:xsi="http://www.w3.org/2001/XMLSchema-instance"
         xsi:schemaLocation="http://maven.apache.org/POM/4.0.0
         http://maven.apache.org/xsd/maven-4.0.0.xsd">

    <groupId>com.masteringselenium.demo</groupId>
    <artifactId>mastering-selenium-appium</artifactId>
    <version>DEV-SNAPSHOT</version>
    <modelVersion>4.0.0</modelVersion>

    <name>Mastering Selenium with Appium</name>
    <description>A basic Appium POM file</description>
    <url>http://www.masteringselenium.com</url>

    <properties>
        <project.build.sourceEncoding>UTF-
        8</project.build.sourceEncoding>
        <project.reporting.outputEncoding>UTF-
        8</project.reporting.outputEncoding>
        <java.version>1.8</java.version>
        <!-- Dependency versions -->
        <appium-java.version>6.1.0</appium-java.version>
        <selenium.version>3.12.0</selenium.version>
```

```xml
                <testng.version>6.14.3</testng.version>
                <assertj-core.version>3.10.0</assertj-core.version>
                <query.version>1.2.0</query.version>
                <!-- Plugin versions -->
                <maven-compiler-plugin.version>3.7.0
                </maven-compiler-plugin.version>
                <!-- Configurable variables -->
                <threads>1</threads>
                <remote>false</remote>
                <enableDebugMode>false</enableDebugMode>
                <appiumServerURL/>
                <screenshotDirectory>${project.build.directory}
                /screenshots</screenshotDirectory>
        </properties>
        <build>
            <plugins>
                <plugin>
                    <groupId>org.apache.maven.plugins</groupId>
                    <artifactId>maven-compiler-plugin</artifactId>
                    <configuration>
                        <source>${java.version}</source>
                        <target>${java.version}</target>
                    </configuration>
                    <version>${maven-compiler-plugin.version}</version>
                </plugin>
            </plugins>
        </build>

        <dependencies>
            <dependency>
                <groupId>io.appium</groupId>
                <artifactId>java-client</artifactId>
                <version>${appium-java.version}</version>
                <scope>test</scope>
            </dependency>
            <dependency>
                <groupId>org.seleniumhq.selenium</groupId>
                <artifactId>selenium-java</artifactId>
                <version>${selenium.version}</version>
                <scope>test</scope>
            </dependency>
            <dependency>
                <groupId>org.testng</groupId>
                <artifactId>testng</artifactId>
                <version>${testng.version}</version>
                <scope>test</scope>
            </dependency>
            <dependency>
```

```
            <groupId>org.assertj</groupId>
            <artifactId>assertj-core</artifactId>
            <version>${assertj-core.version}</version>
            <scope>test</scope>
        </dependency>
        <dependency>
            <groupId>com.lazerycode.selenium</groupId>
            <artifactId>query</artifactId>
            <version>${query.version}</version>
            <scope>test</scope>
        </dependency>
    </dependencies>
</project>
```

This looks very similar to our Selenium POM file, we have a series of dependencies for the libraries that we are going to use in our framework. You will notice that most of them were also in our Selenium framework, the new one is the Appium dependency. Next we need to create a standard directory structure for a Maven project. We are working towards creating this file structure:

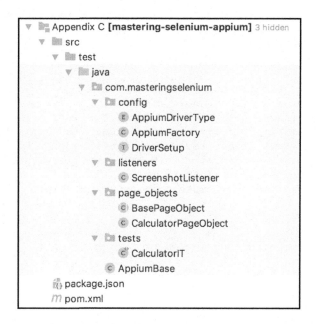

Let's get started on the configuration code. First of all we are going to create an interface called `DriverSetup`:

```
package com.masteringselenium.config;

import io.appium.java_client.AppiumDriver;
import io.appium.java_client.android.Activity;
import org.openqa.selenium.remote.DesiredCapabilities;

import java.net.URL;

public interface DriverSetup {
    DriverSetup createAppiumObject(URL appiumServerLocation,
    DesiredCapabilities capabilities);

    DriverSetup setActivity(Activity activity);

    AppiumDriver getAppiumDriver();
}
```

This sets up our three methods that each type of Appium driver is going to need to implement. Next, we have an `AppiumDriverType` class:

```
package com.masteringselenium.config;

import io.appium.java_client.AppiumDriver;
import io.appium.java_client.android.Activity;
import io.appium.java_client.android.AndroidDriver;
import io.appium.java_client.remote.AndroidMobileCapabilityType;
import io.appium.java_client.remote.AutomationName;
import io.appium.java_client.remote.MobileCapabilityType;
import org.openqa.selenium.Platform;
import org.openqa.selenium.remote.DesiredCapabilities;

import java.net.URL;

public enum AppiumDriverType implements DriverSetup {


    ANDROID {
        public AppiumDriverType createAppiumObject(URL
        appiumServerLocation, DesiredCapabilities desiredCapabilities)
        {
            capabilities = desiredCapabilities;
            serverLocation = appiumServerLocation;
            capabilities.setCapability(MobileCapabilityType.
            PLATFORM_NAME, Platform.ANDROID);
```

```
        capabilities.setCapability(MobileCapabilityType
        .AUTOMATION_NAME, AutomationName.APPIUM);
        capabilities.setCapability(MobileCapabilityType.
        DEVICE_NAME, "Android Device");

        if (ENABLE_DEBUG_MODE) {
            capabilities.setCapability(MobileCapabilityType.
            NEW_COMMAND_TIMEOUT, "3600");
        }

        return this;
    }

    public AppiumDriver getAppiumDriver() {
        return new AndroidDriver(serverLocation, capabilities);
    }

};

    private static final boolean ENABLE_DEBUG_MODE =
    Boolean.getBoolean("enableDebugMode");
    DesiredCapabilities capabilities;
    URL serverLocation;

    public AppiumDriverType setActivity(Activity activity) {
        capabilities.setCapability(AndroidMobileCapabilityType
        .APP_PACKAGE, activity.getAppPackage());
        capabilities.setCapability(AndroidMobileCapabilityType
        .APP_ACTIVITY, activity.getAppActivity());

        return this;
    }
}
```

For this example, we are just going to get up and running with Android. If you look for second-hand Android phones you can easily buy a relatively powerful Samsung phone that is ideal for practising your android scripts on. It's also less hassle to set up because you don't need to worry about creating an Apple developer account. Let's walk through the preceding code. First of all, we have some generic desired capabilities that need to be set all the time. PLATFORM_NAME let's Appium know what sort of device to expect. AUTOMATION_NAME lets Appium know what method to use when running the tests (so, for android, you could have APPIUM, ESPRESSO, SELENDROID, and so on.)

If a particular implementation doesn't work for you, you can always switch over to another one and see if you fare better. Finally, we set a device name; this is a Selenium requirement, the name can be anything as long as it is set.

You will then see that we check to see if we have a boolean flag set called ENABLE_DEBUG_MODE. By default, the Appium server will time out and shut itself down if it doesn't see any commands for 15 seconds. When you are stepping through code trying to work out what has gone wrong you probably want a bit more time than that. This updates the command timeout to be 5 minutes. That should be lots of time to pause for a ponder whilst debugging.

Finally, we have some Android-specific code. You can get Appium to install packages on your device for you, however this can be quite time consuming. If you know the package is already installed, you can also specify the activity to start. That's the method we are going to use.

Now we need to create our `AppiumFactory` class:

```
package com.masteringselenium.config;

import io.appium.java_client.AppiumDriver;
import io.appium.java_client.android.Activity;
import io.appium.java_client.remote.MobileCapabilityType;
import org.openqa.selenium.Platform;
import org.openqa.selenium.remote.DesiredCapabilities;

import java.net.MalformedURLException;
import java.net.URL;
import java.util.Optional;

import static com.masteringselenium.config.AppiumDriverType.ANDROID;

public class AppiumFactory {

    private AppiumDriver driver;
    private AppiumDriverType selectedDriverConfiguration;
    private Activity currentActivity;

    private static final boolean USE_SELENIUM_GRID =
    Boolean.getBoolean("useSeleniumGrid");
    private static final String DEFAULT_SERVER_LOCATION =
    "http://127.0.0.1:4723/wd/hub";
    private static String APPIUM_SERVER_LOCATION =
    System.getProperty("appiumServerLocation",
    DEFAULT_SERVER_LOCATION);
```

```
public AppiumFactory() {
    AppiumDriverType driverType = ANDROID;
    String appiumConfig = System.getProperty("appiumConfig",
    driverType.toString()).toUpperCase();
    if (null == APPIUM_SERVER_LOCATION ||
    APPIUM_SERVER_LOCATION.trim().isEmpty()) {
        APPIUM_SERVER_LOCATION = DEFAULT_SERVER_LOCATION;
    }
    try {
        driverType = AppiumDriverType.valueOf(appiumConfig);
    } catch (IllegalArgumentException ignored) {
        System.err.println("Unknown driver specified,
        defaulting to '" + driverType + "'...");
    } catch (NullPointerException ignored) {
        System.err.println("No driver specified,
        defaulting to '" + driverType + "'...");
    }
    selectedDriverConfiguration = driverType;
}

public AppiumDriver getDriver() throws Exception {
    return getDriver(currentActivity);
}

public AppiumDriver getDriver(Activity desiredActivity)
throws Exception {
    if (null != currentActivity &&
    !currentActivity.equals(desiredActivity)) {
        quitDriver();
    }
    if (null == driver) {
        currentActivity = desiredActivity;
        instantiateWebDriver(selectedDriverConfiguration);
    }

    return driver;
}

public void quitDriver() {
    if (null != driver) {
        driver.quit();
        driver = null;
        currentActivity = null;
    }
}

private void instantiateWebDriver(AppiumDriverType
appiumDriverType) throws MalformedURLException {
```

```
System.out.println("Current Appium Config Selection: " +
selectedDriverConfiguration);
System.out.println("Current Appium Server Location: " +
APPIUM_SERVER_LOCATION);
System.out.println("Connecting to Selenium Grid: " +
USE_SELENIUM_GRID);

DesiredCapabilities desiredCapabilities = new
DesiredCapabilities();
if (Boolean.getBoolean("enableDebugMode")) {
    desiredCapabilities.setCapability(MobileCapabilityType
    .NEW_COMMAND_TIMEOUT, "3600");
}
Optional.ofNullable(System.getProperty("device_id", null))
        .ifPresent(deviceID -> desiredCapabilities.
        setCapability(MobileCapabilityType.UDID, deviceID));
if (USE_SELENIUM_GRID) {
    URL seleniumGridURL = new
    URL(System.getProperty("gridURL"));
    String desiredVersion =
    System.getProperty("desiredVersion");
    String desiredPlatform =
    System.getProperty("desiredPlatform");

    if (null != desiredPlatform && !desiredPlatform.isEmpty())
    {
        desiredCapabilities.setPlatform
        (Platform.valueOf(desiredPlatform.toUpperCase()));
    }

    if (null != desiredVersion && !desiredVersion.isEmpty())
    {
        desiredCapabilities.setVersion(desiredVersion);
    }

    desiredCapabilities.setBrowserName
    (selectedDriverConfiguration.toString());
    driver = new AppiumDriver(seleniumGridURL,
    desiredCapabilities);
} else {
    driver = appiumDriverType.createAppiumObject(new
    URL(APPIUM_SERVER_LOCATION), desiredCapabilities)
            .setActivity(currentActivity)
            .getAppiumDriver();
}
    }
}
```

This will look very similar to the driver factory we were working with previously. When we instantiate `AppiumFactory`, we look for an environment variable called `appiumConfig`. If we find it, we try to convert it into one of our `AppiumDriverType` objects. In our case, we only have a single type defined, our Android one. This will be useful in the future if we expand our implementation to support different devices. The other main thing we do on instantiation is work out where our Appium server is running. We have some error checking around this to make sure that at a minimum, we always try to run against an Appium instance running locally on the default port.

We then have a couple of `getDriver()` methods. One of them allows to start up a specific activity (for example, the *Calculator* app), or switch activity. The other one just returns the current driver object, we are already using. We next have a very similar `quitDriver()` method that closes everything down. Finally, we use our `instantiateWebDriver` method. This is the method that works out if we are connecting to a Selenium-Grid, or a local Appium server and instantiates our driver object.

We are still going to want to get a screenshot when our tests fail, so the next bit of setup that we need to perform is to create `ScreenshotListener`:

```
package com.masteringselenium.listeners;

import org.openqa.selenium.OutputType;
import org.openqa.selenium.TakesScreenshot;
import org.openqa.selenium.WebDriver;
import org.openqa.selenium.remote.Augmenter;
import org.testng.ITestResult;
import org.testng.TestListenerAdapter;

import java.io.File;
import java.io.FileOutputStream;
import java.io.IOException;

import static com.masteringselenium.AppiumBase.getDriver;

public class ScreenshotListener extends TestListenerAdapter {

    private static boolean createFile(File screenshot) {
        boolean fileCreated = false;

        if (screenshot.exists()) {
            fileCreated = true;
        } else {
            File parentDirectory = new File(screenshot.getParent());
            if (parentDirectory.exists() || parentDirectory.mkdirs()) {
                try {
```

```
                fileCreated = screenshot.createNewFile();
            } catch (IOException errorCreatingScreenshot) {
                errorCreatingScreenshot.printStackTrace();
            }
        }
    }

    return fileCreated;
}

private static void writeScreenshotToFile(WebDriver driver,
File screenshot) {
    try {
        FileOutputStream screenshotStream = new
        FileOutputStream(screenshot);
        screenshotStream.write(((TakesScreenshot)
        driver).getScreenshotAs(OutputType.BYTES));
        screenshotStream.close();
    } catch (IOException unableToWriteScreenshot) {
        System.err.println("Unable to write " +
        screenshot.getAbsolutePath());
        unableToWriteScreenshot.printStackTrace();
    }
}

public static void takeScreenshot(WebDriver driver,
String filename) {
    String screenshotDirectory =
    System.getProperty("screenshotDirectory",
    "build/screenshots");
    String screenshotAbsolutePath = screenshotDirectory +
    File.separator + System.currentTimeMillis() + "_" +
    filename + ".png";
    File screenshot = new File(screenshotAbsolutePath);
    if (createFile(screenshot)) {
        try {
            writeScreenshotToFile(driver, screenshot);
        } catch (ClassCastException weNeedToAugmentOurDriverObject)
        {
            writeScreenshotToFile(new Augmenter().augment(driver),
            screenshot);
        }
        System.out.println("Written screenshot to " +
        screenshotAbsolutePath);
    } else {
        System.err.println("Unable to create " +
        screenshotAbsolutePath);
    }
```

```
        }

        @Override
        public void onTestFailure(ITestResult failingTest) {
            try {
                takeScreenshot(getDriver(), failingTest.getName());
            } catch (Exception ex) {
                System.err.println("Unable to capture screenshot...");
                ex.printStackTrace();
            }
        }
    }
}
```

This is a standard TestNG listener and is virtually identical to the one we used before. It does exactly the same thing, when a test fails it takes a screenshot so that we can see what was on the device at the point of failure.

Now that we have all of our config setup we need to create our `AppiumBase` file:

```
package com.masteringselenium;

import com.masteringselenium.config.AppiumFactory;
import com.masteringselenium.listeners.ScreenshotListener;
import io.appium.java_client.AppiumDriver;
import io.appium.java_client.android.Activity;
import org.testng.annotations.AfterSuite;
import org.testng.annotations.BeforeSuite;
import org.testng.annotations.Listeners;

import java.util.ArrayList;
import java.util.Collections;
import java.util.List;

@Listeners(ScreenshotListener.class)
public class AppiumBase {

    private static List<AppiumFactory> webDriverThreadPool =
    Collections.synchronizedList(new ArrayList<AppiumFactory>());
    private static ThreadLocal<AppiumFactory> appiumFactory;

    @BeforeSuite
    public static void instantiateDriverObject() {
        appiumFactory = new ThreadLocal<AppiumFactory>() {
            @Override
            protected AppiumFactory initialValue() {
                AppiumFactory appiumFactory = new AppiumFactory();
                webDriverThreadPool.add(appiumFactory);
```

```
                return appiumFactory;
            }
        };
    }

    public static AppiumDriver getDriver() throws Exception {
        return appiumFactory.get().getDriver();
    }

    public static AppiumDriver getDriver(Activity desiredActivity)
    throws Exception {
        return appiumFactory.get().getDriver(desiredActivity);
    }

    @AfterSuite(alwaysRun = true)
    public static void closeDriverObjects() {
        for (AppiumFactory appiumFactory : webDriverThreadPool) {
            appiumFactory.quitDriver();
        }
    }
}
```

This looks just like our previous `DriverBase` file. We have the same thread pool, the same clean up method and the same `getDriver()` method. The new method that we have is our secondary `getDriver()` method that allows us to switch to a specific activity as noted earlier.

We, now have everything we need to start writing some basic tests.

Automating the Android calculator

We are going to write a basic automation script that will enable us to perform some sums with the build in Android calculator. The first thing we are going to do is configure `BasePageObject` that all future page objects can extend as we did in our Selenium framework:

```
package com.masteringselenium.page_objects;

import com.masteringselenium.AppiumBase;
import io.appium.java_client.AppiumDriver;
import io.appium.java_client.TouchAction;
import org.openqa.selenium.support.ui.WebDriverWait;

public abstract class BasePageObject {

    AppiumDriver driver;
```

```
WebDriverWait webDriverWait;
TouchAction touchAction;

BasePageObject() {
try {
this.driver = AppiumBase.getDriver();
    } catch (Exception ignored) {
    //This will be be thrown when the test starts
    //if it cannot connect to a RemoteWebDriver Instance
    }

    this.webDriverWait = new WebDriverWait(driver, 30, 250);
    this.touchAction = new TouchAction(driver);
  }
}
```

This is going to provide an easy way for our page objects to get an `AppiumDriver` instance as well as giving us a couple of useful objects that will probably be used more than once, a `WebDriverWait` object and a `TouchAction` object. The next job is to create `CalculatorPageObject`, but to do this we are going to need a way to examine the calculator object on a device. To do that we will need to download the Appium desktop application which is available at `https://github.com/appium/appium-desktop/releases`. While you are doing that you will also want to install ADB, this will be useful to query the device you are using to get hold of package names. You can get ADB at `https://developer.android.com/studio/command-line/adb`.

Once you have got these packages installed, you are ready to start up Appium desktop, it will look like this:

First of all you will want to click on **Start Server**, which will provide you with this screen:

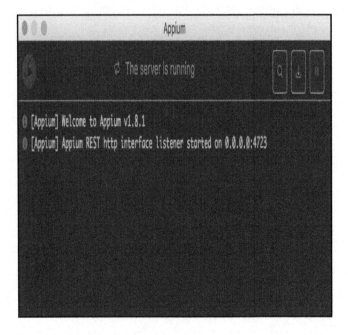

Next we want to click on the magnifying glass icon in the top left. This will pop up a box that looks like this:

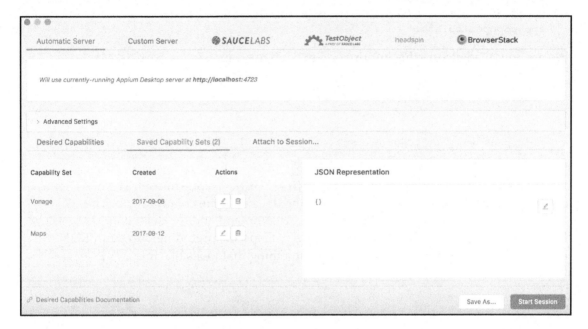

To start a debug session, we need to configure DesiredCapabilities. We can do this by generating a JSON representation of DesiredCapabilities. To do this, we now need to connect our Android device to our machine via a USB cable and find out which calculator package is installed. Samsung bundles their own calculator app so if you are not using a Samsung device you may find a different package.

 Don't forget to put your test device into development mode before trying to use ADB commands. If it isn't in the development mode, it will just ignore the commands. To turn it on you normally go to **Settings | About phone | Build number** and then tap on the build number seven times, different devices may have slightly different way to enable it though.

The command you need to type into your Terminal is:

```
adb shell pm list packages -f |grep calc
```

On a Samsung S6 it returns the following:

```
package:/system/priv-
app/SecCalculator_N/SecCalculator_N.apk=com.sec.android.
app.popupcalculator
```

We are now ready to use this information to configure our `DesiredCapabilities`:

```
{
  "platformName": "Android",
  "deviceName": "Samsung S6",
  "appPackage": "com.sec.android.app.popupcalculator",
  "appActivity": ".Calculator"
}
```

We have an android device, so we are using `platformName` of Android. The `deviceName` can be anything, so I have used the name of the device we are connecting to. The `appPackage` is the one we found using our `ADB` command and the default `appActivity` for calculator apps in Android is `.Calculator`. Copy the preceding into your JSON representation block and you should have something that looks like this:

Now click on **Start Session** and Appium will launch the *Calculator* app, and load a view of what you can see on your device in the session window:

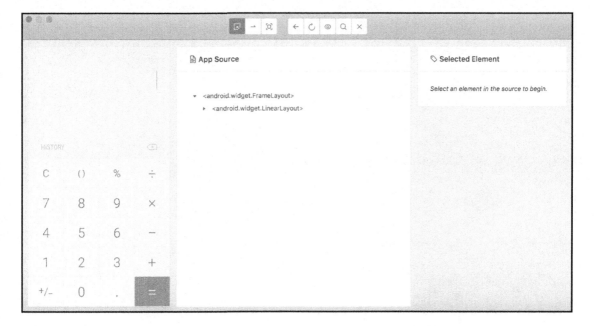

You can now select elements on the screen and get locator information. We are going to use this to build up our page object:

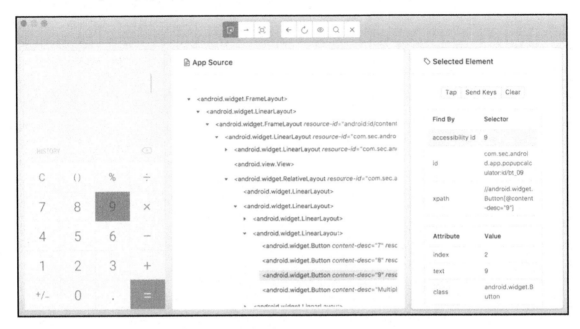

Here is our `CalculatorPageObject`, if you are not using a Samsung device you may have slightly different locators, but generally the page object should look very similar:

```java
package com.masteringselenium.page_objects;

import com.lazerycode.selenium.util.Query;
import io.appium.java_client.MobileBy;
import io.appium.java_client.touch.offset.ElementOption;

import java.util.Collections;
import java.util.HashMap;
import java.util.Map;

import static io.appium.java_client.touch.TapOptions.tapOptions;

public class CalculatorPageObject extends BasePageObject {

    private Query one = new Query(MobileBy.AccessibilityId("1"),
    driver);
    private Query two = new Query(MobileBy.AccessibilityId("2"),
    driver);
    private Query three = new Query(MobileBy.AccessibilityId("3"),
```

```
driver);
private Query four = new Query(MobileBy.AccessibilityId("4"),
driver);
private Query five = new Query(MobileBy.AccessibilityId("5"),
driver);
private Query six = new Query(MobileBy.AccessibilityId("6"),
driver);
private Query seven = new Query(MobileBy.AccessibilityId("7"),
driver);
private Query eight = new Query(MobileBy.AccessibilityId("8"),
driver);
private Query nine = new Query(MobileBy.AccessibilityId("9"),
driver);
private Query zero = new Query(MobileBy.AccessibilityId("0"),
driver);
private Query addButton = new
Query(MobileBy.AccessibilityId("Plus"), driver);
private Query subtractButton = new
Query(MobileBy.AccessibilityId("Minus"), driver);
private Query equalsButton = new
Query(MobileBy.AccessibilityId("Equal"), driver);
private Query result = new
Query(MobileBy.id("com.sec.android.app.popupcalculator:id
/txtCalc"), driver);

private final Map<Character, Query> NUMBERS =
Collections.unmodifiableMap(
        new HashMap<Character, Query>() {{
            put('1', one);
            put('2', two);
            put('3', three);
            put('4', four);
            put('5', five);
            put('6', six);
            put('7', seven);
            put('8', eight);
            put('9', nine);
            put('0', zero);
        }});

public CalculatorPageObject enterNumber(String number) {
    for (Character digit : number.toCharArray()) {
        touchAction.tap(tapOptions()
        .withElement(ElementOption.element(NUMBERS.
        get(digit).findMobileElement())))).perform();
    }

    return this;
```

```
    }

    public CalculatorPageObject add() {
        touchAction.tap(tapOptions().withElement
        (ElementOption.element(addButton.findMobileElement())))
        .perform();

        return this;
    }

    public CalculatorPageObject subtract() {
        touchAction.tap(tapOptions().withElement
        (ElementOption.element(subtractButton.findMobileElement())))
        .perform();

        return this;
    }

    public String equals() {
        touchAction.tap(tapOptions().withElement
        (ElementOption.element(equalsButton.findMobileElement())))
        .perform();

        return result.findMobileElement().getText();
    }

}
```

This is again fairly self explanatory. At the top, we have a series of Query elements that can be used to locate elements on the screen. Then we have a method that will take a number string and convert it into a series of tap events. Then we have some methods that will hit some individual buttons like plugin and minus. Finally, we have an equals method that will hit the equals button and then capture the value currently displayed on the screen. If you are still in your inspector session at this point, you can quit and go back to the running Appium server, we are about to use to run a test.

Before we can run that test, however, we are going to need to write it, but that's very straightforward now that we have our page object. Here it is:

```
package com.masteringselenium.tests;

import com.masteringselenium.AppiumBase;
import com.masteringselenium.page_objects.CalculatorPageObject;
import io.appium.java_client.android.Activity;
import org.testng.annotations.BeforeMethod;
import org.testng.annotations.Test;
```

```java
import static org.assertj.core.api.AssertionsForClassTypes.assertThat;

public class CalculatorIT extends AppiumBase {

    @BeforeMethod
    public void setCorrectActivity() throws Exception {
        String appPackage = "com.sec.android.app.popupcalculator";
        String appActivity = ".Calculator";
        getDriver(new Activity(appPackage, appActivity));
    }

    @Test
    public void AddNumbersTogether() {
        CalculatorPageObject calculatorPageObject = new
        CalculatorPageObject();

        String result = calculatorPageObject.enterNumber("100")
                .add()
                .enterNumber("27")
                .equals();

        assertThat(result).isEqualTo("127");
    }
}
```

We have two pieces to our test. First of all before we start running the test, we invoke the calculator activity in `@BeforeMethod`. We could do this inside the test as well, but the advantage of doing it outside the test is if we have multiple tests, we would want to run them inside the same activity.

Our test is then quite self explanatory. We enter a number, tap add, enter another number, and then tap equals. Finally, we compare the value that was returned after we tapped equals to make sure it matches our expectation.

Congratulations, you have just written your first Appium test.

Running the tests through Maven

We currently have a test that works fine in IntelliJ, but we haven't put any configuration in our POM file yet to enable us to run this test through Maven. Let's create a Maven profile that will allow us to do that. First of all, we need to add a property to define our `maven-failsafe-plugin` version:

```
<maven-failsafe-plugin.version>2.21.0</maven-failsafe-plugin.version>
```

Then we need to add a new profile:

```
<profiles>
    <profile>
        <id>appiumAlreadyRunning</id>
        <activation>
            <property>
                <name>!invokeAppium</name>
            </property>
        </activation>
        <build>
            <plugins>
                <plugin>
                    <groupId>org.apache.maven.plugins</groupId>
                    <artifactId>maven-failsafe-plugin</artifactId>
                    <version>${maven-failsafe-plugin.version}</version>
                    <configuration>
                        <systemPropertyVariables>
                            <appiumServerLocation>${appiumServerURL}
                            </appiumServerLocation>
                            <enableDebugMode>${enableDebugMode}
                            </enableDebugMode>
                        <screenshotDirectory>
                        ${project.build.directory}
                        /screenshots</screenshotDirectory>
                            <remoteDriver>${remote}</remoteDriver>
                            <appiumConfig>${appiumConfig}
                            </appiumConfig>
                        </systemPropertyVariables>
                    </configuration>
                    <executions>
                        <execution>
                            <goals>
                                <goal>integration-test</goal>
                                <goal>verify</goal>
                            </goals>
                        </execution>
                    </executions>
```

```
            </plugin>
        </plugins>
    </build>
</profile>
</profiles>
```

This will look very similar to `maven-failsafe-plugin` that we have set up in our Selenium framework. What is slightly different is the way we are using `<activation>` this time. We are looking to see if a property called `invokeAppium` has been set. If it hasn't, we run this profile. This means that by default this profile will always run. We will explain why we have used activation in this way later on in this chapter. For now, we can try running our tests through Maven.

First of all, we will need to start up our Appium server (if you don't still have it running). Then on the command line you will need to type:

```
mvn clean verify
```

You should see the Maven build start up and it will connect to the Appium server that you have started. It will then successfully complete the tests. This is great, if you are happy starting and stopping an Appium server by yourself, but it's not yet a system that does everything for you. We can make this better.

Starting and stopping Appium with Maven

When we run our tests we want the ability to start and stop everything, so we are going to add another profile and a series of additional plugins. First of all, we need to add some properties into our `<properties>` block in preparation for this new profile with all these new plugins:

```
<appium-maven-plugin.version>0.2.0</appium-maven-plugin.version>
<maven-compiler-plugin.version>3.7.0</maven-compiler-plugin.version>
<frontend-maven-plugin.nodeVersion>v7.4.0</frontend-maven-
plugin.nodeVersion>
<frontend-maven-plugin.npmVersion>4.1.1</frontend-maven-plugin.npmVersion>
<port-allocator-maven-plugin.version>1.2</port-allocator-maven-
plugin.version>
```

Next we have our new profile, this is quite a big one:

```xml
<profile>
    <id>startAndStopAppium</id>
    <activation>
        <property>
            <name>invokeAppium</name>
        </property>
    </activation>
    <build>
        <plugins>
            <plugin>
                <groupId>com.github.eirslett</groupId>
                <artifactId>frontend-maven-plugin</artifactId>
                <version>1.5</version>
                <executions>
                    <execution>
                        <id>install node and npm</id>
                        <phase>process-resources</phase>
                        <goals>
                            <goal>install-node-and-npm</goal>
                        </goals>
                        <configuration>
                            <nodeVersion>${frontend-maven-
                            plugin.nodeVersion}</nodeVersion>
                            <npmVersion>${frontend-maven-
                            plugin.npmVersion}</npmVersion>
                        </configuration>
                    </execution>
                    <execution>
                        <id>npm install</id>
                        <phase>process-resources</phase>
                        <goals>
                            <goal>npm</goal>
                        </goals>
                        <configuration>
                            <arguments>install</arguments>
                        </configuration>
                    </execution>
                </executions>
            </plugin>
            <plugin>
                <groupId>org.sonatype.plugins</groupId>
                <artifactId>port-allocator-maven-plugin</artifactId>
                <version>${port-allocator-maven-plugin.version}
                </version>
                <executions>
                    <execution>
```

```xml
                <phase>validate</phase>
                <goals>
                    <goal>allocate-ports</goal>
                </goals>
                <configuration>
                    <ports>
                        <port>
                            <name>appium.port</name>
                        </port>
                    </ports>
                </configuration>
            </execution>
        </executions>
    </plugin>
    <plugin>
        <groupId>org.apache.maven.plugins</groupId>
        <artifactId>maven-failsafe-plugin</artifactId>
        <version>${maven-failsafe-plugin.version}</version>
        <configuration>
            <systemPropertyVariables>
                <appiumServerLocation>http://localhost:
                ${appium.port}/wd/hub</appiumServerLocation>
                <enableDebugMode>${enableDebugMode}
                </enableDebugMode>
                <screenshotDirectory>${project.build.directory}
                /screenshots</screenshotDirectory>
                <remoteDriver>${remote}</remoteDriver>
                <appiumConfig>${appiumConfig}</appiumConfig>
            </systemPropertyVariables>
        </configuration>
        <executions>
            <execution>
                <goals>
                    <goal>integration-test</goal>
                    <goal>verify</goal>
                </goals>
            </execution>
        </executions>
    </plugin>
    <plugin>
        <groupId>com.lazerycode.appium</groupId>
        <artifactId>appium-maven-plugin</artifactId>
        <version>${appium-maven-plugin.version}</version>
        <configuration>
            <nodeDefaultLocation>
            ${basedir}/node</nodeDefaultLocation>
            <appiumLocation>${basedir}
            /node_modules/appium</appiumLocation>
```

```
                        <appiumPort>${appium.port}</appiumPort>
                    </configuration>
                    <executions>
                        <execution>
                            <id>start appium</id>
                            <phase>pre-integration-test</phase>
                            <goals>
                                <goal>start</goal>
                            </goals>
                        </execution>
                        <execution>
                            <id>stop appium</id>
                            <phase>post-integration-test</phase>
                            <goals>
                                <goal>stop</goal>
                            </goals>
                        </execution>
                    </executions>
                </plugin>
            </plugins>
        </build>
    </profile>
```

The first thing you will notice when you invoke this profile is that we have set a property called `invokeAppium` in the activation block. This is how we ensure that when we are running our Appium tests we, either used this profile or the previous one. We cannot run them both at the same time.

Next, we have `frontend-maven-plugin`. We are using this to install an isolated node and npm that is only used as part of the build for this project. We then use npm to download the Appium server. This also requires us to have `package.json` in the root of our project where we specify the version of Appium that we want to download:

```
{
  "name": "mastering-selenium-appium",
  "private": false,
  "license": "Apache 2",
  "version": "0.0.0",
  "description": "Download appium for automated tests",
  "devDependencies": {
    "appium": "1.8.1",
    "deviceconsole":"1.0.1"
  },
```

```
"scripts": {
  "prestart": "npm install",
  "pretest": "npm install"
}
}
```

The next plugin we have configured is `port-allocator-maven-plugin`. This allows us to search for ports that are currently not in use so that we can ensure that when we start up our Appium server, it doesn't try to use a port that is already in use. We then have our `failsafe-maven-plugin` configuration. It's very similar to the configuration in the previous profile, but this time we need to make sure we are passing in the custom ports being used by the Appium server instance that has been started up as a part of this build. Finally, we have our `appium-maven-plugin` configuration. This has a simple job, it starts Appium before the `integration-test` phase and then shuts it down again afterwards.

We now have everything, we need to download Appium, start it up, run our tests, and then shut down the Appium server again. You can do this using:

```
mvn clean verify -PstartAndStopAppium
```

This may be a bit slow the first time you run it because it has to download node and install it as well as Appium, but once the initial download is complete it will reuse it in future test runs.

Summary

In this appendix, we learnt how to create a basic Appium test framework that is very similar in form to the Selenium framework, we built up throughout the rest of the book. We have used the Appium desktop application to find the locators required for our page objects and we have used ADB to find out package names to use in our Appium tests. Finally, we learnt how to configure our `POM.xml` to download and start up Appium as part of a standard Maven build.

Other Books You May Enjoy

If you enjoyed this book, you may be interested in these other books by Packt:

Selenium Framework Design in Data-Driven Testing
Carl Cocchiaro

ISBN: 978-1-78847-357-6

- Design the Selenium Driver Class for local, remote, and third party grid support
- Build Page Object Classes using the Selenium Page Object Model
- Develop Data-Driven Test Classes using the TestNG framework
- Encapsulate Data using the JSON Protocol
- Build a Selenium Grid for RemoteWebDriver Testing
- Construct Utility Classes for use in Synchronization, File I/O, Reporting and Test Listener Classes
- Run the sample framework and see the benefits of a live data-driven framework in real-time

Selenium WebDriver 3 Practical Guide - Second Edition

Unmesh Gundecha

ISBN: 978-1-78899-976-2

- Begin by learning what Selenium 3 is and how is it better than its predecessor.
- Learn how to use different mobile and desktop browser platforms with Selenium 3.
- Perform advanced actions such as drag-and-drop, double-click, right-click, and action builders on web page.
- Learn to use Java 8 API and Selenium 3 together.
- Explore remote WebDriver and how to use it.
- Learn how to use Selenium Grid to run tests from Cross Browser and distributed testing.
- Explore how to use Actions API for performing various Keyboard and Mouse actions on Web and Mobile Applications.

Leave a review - let other readers know what you think

Please share your thoughts on this book with others by leaving a review on the site that you bought it from. If you purchased the book from Amazon, please leave us an honest review on this book's Amazon page. This is vital so that other potential readers can see and use your unbiased opinion to make purchasing decisions, we can understand what our customers think about our products, and our authors can see your feedback on the title that they have worked with Packt to create. It will only take a few minutes of your time, but is valuable to other potential customers, our authors, and Packt. Thank you!

Index

Made in the USA
Middletown, DE
19 April 2021